PEOPLE, POLITICS, AND PURPOSE

C.D. HOWE SERIES IN CANADIAN POLITICAL HISTORY

Series editors: Robert Bothwell and John English

This series offers fresh perspectives on Canadian political history and public policy from over the past century. Its purpose is to encourage scholars to write and publish on all aspects of the nation's political history, including the origins, administration, and significance of economic policies; the social foundations of politics and political parties; transnational influences on Canadian public life; and the biographies of key public figures. In doing so, the series fills large gaps in our knowledge about recent Canadian history and makes accessible to a broader audience the background necessary to understand contemporary public-political issues. Other volumes in the series are:

Grit: The Life and Politics of Paul Martin Sr., by Greg Donaghy
The Call of the World: A Political Memoir, by Bill Graham
Prime Ministerial Power in Canada: Its Origins under Macdonald, Laurier, and Borden, by Patrice Dutil
The Good Fight: Marcel Cadieux and Canadian Diplomacy, by Brendan Kelly
Challenge the Strong Wind: Canada and East Timor, 1975–99, by David Webster
The Nuclear North: Histories of Canada in the Atomic Age, edited by Susan Colbourn and Timothy Andrews Sayle
The Unexpected Louis St-Laurent: Politics and Policies for a Modern Canada, edited by Patrice Dutil
Canadian Foreign Policy: Reflections on a Field in Transition, edited by Brian Bow and Andrea Lane
The Rowell-Sirois Commission and the Remaking of Canadian Federalism, by Robert Wardhaugh and Barry Ferguson
A Long Way to Paradise: A New History of British Columbia Politics, by Robert A.J. McDonald
A Cooperative Disagreement: Canada-United States Relations and Revolutionary Cuba, 1959–93, by John M. Dirks

The series originated with a grant from the C.D. Howe Memorial Foundation and is further supported by the Bill Graham Centre for Contemporary International History.

C.D. Howe Series in
Canadian Political History

PEOPLE, POLITICS, AND PURPOSE

Biography and Canadian Political History

EDITED BY GREG DONAGHY AND
P. WHITNEY LACKENBAUER

UBCPress · Vancouver · Toronto

32 31 30 29 28 27 26 25 24 23   5 4 3 2 1

Printed in Canada on FSC-certified ancient-forest-free paper (100% post-consumer recycled) that is processed chlorine- and acid-free.

Library and Archives Canada Cataloguing in Publication

Title: People, politics, and purpose : biography and Canadian political history / edited by Greg Donaghy and P. Whitney Lackenbauer.
Names: Donaghy, Greg, editor. | Lackenbauer, P. Whitney, editor.
Series: C.D. Howe series in Canadian political history.
Description: Series statement: C.D. Howe series in Canadian political history | Includes bibliographical references and index.
Identifiers: Canadiana (print) 20220455481 | Canadiana (ebook) 20220455589 | ISBN 9780774866804 (hardcover) | ISBN 9780774866811 (paperback) | ISBN 9780774868020 (EPUB) | ISBN 9780774866828 (PDF)
Subjects: LCSH: Politicians – Canada – Biography – History and criticism. | LCSH: Canada – Biography – History and criticism. | LCSH: Canada – Politics and government – Historiography. | LCSH: Canada – Foreign relations – Historiography.
Classification: LCC FC26.P6 P46 2023 | DDC 324.2092/271 – dc23

Canadä

UBC Press gratefully acknowledges the financial support for our publishing program of the Government of Canada (through the Canada Book Fund), the Canada Council for the Arts, and the British Columbia Arts Council.

This book has been published with the help of a grant from the Canadian Federation for the Humanities and Social Sciences, through the Awards to Scholarly Publications Program, using funds provided by the Social Sciences and Humanities Research Council of Canada.

Printed and bound in Canada by Friesens
Set in Perpetua and Minion by Apex CoVantage, LLC
Copy editor: Robyn So
Proofreader: Sophie Pouyanne

UBC Press
The University of British Columbia
2029 West Mall
Vancouver, BC V6T 1Z2
www.ubcpress.ca

CONTENTS

FOREWORD

It is not an easy task to write an introduction to a volume that celebrates the life and career of John English. One of Canada's pre-eminent political historians over the past half-century, English also wrote extensively on international affairs, while engaging in politics both at the front of the parliamentary stage and in the backrooms where politics is really concocted. English is of course a Canadian Liberal, and the Canadian Liberal party is one of the longest-lived political formations on the planet. The Liberal party was and is an omnibus formulation, embodying a rich variety of self-contradiction, and it is appropriate that a broad-minded and tolerant man like English should find a lifelong home in a party often and justly compared to a broad church, drawing its strength and longevity from its incoherence.

While a party man, English has always reached "across the aisle," as the Americans say, in writing and teaching, and in politics. He brought his political experience, but not his partisanship, into teaching and writing. Though a Canadian nationalist, he is simultaneously an internationalist, which flavours his work with realism and, often, pessimism. He even engaged in diplomacy himself at the end of the 1990s and could ruefully agree with Malcolm Muggeridge's characterization of a British diplomat as "forever Jeeves, to an increasingly demented Bertie Wooster."

Jeeves cast an ironic eye on the world, as English does – on academia, on politics, on the waves of political and intellectual hysteria that engaged many of his colleagues over a long professional lifetime. He followed in his life Pierre Trudeau's summons to intellectuals to become engaged in the broader world, but he always retained a cognitive distance. Reason over passion was the watchword of the passionate Trudeau. A passion for reason is the appropriate characterization for John English.

ROBERT BOTHWELL

***

The C.D. Howe Series on Canadian Political History is supported by a grant from the C.D. Howe Memorial Foundation. The grant was given to promote greater research and publications on Canada's political history. The Bill Graham Centre for Contemporary International History also supports this series, which has already published important biographies and analytical studies that have attracted academic and popular interest.

PEOPLE, POLITICS, AND PURPOSE

INTRODUCTION

Greg Donaghy and P. Whitney Lackenbauer

John English's remarkable breadth of scholarly interest and knowledge, his mastery of archival research, and his ability to cast ideas in evocative, readable prose have made this bestselling author the pre-eminent Canadian political biographer of the last half-century. As an editor of the *Dictionary of Canadian Biography* during some of its most challenging times and an inspiration behind the UBC Press's political history series, English has championed the form. He was first drawn to the biographer's craft as a young historian – his biography of Sir Robert Borden was published in 1977 – and no contemporary Canadian historian has done more to deepen our understanding of Canadian prime ministers. His landmark biographies of Lester B. Pearson and Pierre Elliott Trudeau, products of a mature and seasoned mind, stand as cornerstones of Canadian historiography.

The chapters in this volume offer insights into Canada's place in the world, illuminate the roles and reputations of diverse political actors, and stimulate fresh thinking about the nature and value of political biography. The authors' critical perspectives do not promote a return to the "great man theory" that long animated political biography but celebrate the value of analyzing both macro- and microdynamics toward a better understanding of Canada's past. The essays in this book are reflections by historians on historical actors engaged in and affected by the politics around them.

* * *

John English came to the genre of political history as an undergraduate student at the University of Waterloo (near his hometown of Plattsville, Ontario), where he completed a joint major in history and political science. He ventured to Harvard University with a Woodrow Wilson scholarship in history to pursue his graduate studies, where he switched his earlier plans for a project in German or British history to a study on Robert Borden and political management. By the time he completed his PhD in 1973, he had returned to teach at Waterloo, where he published his first books: a short biography of Arthur Meighen; a longer overview of Robert Borden; and a ground-breaking analysis of the Conservatives and the party system.[1] Over the next decade, while coauthoring a lively two-volume survey of twentieth-century Canadian history,[2] English produced influential articles and chapters on Canadian political history and foreign policy. If the discipline of history in Canada was abdicating ground to political scientists on historical topics,[3] English was certainly not part of this trend. As a board member and then coeditor of the *Canadian Historical Review*, from 1983 to 1989, he also encouraged increasingly diverse and inclusive forms of Canadian history. While others became embroiled in so-called history wars, English remained a colleague whose wide networks – spanning beyond history and indeed beyond the academy – included friends on all sides.

English's research on Lester B. Pearson began with a Social Sciences and Humanities Research Council of Canada grant with his friend Robert Bothwell to publish a selection of Pearson's papers. When that book project fell through, the former prime minister's son, Geoffrey, reminded English that his father needed a biography. English started working on it in earnest in 1983, with a Killam grant from 1985 to 1987 enabling him to capitalize on nearly unfettered access to the Pearson papers at the National Archives of Canada (many of which are now closed). When the first volume covering Pearson's life from 1897 to 1948 appeared in 1989,[4] it drew applause from professional historians and literary critics alike. Accolades included the Canadian Authors Association Literary Award for Non-Fiction, the J.W. Dafoe Prize for best Canadian book on Canadian affairs, and the Sir John A. Macdonald Prize of the Canadian Historical Association. He managed to complete the second volume while teaching, presiding over the Canadian Institute for International Affairs, and being actively involved in Liberal politics. Soon after the publication of *The Worldly Years* in 1993,[5] English was elected as the Liberal Party member of Parliament for the riding of Kitchener. Over the next four years, his roles included parliamentary secretary to the president of the Privy Council, minister of intergovernmental affairs and minister responsible for public service renewal; vice-chair of the House of Commons Standing Committee on Foreign Affairs and International Trade; chair of the Subcommittee on Sustainable Human Development; and vice-president of the Organization for Security and Cooperation in Europe – Parliamentary Assembly. The long-time observer of politics had become a direct participant.

After completing his term as MP in 1997, English returned to university life. To his students, he was a deeply committed teacher and mentor held in the highest esteem. He brought to the classroom an unrivalled knowledge of Canadian politics and history, which he situated effortlessly in the broader historiography on international relations. His undergraduate lectures, always delivered without notes, started at a gentle pace as he jotted an outline on the chalkboard and would rise to a crescendo with a few minutes left in class when, Lackenbauer recalls, the students had to feverishly scribble notes to record the denouement of that day's subject. English also had "enormous respect for different sides," his former PhD student Stephen Azzi explained. "Conservative students might have feared taking a course from a partisan Liberal, but they quickly discovered that they had nothing to worry about."[6] The intellectual climate in the seminar room was set by argumentation and debate, rooted in historical evidence, with the perspicacious professor offering contrary interpretations when needed to foster a more judicious appraisal.

As a supervisor, English never imposed his ideas, instead encouraging students to find their own way. He returned drafts quickly, his written comments penetrating and incisive. He would uncover factual errors, flaws in analysis, and failures to consider other arguments. In a few words he would capture the strengths and weaknesses of a thesis chapter. His knowledge of the academic literature, which ranged far beyond his area of speciality, was astounding. Accordingly, meetings were highly rewarding – and much anticipated. "Visiting him in his office was a challenge, because a line of students was always waiting for him," Azzi recalled. "John was in high demand because he was a scintillating conversationalist: intelligent, compassionate, and humorous, always willing to share the latest gossip from Queen's Park or Parliament Hill."[7]

While teaching, English also held a bevy of important assignments for the federal government (which John Milloy describes in his concluding reflections to this book). He worked as a special advisor to the Canadian minister of foreign affairs on landmines, as principal reviewer of the mandate and future roles of the National Library and National Archives of Canada, as chair of the board of the Canadian Museum of Civilization and the Canadian War Museum, and as special envoy promoting Canada's bid for a seat on the UN Security Council. In 2001, he was seconded from the University of Waterloo to serve as the founding executive director of the Centre for International Governance Innovation and oversaw Canada's largest think tank on international affairs for the next eight years. Concurrent with these leadership responsibilities, he also researched his next major project: the official biography of Prime Minister Pierre Elliott Trudeau. He had been approached by Jim Coutts (whom English knew from his Harvard days) and received permission to peruse the Trudeau papers at Library and Archives Canada. Finding them more extensive than any prime minister's papers except William Lyon Mackenzie King's, of excellent quality, and well organized, English accepted and started his research in 2002.

Four years later, English published the first volume of his biography of Pierre Trudeau[8] and became editor of the *Dictionary of Canadian Biography* (*DCB*). Both solidified his reputation as the foremost historical biographer in Canada. *Citizen of the World* won the University of British Columbia Canadian Biography Prize for best Canadian biography, the Amazon.ca award for best biography, and the Dafoe Prize, and was a finalist for the Charles Taylor Prize for Literary Non-Fiction, the Shaughnessy Cohen Prize for Political Writing, and the Donald Smiley Prize of the Canadian Political Science Association. The second volume of the Trudeau biography, *Just Watch Me*, garnered more acclaim, including another Dafoe Prize.[9] "Brilliant, so perceptive about Trudeau, so well informed on the context, so beautifully written," extolled the distinguished historian Ramsay Cook (a former general editor of the *DCB*).[10]

English's institutional leadership continued after his retirement from the University of Waterloo, in 2009. He served as the founding director of the Bill Graham Centre for Contemporary International History at Trinity

College from 2013 to 2019, before turning the reins over to his former student Greg Donaghy. English continues to serve as an advisory board member for the Trudeau Centre for Peace, Conflict and Justice, and remains a sage mentor, trusted advisor, and cherished friend to many scholars, politicians, and pundits across our country.

* * *

Biography flourished in nineteenth-century Canada, as measured by production *and* consumption. Readers looked for inspiration and exemplars, and biographers – British and American, supplemented by translations from Europe – supplied the need. Great men and Florence Nightingale predominated. But "the pages of Canadian history are [also] rich in picturesque and striking figures about whom cluster the great events in the evolution of our national institutions," W.J. Karr wrote in introducing a volume of vignettes, which "through the stories of the lives of these notable men and women, one may obtain … a clear and comprehensive grasp of the history of their times."[11] Discussing Canadian biography in 1980, Robert Craig Brown noted that the earliest examples generally conformed to simple hagiography, "tendentious and didactic tomes, unburdened by a respect for evidence, in which heroes and heroines could do no wrong."[12] Theirs were "exemplary lives" for a generation that craved heroism, especially if infused with contemporary versions of morality – and that advanced thought, as the writers interpreted it.

The subsequent "life and times" form of biography, exemplified in the Canadian canon by O.D. Skelton's graceful *Life and Letters of Sir Wilfrid Laurier* (1921),[13] adopted more assiduous research and an increasingly scholarly tone about the lives of public men. But Skelton demonstrated a fervent commitment to both Laurier the man and the liberal nationalist project that he espoused,[14] narrating the life of his central figure through the political and economic challenges that his "hero" had to overcome. Unlike English's work, however, the life and times biographers emphasized circumstance over "portraiture of character."[15] Contradictions in, unsavoury aspects of, and confusing elements about a subject's life were either downplayed or suppressed. Furthermore, practitioners of this form only partially grappled with core questions about the relationships between individuals in specific sociocultural and political environments, their autonomy and agency to shape their world, and the influences on the development of personality that shape a person's life.[16]

Canadian political biography in the 1950s and early 1960s sought to correct this imbalance between character and circumstance, recreating the lives of politicians to reveal their hopes, intentions, and motivations as embodiments of the nation itself.[17] "In a biography, as in a novel," Donald Creighton suggested, history does not wallow "in generalities and abstractions" but in "a central, main character, a set of subordinate characters, and a series of particular situations."[18] Published in 1952 and 1955, Creighton's epic two-volume biography of John A. Macdonald embodied both meticulous research and elegant writing that drew on the techniques of fiction. In so doing, biographer Donald Wright noted that Creighton "put thoughts into Macdonald's head," invented dialogue, and imagined scenes to evoke emotion in his reader.[19] Through Creighton's biography, Carl Berger observed, "an entire age and its political history were not merely ordered around Macdonald, but ... readers saw the whole scene through his eyes alone."[20]

The George Brown who emerged in J.M.S. Careless's magisterial biography saw the same historical events rather differently from Creighton's Macdonald,[21] but it was not because the biographers disputed the facts. It was their selection and imaginative configuration of the evidence, their interpretation and fashioning of a political narrative that explained their distinct portrayals of their subjects and, by extension, of nineteenth-century Canada. As historian Penny Bryden explains in her recent reflection on the changing shape of English Canadian political history, most historians in the first seven decades of the twentieth century were hedgehogs committed to knowing "one big thing" and telling "a single story" – what twenty-first century scholars might label "empire," "nation building," or "compromise."[22] Most of the "great man" or heroic biographies produced in the three decades after the Second World War followed one of these linear trajectories, tracing stories from beginning to end – often with a tidy teleological arc – through the lives of their chosen protagonist.

As intellectual, labour, business, social, and women's and gender historians broadened and deepened Canadian historiography from the 1960s onward, their theoretical and methodological focus on structures left little room for individual character as a fundamental political determinant. "In trying to write history from below, in moving beyond the top-down decision-making of "great men," the new social historians sought to uncover the experiences and impact of ordinary people," Adele Perry and Brian Lewis observe. "These historians emphasized collectivities over individuals, marching classes, ethnicities, and genders up and down the pages of their texts."[23] It is also telling that French Canadian and Québécois historians produced few political biographies (with the exception of the prolific Robert Rumilly),[24] preferring instead to emphasize collective identities and, in due course, seeking to "normalize" Quebec society's historical experience.[25]

While political biography no longer occupied a dominant position in the Canadian academic discipline, it would be wrong to paint too grim a picture of the state of political biography in the 1970s and 1980s. The number of academic and popular titles surged,[26] with biography offering an enticing alternative to dehumanizing collectivism by highlighting human agency (a core element of liberal democratic thought) and the importance of individual character and beliefs to meet the challenges of modernity.[27] Situating the individual as an agent of history restored narrative approaches that framed history as literature and, by putting a human face on Canadian political history, expanded its popular appeal, attracting a readership that often extended beyond academia.[28] Post-Confederation prime ministers and Opposition leaders, provincial premiers, and other politicians and policy makers received individual attention in a stream of books and doctoral dissertations.[29] The bilingual *DCB*, launched in 1966, provided a permanent portal that encouraged scholars to explore Canada's political and social evolution using a biographical approach. Toronto businessman James Nicholson's bequest to the University of Toronto to create "a biographical reference work for Canada of truly national importance"[30] meant a disproportionate emphasis on political figures, given the traditional association of national significance with public life. Peter Waite described it as "perhaps the largest, longest-sustained, and most concentrated of any collective historical endeavour yet undertaken in this country." Its founders emphasized how biographies should not simply catalogue events but "appraise circumstances which shaped careers." Instead, authors should "leave the reader with a definite impression of the personality and achievements of the subject," while upholding ideals of objectivity, balance, and fairness.[31] A widening array of professional and nonprofessional historians have typically embraced the detached, objective/academic style of factual narrative to ground their interpretations, rather than more dramatic or expressive forms.[32] (Fittingly, John English – a long-time reader of and contributor to the *DCB* – became general editor from 2006 to 2013, during which time the *DCB* was recognized with the Governor General's History Award for Popular Media: The Pierre Berton Award.[33])

The *DCB* also offers strong insight into broader Canadian historical currents and how these have carried the genre of political biography. As new generations of historians expanded their gaze to encompass a more diverse cast of political actors – from woman suffragists and clergy to Indigenous leaders and civil service mandarins – the *DCB* became increasingly diverse in subject matter, sources, and styles of writing.[34] Labour and social historians brought their perspectives to political biography, contributing entries (and books) on prominent union leaders, progressive reformers, and entrepreneurs. Despite a selection bias toward men with public profiles (and with ample primary sources to back their stories), biographies of more than five hundred women have appeared in the *DCB,* most prominently in those volumes covering the twentieth century.[35] "Without ever setting out to do anything but tell one story as he or she saw fit," Francess Halpenny observes, "each and every author [who has contributed to the *DCB*] has added a segment to what now constitutes a monumental yet pulsing biography of Canada."[36] The *DCB* is not just a monument to Canadian history; its pages also reveal a who's who of many of Canada's finest scholars.

The rising tide of regionalism in Canadian political studies also brought a surge of biographies of provincial politicians. For example, when a group of prominent Toronto-based historians established the Ontario Historical Studies Series in the early 1970s, they lamented how "Ontario has many fine historians, but much of their work has been focused on national themes."[37] A series of biographies of Ontario premiers sought to capture the province's distinctive history, as did similar books by political historians across the country. Thomas Flanagan's reassessment of Louis Riel, Hugh Dempsey's biographies of Crowfoot (Isapo-muxika), Red Crow (Mékaisto), and Big Bear (Mistahimaskwa), and Murray Dobbin's profile of Jim Brady and Malcolm Norris also raised the profile of Indigenous political leaders who shaped the course of their people – and of modern Canada.[38]

While treatments of prime ministers and other federal politicians incorporated new historiographical currents, H. Blair Neatby noted in 1993 that their biographers continued to write in prose deliberately crafted to appeal to nonacademic audiences – a contrast from most academic historians who now published specialized studies for other scholars.[39] John English's masterful two-volume biography on Lester Pearson – *Shadow of Heaven* (1989) and *The Worldly Years* (1993) – blurred the lines between the public and private person, carefully analyzing political events throughout Pearson's life while situating these in sophisticated sociocultural contexts. Academic and nonacademic audiences, as well as various national award committees, approved.[40]

Since then, an increasingly diverse array of subjects associated with political history have invited changes in scope and methodology. In their introduction to a 2010 special issue of the *Journal of the Canadian Historical Association* on "The Biographical (Re)Turn," Adele Perry and Brian Lewis note how "renewed interest in the individual and in agency" has revitalized "the contextualized biography as an entry-point to a study of a broader world."[41] By embracing subjectivities, identity construction, and "performances" of self, however, biographers can claim a place in "restoring a sense of human agency to the historical process."[42] After all, as Peter Waite emphasized, without humans, there "are no forces; there are no movements; there are no trends. Different people may behave differently as individuals, groups, or crowds; but ... they are all human."[43]

The breadth of academics writing historical biography also reinforces that it is hardly a genre of "disrepute."[44] Methodological and theoretical diversity, coupled with a broadening and deepening of the subject areas (and thus the range of actors), has fragmented traditional national political narratives and produced a "new political history" that expands beyond the study of "great men," "great events," and state politics.[45] Accordingly, traditional political biography now coexists alongside more experimental forms featuring a rich plurality of approaches, themes, and subjects. "There is no reason why biography cannot serve as a legitimate way to look carefully at individual and collective lives, great and laboring men, or maids and duchesses," British historian Lucy Riall observes. "The structure of a life may be remembered and recounted as a sketch or in fragments, or as a chronological narrative with origin, purpose, or end, or as some combination of all these forms."[46]

Few Canadian historians writing in the genre have proven willing to dispense with conventional considerations of chronology, consistent with Robert Rotberg's insistence that "biographical treatments must never be divorced from their temporal or spatial contexts. Choice, and rational action, occurs only within such a framework."[47] Even this logic, however, cannot reveal the full inner life of a subject. As John English noted in the introduction to his first volume on Pearson, *Shadow of Heaven:*

> Lester Pearson has not been easy to know. He had a Victorian reserve that made revelation about one's private life difficult. In writing this biography, especially on those occasions when I had to divine Pearson's private thoughts and motives, I often recalled Virginia Woolf's comment about her sighting of a kingfisher on a cold September day that awakened a special feeling in her. No biographer, she rightly warned, could ever know that important fact about her life in the late summer of 1926 and no biographer should pretend to do so.[48]

As such, the biographer bears a heavy burden of creative responsibility when discerning and finding motives for their subject's decisions and actions – even if this entails reinventing as well as reconstructing the past.[49]

Ged Martin asked in 1992: "Have we passed from an era of heroic biography into an era more interested in the archaeology of humbler lives?"[50] Perhaps not, as traditional forms of heroic biography have continued to thrive in Canada as elsewhere.[51] Nonetheless, historians increasingly blend careful archival research and methodological analysis of secondary sources with oral histories and other sources to weave together political and cultural themes into what some commentators describe as "the new biography."[52] Accordingly, the new political biography in Canada also reflects the shift in political history toward multidimensional approaches that are less teleological or certain, embrace complexity, and are expected to "consider more complicated ways of engaging individual lives and nation states."[53]

Reappraisals of the life and times of Prime Minister Pierre Elliott Trudeau reflect the ongoing appeal of political biography in Canada, both in their contributions to historiography and in book sales. Although Trudeau was the subject of various biographies while in office and in retirement[54] (as well as a thin autobiography[55]), a deluge of writings on his intellectual influences, ideological predilections, political and cultural appeal, and contributions to Canada have appeared since his death in 2000, renewing vigorous debate about his legacies.[56]

English, as official biographer, enjoyed unfettered access to Trudeau's personal papers, leading him to dramatically revise our understandings of the prime minister's early life. "In reading Trudeau's own words, I came to realize that the seeming contradictions in his life were more often consistencies," English explained.[57] Trudeau's papers revealed youthful adherence to socially conservative Catholic and radical separatist ideas that he avoided in his memoirs – ideas expunged through education in the United States, Britain, and France. Unlike many earlier prime ministerial biographies, English emphasizes how intellectuals around Trudeau influenced his professional life, shaping his ideas and the constitutional, economic, foreign, and domestic policies that he promoted.[58] By carefully situating Trudeau in Quebec society of the 1930s–40s and then broader international currents, English demonstrates how, at various stages of life, the intellectual-cum-politician reflected the world of ideas around him. Trudeau's letters to his mother and female friends provide insight into the private side of a person who, English reveals, always anticipated a life in politics. The Trudeau that emerges "is a far more complex, conflicted, and challenging character than we have ever known before."[59] In engaging this complexity, "English is even-handed, rarely praising, blaming or psychologizing, but he explains and invokes all the different views on the events recounted," William Johnson noted in a *Globe and Mail* review. "And it's a good read."[60] Again, book prize committees agreed.[61]

English's biographies of Pearson and Trudeau affirm how recent political biography in Canada is informed by scholarship from the social sciences but retains its close affinity with literature in its narrative form and content. "Biography … is a branch of history but it is not the same thing as history," Carl Berger asserts. "History deals in generalizations about groups, institutions, and movements in time and is more than a mosaic of lives. Biography deals with the particularities of a human being and seeks to simulate, through narrative, an individual's life."[62] This categorical statement draws a clear distinction between history and biography, although vigorous debate continues about whether biography should be considered a genre distinct from history, an approach to it, or a field within it.[63] Whatever the verdict, the biographer's intent is to furnish a sophisticated view of the role of individuals, perceptions of them, and the people, movements, and forces that influenced them.

"Historians are not interested in simply charting the course of individual lives," American historian David Nasaw argues, "but in examining those lives in a dialectical relationship to the multiple social, political, and cultural worlds they inhabit and give meaning to."[64] The chapters in this book not only reveal how individuals have contributed to the shaping of Canadian history, but also how they have been shaped in and shaped by particular historical, political, and sociocultural contexts.

* * *

"Biography is the most common form of history," English and Robert Bothwell observe in their foreword to a recent monograph in the field. "Some subjects anticipate their immortality and compose their own versions of their lives."[65] The opening chapter of this collection, by historians Bothwell and Norman Hillmer, opens up an important question in this collection: What do memoirs and diaries contribute to understanding Canada's history? While their focus remains autobiography, the chapter embraces the field of life-writing, which includes diaries, as means of contextualizing the writing of history. Their chapter explores the numerous published and unpublished texts of Canada's many diplomatic autobiographers, suggesting that these sources personalize history for the reader and make use of the reader's understanding of others' personal traits as a bridge to the unfamiliar worlds of the past.

Personal diaries, Bothwell and Hillmer argue, "act, like memoirs, as self-promotion, self-justification, or self-explanation – sometimes all three – but they have the advantage of not having travelled through the filter of too much reflection." Beginning with the exceptionally literate group of diplomats that staffed the Department of External Affairs in the 1920s, Canada's foreign service officers stand out as sharp observers of the country's growing independence. Despite their inherent limitations, the products of ego and spite, their memoirs and autobiographies add vital nuance to our historical narratives, especially with their insights into the personalities and personal relationships that shaped policy. Locating their own experiences within the broad currents of contemporaneous national and international history, these writers facilitate a deeper comprehension of Canada's international history.

While diaries and autobiography embody how people portray themselves, biographers and historians apply their own narrative devices to shape how readers see individuals in their historical context. In Chapter 2, Galen Perras and Asa McKercher remind us, as English insists, that history is determined by the "intersection of people and policy." Their investigation into American perceptions of Pearson throughout his diplomatic and political career reveals the way American policy makers saw Pearson as a function of their perceptions of Canadian foreign policy in the decades after the Second World War. American opinions of Pearson were linked to a growing suspicion of Canada's increasingly independent postwar foreign policy. Perras and McKercher argue that while many Washington insiders welcomed Pearson's steady rise, some were irritated and disappointed by his readiness to forge an independent course in international affairs. The authors identify the emergence of this trend long before Pearson's 1965 proposition to suspend US strategic bombing in Vietnam – an event that led to a falling out with US president Lyndon B. Johnson.

Political biography "personalizes" historical figures in time and space but risks overlooking the collective experiences of ordinary people. In Chapter 3, Angie Sauer offers a "history from below" that decentres political biography by emphasizing the social, cultural, and transnational aspects of migration along the Canada-US border. Using the 1943–44 "lumberjack wars" as a case study, she explores how individual stakeholders – woodworkers, newspaper editors, and industry lobbyists – defied government expectations in search of economic advantage. While acknowledging that political decision makers are important, she reminds us that they work within and are constrained by a web of social and cultural connections. By collectivizing experience and prioritizing circumstance over character, she offers an interpretation of Canada-US relations that questions what political borders and boundaries meant for itinerant workers. The history of cross-border labourers in the forest, mining, and milling sectors reminds readers of the interdependence of traditional forms of agriculture and industrialization, as well as offers insight into the gendered, social, and cultural dynamics of the workers' family economies. Taken as a whole, such contexts are overlooked in broader historical accounts of high-level diplomacy focused on national interests rather than the socioeconomic interests of citizens.

The dramatic resurgence of Indigenous Peoples as a political force in Canada since the Second World War also invites more biographical attention to Indigenous leaders who have reshaped Indigenous-Crown relations through interactions with and within Canadian institutions. In Chapter 4, P. Whitney Lackenbauer investigates the selection of Canada's first Indigenous senator, James Gladstone, of the Blood Tribe, also known as the Kainai Nation. Situating the process that led to his appointment within shifting discursive and federal policy contexts on Indigenous Peoples after the Second World War, Lackenbauer parses how political and media commentators at the time framed biographies of the leading nominees for the Senate seat that Conservative prime minister John Diefenbaker designated for a First Nations man. Gladstone's appointment represented a much-celebrated step toward the formal recognition of Indigenous political rights, Lackenbauer observes. His chapter also reveals the ways that supporters and critics described the nominees – Gilbert Monture, Chief Andy Paull, and Gladstone – and testifies to the "constructed and contested nature of political appointments," biography, and history more broadly.

In Chapter 5, Stephen Azzi adopts a more traditional biographical frame to analyze Lester Pearson as political leader. Echoing Michael Holroyd, Azzi laments that political biography has been recast as the "shallow end of history" for the past half-century. This unfair characterization overlooks important contributions to our understanding of Canadian politics. English's work on Pearson, for example, outlines a uniquely Canadian style of leadership, one which "combines seemingly contradictory qualities – at once transformational and uninspiring." Azzi argues that perhaps no other Canadian prime minister has captured this paradox more fully than Pearson, noting the tendency of his contemporaries and historians to dismiss him as an indecisive, uncourageous, and weak leader. Insisting that these critics have a limited grasp of the meaning of leadership, Azzi draws on a literature of leadership typically confined to business schools to demonstrate that Pearson's prescience and persistence in legislative and electoral affairs more than offset his cautious style. Furthermore, Pearson showed toughness and decisiveness as both party leader and prime minister, while cultivating future leaders and talent in caucus and cabinet. These qualities enabled Pearson to revitalize the Liberal Party in the early 1960s and emerge as head of an exceptionally accomplished government that adopted transformative legislation and modernized the Canadian state.

Like Azzi, Penny Bryden credits English with rejuvenating Canadian political biography by broadening the scope beyond the life of the single subject and using his studies of Pearson and Trudeau to illuminate questions of identity and culture. In Chapter 5, Bryden focuses on Gerda Munsinger, whose affairs with Progressive Conservative cabinet ministers erupted into a full-blown sex scandal in the mid-1960s. Bryden uses domestic and international media, as well as court documents, to show how Munsinger's story was presented to the public. Though it is usually treated by historians as simply a sorry episode in Prime Minister Pearson's political career, Bryden illustrates how Munsinger's life was shaped and reshaped to fit within the narrative of scandal. Her work invites us to shift our historical focus from the centre to the periphery, demonstrating how political biography can help to refine our understanding of the gendered social and political realities of 1960s Canada.

A close reading of a single policy maker's life can overturn long-established historical understandings. This is the case, for instance, with Jennifer Bonder's chapter on the politics of long-time Windsor member of Parliament and cabinet minister Herb Gray. Typically, Gray is portrayed as a staunch and unyielding Canadian nationalist in his approach to foreign investment and Canada-US relations. Biography, Bonder suggests, can be "the lens that adjusts the image from demagogue to pragmatist." Situating Gray in a specific place and time – Windsor during the heyday of the cross-border auto trade in the 1960s and 1970s – changes our understanding of Gray's brand of nationalism and the Trudeau government's policies. Using Gray's recently opened personal papers, Bonder argues that Gray was no firebrand economic nationalist but a careful and pragmatic compromiser. This judgment is borne out in Bonder's examination of the bureaucratic and political tensions surrounding Gray's efforts to shape industrial policy and control US investment. Through a close reading of his early political speeches and his important report promoting a foreign investment review agency, she demonstrates the way Gray balanced the need for American capital in specific sectors and regions with nationalist concerns about foreign direct investment. Dogmatic politicians seldom enjoy long political careers like Gray's, and his flexible and measured approaches in the early 1970s help to explain why he held elected office for forty years.

In another biographical approach to understanding Canada's international policy, Greg Donaghy provides an in-depth look at the Middle East policy of Allan MacEachen, Trudeau's minister of external affairs from 1974 to 1976 and from 1982 to 1984. Chapter 8 reveals the way the policy preferences of key individual decision makers, fixed in their personal belief systems and worldviews, were crucial determinants of Canadian diplomacy in the Middle East. The prime minister turned Canada's attention southward in 1974, challenging MacEachen to develop policies that reflected his progressive ideals. The result was a long *pas de deux* between MacEachen and Trudeau as they fenced with each other over Canada's Middle East policy against a backdrop of ceaseless Arab-Israeli conflict and bitter cabinet dissension over the path ahead.

Recent calls to reorient the study of Canadian international history away from the North Atlantic Triangle to Asia and other parts of the world also invite detailed studies of diplomats who served in distant corners of the world.[66] "While the question of an individual's influence over government policy is central to political biography, the most effective biographies, political or otherwise, transcend their subjects to tell a larger story about the times in which their subjects lived," historian Brendan Kelly suggests. "This is especially true of the biographies of diplomats who, by the very nature of their work, straddle national and transnational environments and thus offer insights into both their country of origin and the wider world."[67]

In Chapter 9, Ryan Touhey tackles the diplomacy of John Hadwen, Canada's high commissioner to India from 1979 to 1983. Canadian hostility to India's nonaligned diplomacy and bilateral tensions over India's use of Canadian technology to detonate a nuclear explosion in 1974 had left bilateral relations in tatters by the mid-1970s.[68] Hadwen was sent to pick up the pieces. Touhey focuses on Hadwen's approach to his role, suggesting that he deployed a pragmatic diplomacy to convince senior officials in Ottawa of the value of forging positive relations with New Delhi in the aftermath of India's emergence as a regional nuclear power. Touhey uses a close look at Hadwen's personal papers and life story to demonstrate that Hadwen himself was vital in strengthening and redirecting Canada-India relations, while he also explores the ways individual diplomats can influence national policy and shape bilateral relations.

Each of the essays contained in this collection attest to the importance of individuals in how we understand and make sense of history and in how we experience the present. John Milloy reaffirms this point in the concluding chapter of this book: a short reflection on English's own life story. Milloy draws on his experiences working with English, who acted as his informal academic advisor in graduate school and later as a political mentor on Parliament Hill and in the Liberal backrooms of Kitchener-Waterloo. Documenting English's political involvement at the local, regional, and national levels, Milloy argues that English embodies the four Rs of academic activism: he is relatable, respectful, realistic, and relevant. These traits allow English to transcend academia and contribute to Canadian public life as a consummate political activist.

The contributors to this volume, all of whom are close colleagues or former students of John English, would agree with Waite that biography is "not on the periphery of history; it is in the middle of it."[69] They bring the historian's many tools to bear on past lives as they were lived and self-constructed, constructed by contemporaries, or reconstructed by historians. The authors show the ongoing relevance of discerning individual character traits, motivations, and justifications for action with careful respect for robust historical context. Rather than simply offering "minutiae without meaning" (as pundit and professor Stanley Fish provocatively characterized biography),[70] this collection not only provides rich detail – the *what* of biography – but also addresses the larger *so what* that drives history. The chapters stand as eloquent tributes to John English's transformative role in shaping contemporary political biography in Canada.

NOTES

1 John English, *Arthur Meighen* (Don Mills, ON: Fitzhenry & Whiteside, 1977); *Robert Borden, His Life and World* (Toronto: McGraw-Hill Ryerson, 1977); *The Decline of Politics: The Conservatives and the Party System* (Toronto: University of Toronto Press, 1977).

2 Robert Bothwell, Ian Drummond, and John English, *Canada, 1900–1945* (Toronto: University of Toronto Press, 1990) and *Canada since 1945: Power, Politics, and Provincialism* (Toronto: University of Toronto Press, 1981, 1989).

3 John English, "The Second Time Around: Political Scientists Writing History," *Canadian Historical Review* 67, 1 (1986): 1–16.
4 John English, *Shadow of Heaven: The Life of Lester Pearson*, vol. 1, *1897–1948* (Toronto: Lester and Orpen Dennys, 1989).
5 John English, *The Worldly Years: The Life of Lester Pearson*, vol. 2, *1949–1972* (Toronto: Vintage Canada, 1993).
6 Azzi, email to the editors.
7 Ibid.
8 John English, *Citizen of the World: The Life of Pierre Elliott Trudeau*, vol. 1, *1919–1968* (Toronto: Vintage Canada, 2006).
9 John English, *Just Watch Me: The Life of Pierre Elliott Trudeau*, vol. 2, *1968–2000* (Toronto: Knopf, 2009).
10 Citation inside of English, *Just Watch Me*.
11 W.J. Karr, *Explorers, Soldiers and Statesmen: A History of Canada through Biography* (Toronto: J.M. Dent, 1929), ix. He continued:

> Not only do the stories of their careers give a picturesqueness and romance to our history, but they also set before us ideals of the highest type. Who can read the tales of their achievements for the good of Canada without being inspired with admiration, and who can admire without a desire to be worthy of the heritage which we owe to their labours.
>
> Karr, *Explorers, Soldiers and Statesmen*, ix.

12 Robert Craig Brown, "Presidential Address: Biography in Canadian History," *Historical Papers/Communications historiques* 15, 1 (1980): 4.
13 Oscar D. Skelton, *The Life and Letters of Sir Wilfrid Laurier* (Toronto: Oxford University Press, 1921).
14 Thanks to Norman Hillmer for this idea. For more on Skelton, see Hillmer, *O.D. Skelton: A Portrait of Canadian Ambition* (Toronto: University of Toronto Press, 2015).
15 Brown, "Presidential Address: Biography in Canadian History," 4. See also Donald Creighton, "Sir John Macdonald and Canadian Historians," in *Approaches to Canadian History*, ed. Carl Berger (Toronto: University of Toronto Press, 1967), 53.
16 Roderick Barman, "Biography as History," *Journal of the Canadian Historical Association* 21, 2 (2010): 68.
17 See John S. Moir, ed., *Character and Circumstance: Essays in Honour of Donald Grant Creighton* (Toronto: Macmillan, 1970).
18 Donald Creighton, "Sir John Macdonald and Canadian Historians," *Canadian Historical Review* 29, 1 (1948): 3.
19 Donald Wright, "His Macdonald, My Creighton, Biography, and the Writing of History," *Canadian Historical Review* 98, 2 (2017): 342, 344. See also Wright, *Donald Creighton: A Life in History* (Toronto: University of Toronto Press, 2015).
20 Carl Berger, *The Writing of Canadian History: Aspects of English-Canadian Historical Writing: 1900–1970* (Toronto: University of Toronto Press, 1976), 223.
21 J.M.S. Careless, *Brown of the* Globe, 2 vols. (Toronto: University of Toronto Press, 1959 and 1963).
22 Penny Bryden, "Foxes, Hedgehogs, and the Changing Shape of English-Canadian Political History," *Canadian Historical Review* 100, 4 (2019): 589–90.

23 Adele Perry and Brian Lewis, "Introductory Remarks: Special Issue on 'The Biographical (Re)Turn,'" *Journal of the Canadian Historical Association* 21, 2 (2010): 3. See also Perry, "Beyond Biography, Beyond Canada," *Canadian Historical Review* 98, 2 (2017): 321–37.

24 See, for example, Robert Rumilly, *Mercier* (Montreal: Édition du Zodiaque, 1936); *Henri Bourassa: la vie publique d'un grand Canadien* (Montreal: Éditions Chantecler, 1953); and *Maurice Duplessis et son temps,* 2 vols. (Montreal: Fides, 1973). For a list of other biographies, see Martin Pelletier, ed., *Portraits de L'Histoire: Les biographies politiques* (Quebec: Assemblée nationale du Québec, 2007), https://bibliotheque.assnat.qc.ca/DepotNumerique_v2/AffichageFichier.aspx?idf=75205.

25 See, for example, Serge Gagnon, *Quebec and Its Historians: The Twentieth Century,* trans. Jane Brierly (Montreal: Harvest House, 1985); Jean Lamarre, *Le devenir de la nation québécoise selon Maurice Séguin, Guy Frégault et Michel Brunet, 1944–1969* (Quebec: Septentrion, 1993); and Ronald Rudin, *Making History in Twentieth-Century Quebec* (Toronto: University of Toronto Press, 1997).

26 See Clara Thomas, "Biography in Canada," in *Literary History of Canada,* 2nd ed., ed. Carl Klinck (Toronto: University of Toronto Press, 1976), 3:180; Donald Swainson, "Trends in Canadian Biography: Recent Historical Writing," *Queen's Quarterly* 87 (Autumn 1980): 432; and a survey of reviews in the *Canadian Historical Review* from 1965 to 1990.

27 See Philip Massolin, *Canadian Intellectuals, the Tory Tradition, and the Challenge of Modernity, 1939–1970* (Toronto: University of Toronto Press, 2001).

28 Berger, *Writing of Canadian History,* 220–21.

29 For a useful sample, see J.L. Granatstein and Paul Stevens, eds., *A Reader's Guide to Canadian History,* vol. 2, *Confederation to Present* (Toronto: University of Toronto Press, 1982); and John English, "National Politics and Government," in *Canadian History: A Reader's Guide,* ed. Doug Owram, vol. 2, *Confederation to the Present* (Toronto: University of Toronto Press, 1994), 3–50.

30 Entries in the *Dictionary of Canadian Biography,* copublished by the University of Toronto Press and Laval University, are available online at http://biographi.ca/. See also Dictionary of Canadian Biography, "About Us," http://biographi.ca/en/about_us.php.

31 Peter B. Waite, "Journeys through Thirteen Volumes: The Dictionary of Canadian Biography," *Canadian Historical Review* 76, 3 (1995): 468.

32 On forms of biographical narration, see Ira B. Nadel, *Biography: Fiction, Fact and Form* (New York: St. Martin's Press, 1984).

33 Kim Luke, "John English Resigns as General Editor," University of Toronto press release, 24 June 2013, http://www.biographi.ca/en/article/john_english_resignation.html.

34 Waite, "Journeys through Thirteen Volumes"; Andrew J. Ross and Andrew D. Smith, eds., *Canada's Entrepreneurs: From the Fur Trade to the 1929 Stock Market Crash: Portraits from the Dictionary of Canadian Biography* (Toronto: University of Toronto Press, 2011); and David Wilson, "The *Dictionary of Canadian Biography* and the Irish Diaspora," in *'True Biographies of Nations?': The Cultural Journeys of Dictionaries of*

National Biography, ed. Karen Fox (Canberra: Australian National University Press, 2019), 209–24.

35 Dictionary of Canadian Biography, "Women in the Dictionary of Canadian Biography," http://www.biographi.ca/en/theme_women.html.

36 Francess Halpenny, "Expectations of Biography," in *Boswell's Children: The Art of the Biographer*, ed. R.B. Fleming (Toronto: Dundurn, 1992), 23.

37 Goldwin French, Peter Oliver, and Jeanne Beck, "The Ontario Historical Studies Series," in David Gagan, *Hopeful Travellers: Families, Land, and Social Change in Mid-Victorian Peel County, Canada West* (Toronto: University of Toronto Press, 1981), xv.

38 Thomas Flanagan, *Louis 'David' Riel: Prophet of the New World* (Toronto: University of Toronto Press, 1979); Hugh Dempsey, *Crowfoot: Chief of the Blackfeet* (Edmonton, AB: Hurtig, 1972); Dempsey, *Red Crow, Warrior Chief* (Saskatoon, SK: Western Producer Prairie Books, 1980); Dempsey, *Big Bear: The End of Freedom* (Vancouver: Douglas and McIntyre, 1984); and Murray Dobbin, *The One-and-a-Half Men: The Story of Jim Brady and Malcolm Norris, Métis Patriots of the Twentieth Century* (Vancouver: New Star Books, 1981).

39 H. Blair Neatby, "'Character and Circumstance': Political Biography in the 1990s," *Acadiensis* 22, 2 (1993): 154.

40 English, *Shadow of Heaven*; and English, *The Worldly Years*. Both volumes were awarded the John A. Macdonald Prize of the Canadian Historical Association, the Canadian Author's Association Prize for best nonfiction book in Canada, and the Dafoe Prize for best Canadian book on Canadian affairs, and both were finalists for the Trillium Prize and the Lionel Gelber Prize.

41 Perry and Lewis, "Introductory Remarks: Special Issue on 'The Biographical (Re)Turn,'" 3. See, for example, Adele Perry's *Colonial Relations: The Douglas-Connolly Family and the Nineteenth-Century Imperial World* (Cambridge: Cambridge University Press, 2015).

42 Lucy Riall, "The Shallow End of History? The Substance and Future of Political Biography," *Journal of Interdisciplinary History* 40, 3 (2010): 381.

43 Peter B. Waite, "Invading Privacies: Biography as History," *Dalhousie Review* 69, 4 (1990): 493.

44 Elsbeth Heaman, "Character versus Circumstance in Recent Canadian Historical Biography," *Journal of Canadian Studies* 43, 3 (2009): 234.

45 For reflections on these changes, see Ian McKay, "The Liberal Order Framework: A Prospectus for a Reconnaissance of Canadian History," *Canadian Historical Review* 81, 4 (2000): 616–78; Larry A. Glassford, "The Evolution of 'New Political History' in English-Canadian Historiography: From Cliometrics to Cliodiversity," *American Review of Canadian Studies* 32, 3 (2002): 347–67; Michel Ducharme and Jean-François Constant, eds., *Liberalism and Hegemony: Debating the Canadian Liberal Revolution* (Toronto: University of Toronto Press, 2009); Kevin Anderson, "Canadian Political History and Ideas: Intersections and Influences," *History Compass* 12, 5 (2014): 444–54; and Matthew Hayday, Mary-Ellen Kelm, and Tina Loo, eds., "From Politics to the Political: Historical Perspectives on the New Canadian Political History," special issue of the *Canadian Historical Review* 100, 4 (2019): 564–653.

46 Riall, "Shallow End of History?" 396.

47 Robert I. Rotberg, "Biography and Historiography: Mutual Evidentiary and Interdisciplinary Considerations," *Journal of Interdisciplinary History* 40, 3 (2010): 306. On the persistence of narrative forms and content in Canadian political biography, see also Neatby, "Character and Circumstance," 154.

48 English, *Shadow of Heaven,* ix-x.

49 On reinvention rather than reconstruction, see Nadel, *Biography: Fiction, Fact and Form,* 8.

50 Ged Martin, "Foreword: Biography and History," in *Boswell's Children: The Art of the Biographer,* ed. R.B. Fleming (Toronto: Dundurn, 1992), xiv.

51 On the ongoing vitality of biography, see Paula Backscheider, *Reflections on Biography* (Oxford: Oxford University Press, 1999); Nigel Hamilton, *Biography: A Brief History* (Cambridge, MA: Harvard University Press, 2007); and Hans Renders and David Veltman, eds., *Different Lives: Global Perspectives on Biography in Public Cultures and Societies* (Leiden, Netherlands: Brill, 2020).

52 See, for example, Jo Burr Margadant, ed., *The New Biography: Performing Femininity in Nineteenth-Century France* (Berkeley: University of California Press, 2000); Charlotte Gray, "The New Biography," *Queen's Quarterly* 108, 2 (2001): 242–57; Laura Marcus, "The Newness of the 'New Biography': Biographical Theory and Practice in the Early Twentieth Century," in *Mapping Lives: The Uses of Biography,* ed. Peter France and William St. Clair (New York: Oxford University Press, 2002), 193–218; and Lois Banner, "AHR Roundtable: Biography as History," *American Historical Review* 114, 3 (2009): 579–86.

53 Perry, "Beyond Biography, Beyond Canada," 321.

54 The most memorable include George Radwanski, *Trudeau* (Toronto: Macmillan, 1978); Richard Gwyn, *The Northern Magus: Pierre Trudeau and Canadians* (Toronto: McClelland and Stewart, 1981); and Stephen Clarkson and Christina McCall, *Trudeau and Our Times,* 2 vols. (Toronto: McClelland and Stewart, 1990–1994) .

55 Pierre Elliott Trudeau, *Memoirs* (Toronto: McClelland and Stewart, 1993). See also Thomas S. Axworthy and Pierre Elliott Trudeau, eds., *Towards a Just Society: The Trudeau Years* (Toronto: Viking, 1990); Ivan Head and Trudeau, *The Canadian Way: Shaping Canada's Foreign Policy, 1968–1984* (Toronto: McClelland and Stewart, 1995); and Trudeau, *Against the Current: Selected Writings, 1939–1996,* ed. Gérard Pelletier (Toronto: McClelland and Stewart, 1996).

56 Examples in English include Andrew Cohen and J.L. Granatstein, eds., *Trudeau's Shadow: The Life and Legacy of Pierre Elliott Trudeau* (Toronto: Vintage Canada, 1998); Ramsay Cook, *Teeth of Time: Remembering Pierre Elliott Trudeau* (Montreal/Kingston: McGill-Queen's University Press, 2006); Max Nemni and Monique Nemni, *Young Trudeau: Son of Quebec, Father of Canada, 1919–1944,* trans. William Johnson (Toronto: McClelland and Stewart, 2006); Nemni and Nemni, *Trudeau Transformed: The Shaping of a Statesman, 1944–1965* (Toronto: McClelland and Stewart, 2011); Nino Ricci, *Extraordinary Canadians: Pierre Elliott Trudeau* (Toronto: Penguin Canada, 2009); Bob Plamondon, *The Truth about Trudeau* (Ottawa: Great River Media, 2013); and Allen Mills, *Citizen Trudeau: An Intellectual Biography, 1944–1965* (Don Mills, ON:

Oxford University Press, 2016). More specialized studies include John English, Richard Gwyn, and P. Whitney Lackenbauer, eds., *The Hidden Pierre Elliott Trudeau: The Faith behind the Politics* (Ottawa: Novalis, 2004); Paul Litt, *Trudeaumania* (Vancouver: UBC Press, 2016); Robert Wright, *Trudeaumania: The Rise to Power of Pierre Elliott Trudeau* (Toronto: HarperCollins, 2016); and Christo Aivalis, *The Constant Liberal: Pierre Trudeau, Organized Labour, and the Canadian Social Democratic Left* (Vancouver: UBC Press, 2018).

57 English, *Citizen of the World*, 3.

58 See Kurt Heinrich, "Just Watch Me: Book Review," Active History.ca, http://activehistory.ca/book-reviews/review-5/.

59 English, *Citizen of the World*, 3.

60 William Johnson, "Review: Just Watch Me," *Globe and Mail*, 30 October 2009.

61 The first volume, *Citizen of the World* (2006), won the University of British Columbia Canadian Biography Prize for best Canadian biography, the Amazon.ca award for best biography, and the Dafoe Prize. The second volume, *Just Watch Me*, won the 2009 Shaughnessy Cohen Prize for Political Writing. Both volumes were also shortlisted for the Governor General's Non-Fiction Literary Award and the Charles Taylor Prize for Literary Non-Fiction.

62 Berger, *Writing of Canadian History*, 222.

63 See R.B. Fleming, "The Two Solitudes of History and Biography," in *Boswell's Children: The Art of the Biographer*, ed. R.B. Fleming (Toronto: Dundurn, 1992), 259–66.

64 David Nasaw, "AHR Roundtable Historians and Biography: Introduction," *American Historical Review* 114, 3 (2009): 574.

65 John English and Robert Bothwell, foreword to *The Good Fight: Marcel Cadieux and Canadian Diplomacy*, by Brendan Kelly (Vancouver: UBC Press, 2019), ix.

66 Recent calls on Canadian historians to more deliberately embrace global and transnational turns, critically examine race and gender in foreign affairs, and carefully parse the myriad domestic political, cultural, and socioeconomic drivers behind foreign policy also invite critical studies that engage with the views of Canadian decision makers and diplomats abroad. See, for example, Laura Madokoro, Francine McKenzie, and David Meren, eds., *Dominion of Race: Rethinking Canada's International History* (Vancouver: UBC Press, 2017); and Asa McKercher and Philip Van Huizen, eds., *Undiplomatic History: The New Study of Canada and the World* (Montreal/Kingston: McGill-Queen's University Press, 2019). David Meren's call for more complex narratives that expose Canada's complicity in British and American imperialism, engage in critical revisionism, and move beyond "romanticized notions of Canada's international action," also encourages re-engagement, and potential reappraisal, of the diplomatic memoirs discussed by Bothwell and Hillmer in Chapter 1. Meren, "The Tragedies of Canadian International History," *Canadian Historical Review* 96, 4 (2015): 534–66. See also the responses in the same issue: John English, "The Tragedies of Canadian International History: A Comment," *Canadian Historical Review* 96, 4 (2015): 567–75; Adam Chapnick, "Confessions of a Teacher, and Historian, of Canadian Diplomacy,"

Canadian Historical Review 96, 4 (2015): 576–82; and Dominique Marshall, "Réponse à 'The Tragedies of Canadian International History' : un autre survol historiographique," *Canadian Historical Review* 96, 4 (2015): 583–89.

67 Brendan Kelly, "'Six mois à Hanoi': Marcel Cadieux, Canada, and the International Commission for Supervision and Control in Vietnam, 1954–5," *Canadian Historical Review* 99, 3 (2018): 397.

68 For more on this theme, see Ryan Touhey, *Conflicting Visions: Canada and India in the Cold War World, 1946–76* (Vancouver: UBC Press, 2015).

69 Waite, "Invading Privacies," 494.

70 Stanley Fish, "Just Published: Minutiae without Meaning," *New York Times*, 7 September 1999, A23.

CHAPTER 1

CANADA'S DIPLOMATIC AUTOBIOGRAPHERS AND THE BURDEN OF HISTORY, 1928–84

Robert Bothwell and Norman Hillmer

Autobiography may have begun in Neolithic pictographs, or as a self-glorifying mammoth-slaying tale by the fire. The pharaonic statues at Abu Simbel are a kind of autobiography – huge, impressive, eternal. Most of us, though, understand autobiography to be a literate discipline. In the century before the birth of Christ, we find Julius Caesar shaping memoir into a propaganda tool to further his political career. By classical times, "lives lived" were a well-established form of sententiousness, moral fables in biographical guise. Whatever the motive, there has always been what we could call "active autobiography," a kind of animal spirits, an irrepressible human force. That is how Saint Augustine saw it, and used it, in his *Confessions* to encourage his audience to believe that more was to come. Diaries, the first drafts of autobiography, go deeper, or ought to. They act, like memoirs, as self-promotion, self-justification, or self-explanation – sometimes all three – but they have the advantage of not having travelled through the filter of too much reflection. They give the immediacy of the first-hand, not the careful reshaping of a life to lend it purpose and coherence. We take heart from how much human memorialization has survived: Samuel Pepys's diary or the letters of Madame de Sévigné; the worthy and the unworthy; the profound and the trivial; the truth tellers, the liars, and the fantasists.

Our tribute to John English investigates the contribution of autobiography to the understanding of Canada's international history, the field that he has illuminated. English's biographies of Lester B. Pearson and Pierre

Elliott Trudeau suggest a chronology – from 1928, when Pearson entered the Department of External Affairs, to 1984, when Trudeau took his walk in the snow, the night before he announced his retirement as prime minister. We talk about memoirs and their raw materials, with occasional biographical asides. In doing so, we trace a rich literature of recollection, but one dominated by English Canadian men of senior rank and function writing diplomatically about their pasts. For less discretion, we turn to an important grouping of diaries that have more forthright stories to tell. "Nothing," the British author Alan Bennett says of his diary when it is at its most truthful, "is ever quite so bad that one can't write it down or so shameful either."[1]

Canada's diplomacy from 1928 into the Second World War belonged mostly to William Lyon Mackenzie King and his foreign policy partner, O.D. Skelton. Both King and Skelton left diaries. Skelton's diary is sparse. King's is anything but, page after page tumbling out on almost every day for more than a half-century. The Skelton journal, begun when he was in university but not taken up again until he thought himself on the cusp of history when he teamed up with King in the early 1920s, has been published in part by the Champlain Society.[2] Skelton's diary discloses a man intent on carving out a reputation for his country and himself, as if one could not be distinguished from the other. It also shines crucial light on the mercurial Prime Minister R.B. Bennett's leadership from 1930 to 1935, because King was not always in power – it just seemed that way. King's diary has appeared in different formats and is online and searchable.[3] The relentless daily detail, larded with the leader's insecurities, is stultifying, but the reporting of events is usually reliable. There is nothing like it as a record of Canada's world from the 1920s to the 1940s.

Britain and the British Empire are everywhere in the King and Skelton diaries, as they once were in the lives of so many Canadians. Often there is admiration. More often there is resistance. Alone with their thoughts, the prime minister and the adviser warned London not to tread on them or their Canada. King did not quite mean it. Skelton did, with a vengeance. The two men entered the Second World War in 1939 together and apart. Skelton was angry at what he thought was Canada's and King's too-easy rush to Britain's side, a jettisoning of autonomy in the name of loyalty. King was determined to stand for Anglo-Canadian values of democracy and human rights and to respect the views of those who did not feel his fervour. He reflected where Canada was, poised between an old empire and a new world. Skelton knew where Canadians were going: toward an independent country and foreign policy in a North America that was Canada's inevitable destiny.

Raoul Dandurand's autobiography, originally written for his grandchildren and published posthumously, occupies the nationalist ground that Skelton was busily tilling. He counted Dandurand as a staunch anti-imperialist ally, "really Canadian," and "opposed to any cooperation whatever" with the British.[4] Dandurand's memoirs underline the point. Canadians could not be forever "'colonials,' toujours en tutelle"; he refused "d'être un Canadien de seconde zone."[5] A senator appointed by Prime Minister Sir Wilfrid Laurier at the end of the nineteenth century, Dandurand was the face of the Liberal government at the League of Nations in the interwar years. He was elected president of the League Assembly in 1925 and was a factor in Canada's successful bid for a three-year seat on the Council in 1927. He was inclined to do the bidding of his suspicious prime minister, memorably pointing out that the risks undertaken by League members were not equal: Canadians lived "in a fire-proof house, far from inflammable materials."[6] Yet Dandurand cared deeply about the League. His memoirs fail to mention the fireproof house speech, which was almost certainly written by Skelton. Instead, Dandurand catalogues his efforts to foster international cooperation in the name of collective security, the protection of European minority rights, and the Permanent Court of International Justice.[7] Dandurand was never in the front rank of Canadian politicians. He did not have the full confidence of King, or the influence in cabinet wielded by Ernest Lapointe and Louis St. Laurent. But Lapointe and St. Laurent did not write their memoirs. Thin and haphazardly edited though they are, Dandurand's are the only published reminiscences of a francophone Quebec politician on the federal level in the Mackenzie King era.

Unlike Dandurand, but like most English Canadians, Vincent Massey divided his patriotisms. He split his allegiances between his native Canada and a beloved Britain, where he served as high commissioner at Canada House in wartime London. From the vantage point of Charles Ritchie's position as Massey's private secretary, the young diplomat saw that his chief had his legacy on the brain. Massey was worried that the National Archives in Ottawa might not have reports from the High Commission on what he called the greatest war in history, but he censored anything that was critical of England or might weaken resolve on Canada's home front. He could not tell the truth, even with his diary in front of him.[8]

"Some day," Ritchie wrote perceptively in his own diary, Massey would "publish his memoirs. In fact he is looking forward to doing so – but they will be composed in the prose he loves best – that of a *Times* leading article. It is a pity, because he has in conversation the vivacity of phrase to produce a vivid, if superficial, account of the London scene. Alas, his reverence is too much for him."[9] The eventual Massey memoir,[10] published in 1963, was as Ritchie expected. Written de haut en bas, moderately repellent but unquestionably useful, the volume includes long sections on Massey's service as the first Canadian diplomatic representative in the United States and on his years as high commissioner to Great Britain from 1935 to 1946. It was completed with the help of a smooth-writing professor, James Eayrs, but it has none of his flair. For Massey's many critics, the autobiography reinforced the image that he built up while he was the country's first Canadian governor general: that of a dried-up relic of bygone days, an imperial Canadian in a place that no longer valued the empire. Biographer Claude Bissell declared that Massey's autobiography "struggles for life in an atmosphere of pallid remoteness."[11]

Ritchie mistook Massey's diary, which was frequently little more than a list of appointments, for a confessional. Ritchie's own diary was just that, at one with his search for an intensity of experience that Massey might aspire to but could not express and that Ritchie saw always on the horizon: to seize life before it was too late; to escape the arid, the false, and the conventional in the drudgery of diplomacy, a profession he deeply respected, making the diary's flights of passion and poetry all the more of a release. Ritchie's diplomatic colleagues, or some of them, were unimpressed. When he was Canada's permanent representative to the United Nations, Britain's UN delegation dismissed him as "something of a dilettante, who, though he 'gets around' socially a great deal, lacks drive and determination."[12]

Ritchie's thoughts were for him alone, he always said. But there are hints in the diary that he was unwilling to see all his efforts disappear before they were opened up to the light of day.[13] He was unable, though he threatened it, to destroy his handwritten jottings. Soon enough (in his phrase) he went "public, or partly public,"[14] in four rapturously received published volumes, the frustrated novelist in him unable to leave the diaries exactly as he had written them. Things are left out, things are put in. The diary flirts with fiction.

Ritchie could empathize with Massey's British bias.[15] He grew up not just a Nova Scotian, but also a product of Halifax society, closer geographically to Britain than other Canadians and closer spiritually than other Nova Scotians. He learned from his family's colonial history to be half in one place, half in another,[16] and in his various guises as diplomat, lover, bon vivant, and diarist, he lived ambivalently. Ritchie said that he approached England as an outsider-insider who knew the country instinctively but was not an Englishman.[17] His Second World War sympathies lay there, not with the Americans who were about to take over the world, yet Ritchie maintained distance. He knew that many English Canadians thought of Britain as their mother country, but he observed that their strong feelings were seldom reciprocated. Ritchie wrote in 1941 that the English had a genius for making use of people – people like Canadians.[18]

Lester Pearson and Hugh Keenleyside joined Ritchie in keeping diaries and publishing informative depictions of the Department of External Affairs in the 1930s and 1940s.[19] They remembered a small place: ramshackle, writerly, full of professors and near professors. Keenleyside was one of the professors. He freighted his weighty two-volume autobiography with footnotes. Keenleyside never cracked External's inner circle. He did not qualify as one of J.L. Granatstein's Ottawa men.[20] He was not in the Skeltonian mould of relaxed intellectualism; he was pious and stiff, and his principled stand on behalf of fair treatment of the Canadian Japanese in the Second World War made him toxic to Mackenzie King. Keenleyside's autobiography can hardly contain its bitterness that Norman Robertson, an incompetent administrator without personal empathy, reigned over External Affairs after the loss of Skelton in 1941.[21]

Pearson also taught briefly at the University of Toronto, but he had the lightest of touch with people and prose. The parts of his three-volume memoir that he was able to finish before he died are the self-assured reminiscences of a global man who gave his name to Canada's post–Second

World War foreign policy successes and topped them off with the prime ministership – ever upward the Pearsonian trajectory. The first volume of his memoirs, the only one with his full stamp on it, is graceful, fluent, funny, and as elusive as the man himself. There is little in the slim posthumous memoirs of Pearson's colleague Arnold Heeney, but one note from his personal journal is telling. Pearson was "a deep one whose secret self very few, if any, can know."[22] John English points out that Pearson did not tell all in his autobiography, and he did not intend to tell all.[23] Contrast the way that Pearson's memoirs breeze over the choice of Robertson, not Pearson, to succeed Skelton as undersecretary of state for external affairs in 1941 with English's detailed version of how devastated Pearson was by the decision.[24] Nor, more importantly, was the evolution of Pearsonian internationalism as straightforward as the memoirs indicate. The trajectory did not always lead upwards.

Pearson had allies in keeping his (and their) flame burning. Like Pearson, his fellow diplomats Escott Reid, George Ignatieff, and John W. Holmes drew a sharp line between the period before the Second World War and the 1940s and 1950s – between Skeltonism and Pearsonianism. Norman Hillmer's biography of Skelton attempts to make the opposite case, that the long-lasting deputy minister of external affairs was a covert internationalist who looked to the day when Canada would do the world's work.[25] The transition from liberal nationalism to liberal internationalism was not seamless, but there was a logic to it.

That is not the view of the memoirists. Ignatieff and Reid invoke a golden age of Canadian activist internationalism. "For the first time," Ignatieff writes of the arrival of Pearson and Prime Minister Louis St. Laurent at the summit of government, "there was a sense of mission in our foreign policy, a conviction that, as a middle-sized power with a good deal of economic clout and international prestige, Canada had both an obligation and the ability to act as an architect of peaceful solutions to intractable problems."[26] Reid dates his golden age earlier, conveniently coinciding with his years in Ottawa and Washington[27] and boasting of Canada's membership in "an inner group of ... countries which moulded the shape of the future." The idea of Canada as "a nation with a mission," he insists, was a "widely held belief" that doubled as "a sustaining myth," defining Canadians as a people and strengthening "our will to endure."[28]

The "young Lochinvar who came out of the North ... to put the world right" was how John Holmes characterized golden age thinking.[29] He claimed to his friends that he was indulging in whimsy, and his narratives in *The Shaping of Peace, 1943–1957* volumes suggest that he was, because no one understood the "ruthless pragmatism" of Pearsonian diplomacy better than Holmes did.[30] But his colourful allusion to Sir Walter Scott's romantic warrior captures the view of many of the External Affairs men who wrote about the 1940s and 1950s.[31]

As full of words outside External Affairs as he was in it, Reid in retirement created a bookshelf all of his own: four volumes that centre on the high points of his diplomatic career and an autobiography, titled unrepentantly *Radical Mandarin*.[32] All five are referenced in the style of a professional historian and purport to be scholarship. In a way they are, but not masked is the loud voice of a crusader – for the United Nations, NATO, and the Commonwealth, and ultimately for a more ordered and moral world. Reid knew that he was an imperfect diplomatic messenger, too demanding, too arrogant, too (in the words of Pearson in his memoirs) single-mindedly intense.[33] The reader sees the ferocious work ethic and clarity of written expression that made him invaluable to Pearson, but also the lack of perspective and judgment that kept him from ever being fully trusted and from succeeding Robertson and Pearson as the civil service head of the Department of External Affairs.

John Holmes, in *The Shaping of Peace,* ventures further in an effort to treat international history as a scholar would. He claims that he is not writing a memoir, but the years covered by the book again fit almost precisely with the author's service in the Department of External Affairs. They are indelibly marked by his commitment to the Pearson project. Holmes rebuffs Reid. The quality of Canada's diplomacy, Holmes declares, "such as it was, is to be found not in the proposing of grand designs but in the responses, in constructive amendments and imaginative formulas, in the exploiting of occasions, and in the insistence, usually in company, on certain basic principles."[34] "Such as it was"; "in the responses"; "usually in company": how Pearsonian those phrases.

In the thirty years that stretched from King's 1920s to Pearson's 1950s, the world changed more than Canada did. The British Empire faltered, the United States loomed, a Cold War came, and the diplomatic dangers and the opportunities for Canada were amplified. But the premium remained on the familiar verities of balance, brokerage, and improvisation.[35] Pragmatism ruled the day, as it did during the 1956 Suez Crisis.[36] In his pioneering analysis of the early Cold War, John English wrote that "Canadian diplomats were cautious, careful in their actions, and hewed closer to the approach followed by Prime Minister W.L. Mackenzie King in the 1930s than they later confessed."[37] One who did confess it was Charles Ritchie, who confided to his diary in 1953 that policy-making was "the tortuous approach to an ill-defined objective. All-out decisions, unqualified statements, irreconcilable antagonisms are foreign to my nature and my training. In these ways I reflect my political masters, the inheritors of Mackenzie King, and I am fitted to work with them."[38]

If the golden age does not gleam still under the microscope of historians,[39] Canada's reputation and influence were nonetheless at their apogee from the late 1940s to the mid-1950s. The government of the day, under Louis St. Laurent, was unusually competent and effective, its standing at home and abroad reflecting Canada's increased economic strength and a steadily rising standard of living. St. Laurent's papers were culled after his electoral defeat in 1957, so that a full reconstruction of his life has been and remains a very doubtful proposition. Dale Thomson's biography of St. Laurent perhaps does the best it can with the limited resources at his disposal.[40]

Among the St. Laurent ministers, few bequeathed their memoirs to posterity. Pearson kept a sporadic diary that was very useful to the team that finished his memoirs after his death. Jimmy Gardiner, the minister of agriculture, who occasionally conducted his own eccentric foreign agricultural policy, recorded a series of interviews after the electorate retired him. These are located at the Glenbow Museum Archives in Calgary.[41] Brooke Claxton, the long-serving minister of national defence, penned a giant memoir in the last months of his life, after being diagnosed with cancer.[42] Claxton has a nice turn of phrase and a sardonic wit. He describes Mackenzie King's interference in the St. Laurent-Pearson policy on Korea in 1947 as the last bellows of the leader of the herd before he cashed in his cheques. A sergeant major in the First World War, Claxton retained a certain skepticism where officers and especially generals were concerned, though he kept his most piercing shafts for the American variant, most of whom he considered to be professional liars. Claxton also lived, and lives today, through the abundant correspondence that flowed daily from the minister to his friends outside the capital. His writings have the stamp of authenticity and the snap of authority, so unlike the dreadful flow of treacle emitted by ministerial offices today – the twaddle of Twitter. Reading Claxton, one regrets the book that never was.

Other ministers, longer-lived, left a printed impression in a multiplicity of memoirs. There was Pearson, of course, who formed his own cabinets as prime minister from 1963 to 1968, and there was his erstwhile student, younger cabinet colleague and leadership rival, Paul Martin. St. Laurent's youngest minister, Paul Hellyer, played a prominent part in the Pearson government, reorganizing the armed forces, a process he recounts in a less than scintillating memoir.[43] It cannot be ignored, but by the end of this not very long book one wishes it could be. Hellyer may well have been the most prolific of politician-authors, with thirteen books at last count, and he certainly holds the record for membership in the most political parties, some of which he invented himself.

And there was the joyously political Jack Pickersgill. "Jack thought St. Laurent was his father," one of St. Laurent's staff waspishly commented.[44] It suited Pickersgill for his eventual role as one of St. Laurent's few biographers. Trained as a historian, and briefly a teaching one too, he improved his status and his salary by joining the Department of External Affairs in the 1930s, where Undersecretary Skelton wisely seconded him to Mackenzie King's small office. According to Pickersgill, Skelton advised him that he was to do whatever the prime minister wanted, including what by any standard were political functions, but to be careful not to allow it to become public. In other words, Pickersgill should do what Skelton had done: obliterate the line between the civil service and partisan service to the prime minister. Pickersgill eventually became clerk of the Privy Council under King's successor, St. Laurent, and made an easy transition to his cabinet, becoming secretary of state and then minister of citizenship and immigration. As a public servant and as a junior minister, he was much more. "Clear it with Jack" was the watchword around Ottawa, if petitioners were seeking to know what the prime minister could do, would do, or was willing to do.[45]

Pickersgill soldiered on in Opposition after John Diefenbaker became prime minister in 1957 and in the Pearson cabinet as secretary of state and government leader in the House of Commons and then as minister of transport. The Opposition years were notable because of Pickersgill's ability to infuriate Diefenbaker, who gave as good as he got. Pickersgill, said Diefenbaker, was the only member of the House of Commons "I've known who could strut sitting down."[46] In their later years, they lived in houses close by in Rockcliffe Park on the edge of Ottawa. Pickersgill, Scotch in hand, gazed out the window to observe his rival's daily promenades with his dog, Happy. Poor creature, Pick would say, meaning the dog.

Pickersgill found that being in Opposition was financially challenging, and to make money, he edited four volumes of extracts from Mackenzie King's diary.[47] He had special access to the King Papers and thus to the diary in its original form, as one of the former prime minister's literary executors. Pickersgill was aware that the disposition of the diary had become a matter of some public controversy, and he hoped to allay criticism that the keepers of King's memory were not sharing his private thoughts. The first book of diary entries, appearing in 1960, was carefully curated to protect those who were innocent and some who were not. Pickersgill's further volumes were more detailed and less reticent, but they only whetted appetites, scholarly and otherwise, for further revelations. The pressure built to open the whole diary, a demand with which Pickersgill and King's official biographer, Blair Neatby, were sympathetic. In 1971, Pickersgill and his executor colleagues decided that the (almost) complete diary would be released to the public, although not all at once.[48] Once that process was completed in 1980, the Pickersgill volumes became obsolete, although they do contain the odd comment or explanation that makes them useful as the testimony of someone who witnessed the events that King was relating in his diary.

Released by retirement and equipped with an office in downtown Ottawa thanks to the largesse of a well-endowed friend or friends, Pickersgill fashioned the aptly titled *My Years with Louis St. Laurent*. Anyone seeking insight into St. Laurent's character and behaviour from a very close eyewitness should start, but not stop, with this book.[49] Later, fully retired and with his wife Margaret as his typist, Pickersgill wrote his own memoir, *Seeing Canada Whole*, which takes a young Canadian from rural Manitoba to Oxford University.[50] Oxford made an impression that was never wholly lost, but which did not interfere with Pickersgill's Canadianism – a trait that attracted him to St. Laurent, whose nationalist feelings he shared.

The Liberals were in power most of the time from 1935 to 1984. They and their connections necessarily predominate and make it difficult to achieve balance in assessing the monuments of Canada's foreign policy past. However, the Conservative John G. Diefenbaker was prime minister for just short of six years, and he made himself hard to forget, then and later. He signed off with three books of autobiography,[51] and in his will he left money to supply school libraries across Canada with a set. Diefenbaker was, notably, defiantly unilingual in English, and his memoirs, *One Canada,* preached his monochromatic if polysyllabic political vision to a country that had already rejected it. We cannot say whether francophone schools received the Diefenbaker bequest but if they did, it is not hard to imagine their trajectory en route to the pulping machine.

Diefenbaker is remembered for his foreign policy mishaps in dealing with the British and the Americans and, though there were some bright spots, he is not usually thought to have revealed a master touch when it came to dealing with other countries. His literary output was evidently insufficient to secure his fame, so much so that a later Conservative foreign minister renamed one of his department's Sussex Drive structures – once Ottawa's city hall – the John G. Diefenbaker Building, supplementing the existing and better-known Lester B. Pearson Building. They are incongruous twins architecturally, but also spiritually. In death as in life, Diefenbaker and Pearson glare at one another, though at a safe distance. The Rideau River flows between them.

Despite Diefenbaker's autobiographical efforts, which succeeded only in producing self-caricature, there is more to our first-hand knowledge of his foreign policy courtesy of Basil Robinson, the Department of External Affairs assistant in Diefenbaker's office. Robinson acted as the uneasy but skilled liaison between his department and the prime minister, while soothing his foreign adversaries – some of them former friends – or, if necessary, being the first recipient of their resentments. No man is a hero to his valet, it is said, and without seeking in the least to put Robinson into the valet category, he certainly did not think Diefenbaker a hero. Robinson's is a humane and sympathetic account,[52] but the effect is rather like a narrator inserted into a road show of *Macbeth*, periodically turning to the audience to explain and comment on the Scottish king's odd behaviour.

The thick two-volume memoir of Donald Fleming, Diefenbaker's finance minister, is surely the most pompous ever written by a Canadian politician – he informs us that he felt a "compelling duty" to commit autobiography – and he contributes little to an understanding of diplomacy where Robinson contributes so much. Fleming, however, does reinforce the common assessment of Diefenbaker's leadership as increasingly petulant, weak, and undisciplined.[53]

Facing Diefenbaker across the floor of the House of Commons, in Opposition, and while Pearson governed, was the publicly unflappable Paul Martin. It was believed that Martin could make a speech on anything, and especially in the Diefenbaker years he did. Martin's name was a byword for the old-fashioned politician, orotund and unstoppable, but the mannerism masked a breadth of knowledge and experience and a perceptive mind. For the most part, Martin kept his wit at home. Together, Martin and Pearson dominated the high policy of Canada's external affairs in the middle 1960s, parallel, compatible, but not entirely comfortable one with the other.

Foreign minister for five years, from 1963 to 1968, Martin had plenty to tell in his memoirs, based on his papers and on interviews done with him during his career, which stretched from the League of Nations through the United Nations, and from student life at Cambridge and in Geneva to diplomatic service as Canadian high commissioner in London.[54] His two-volume autobiography is not without value or perception or extensive coverage of the issues, in part because Martin engaged a talented historian, William Young, to assist him. Yet it does demonstrate that a 1,198-page memoir is too long for the capacity or interest of even professional students of Canadian foreign affairs. At the High Commission in London, Martin kept a diary that he would occasionally read to his guests before dinner at his official residence. Published in an edited form many years later,[55] the diary is a testament to the author's earnestness and intelligence. He was a well-read man who always claimed that people got him and Pearson wrong: Martin, who had a large and diverse library, was the intellectual, Pearson the consummate pol.

Another angle on Paul Martin is provided by the quasi-diary of Marcel Cadieux, the external affairs undersecretary during the Martin era. Cadieux was the second francophone to become the professional head of the department. He took the term "professional" very seriously, even fanatically. He had a combustible personality that he expressed in dictation to his secretary, producing a volatile set of memoranda – explosions in prose, so to speak. Martin was in Cadieux's line of fire and unconsciously made the problem worse by producing regular verbal bromides. "Une autre perle pour la collection," Cadieux would fulminate.[56] Exaggerated and extravagant, Cadieux's perceptions were not always or even mostly wrong, and they highlight the sometimes-fraught relationship between a minister and his deputy. Cadieux's diplomatic career is evidence that francophone civil servants were sometimes able to make their mark in Ottawa in the days before official bilingualism.[57] The celebrated "mandarin" class was not exclusively anglophone.[58]

Cadieux was an indispensable player in the Canadian government's riposte to Quebec separatism in the 1960s. A passionate federalist, and a fervent believer in a bilingual country, Cadieux devised the winning strategy to maintain Ottawa's authority over foreign relations, to the dismay of Claude Morin, his Quebec counterpart and antagonist. Morin is the author of frequent contemplations about Ottawa's foreign policy from someone who engaged in it from outside. His *L'art de l'impossible* is a representation of Quebec's international initiatives from 1960 to 1971 that is autobiographical history, eagerly promoting Morin's part in advancing the province's various forays into diplomacy while overdoing his and his government's achievements and downplaying (or ignoring) the failures. Morin later wrote a formal memoir, repeating his almost limitless praise of self.[59]

Mitchell Sharp, Pearson's minister of trade and commerce and minister of finance, was careful and compact in his words. Sharp had been an early casualty of John Diefenbaker's marked distrust of senior civil servants, the "Pearsonalities" who had served King and St. Laurent. By 1957, Sharp was a twenty-year veteran of the civil service, but no matter. Fired rapidly by Diefenbaker, Sharp took a variety of corporate appointments and on the side directed the Kingston Conference of 1960, which rejuvenated the Liberals. As a deputy minister, Sharp represented Canada at international trade talks, and his memoirs[60] contain one of the few personal accounts of what Canada said and did in this sector, since Canada's trade negotiators have generally not written about the secrets of their craft.[61] This much is clear: there is a Canadian negotiating style, appealing to facts, rules, and rationality. It was on duty in the Canada-US trade negotiations of the 1980s and 1990s, and again in the North American Free Trade Agreement negotiations with President Donald Trump's America.

As finance minister, Sharp dealt with the international economic file, but it receives only limited treatment in his autobiography. His finance department's main concerns were internal. He also has relatively little to say about his contentious relationship with Walter Gordon, who preceded him in the finance portfolio. They clashed over Gordon's preoccupation with the presence of foreign-owned (especially American) firms in Canada. Gordon believed that the government had to act to limit new foreign investment and even to encourage the foreign owners to sell some of their holdings to Canadians. In Sharp's words, the return of the Canadian economy to Canadian control was for Gordon the acid test of national sovereignty. Sharp's reminiscences deliver his response with understatement: "I found this far too narrow a focus within which to judge policy."[62] His point of view prevailed. Gordon's memoirs give more detail about Sharp and are less generous toward his colleague. Gordon presents himself as little more than a colourless, earnest accountant – a logical, dispassionate patriot, concerned only with the future of his country.[63] The authority on Gordonian economic nationalism, Stephen Azzi, rightly concludes that the Gordon autobiography never digs below the surface.[64]

Sharp was one of Pierre Trudeau's most prominent supporters for the Liberal leadership in 1968. He virtually had his choice of portfolios in the Trudeau cabinet and opted for secretary of state for external affairs. He would remain in that office for six years which, as it happened, were eventful, from the halving of Canadian forces stationed with NATO in Europe to the diplomatic recognition of the People's Republic of China and the kidnapping of the British trade commissioner in 1970 to entering into and quickly exiting from a Vietnam supervisory commission. Sharp's autobiographical analysis is cool and reasoned, what one would expect from a senior bureaucrat used to writing policy papers for his ministers. Sharp was one of the very few political memoirists to have been able to take advantage of a rule that gave ex-ministers access to cabinet minutes from their time in office, long before their release to the public. Alarmed bureaucrats quickly worked to close that loophole, so that the service is no longer available.

Allan MacEachen, who succeeded Sharp as external affairs minister in 1974, had been a university professor before he took up politics, basing himself in the Gaelic fragment of Cape Breton Island. MacEachen never forgot his Scottish roots or the people who elected him. He used his office to help establish a Canadian Studies program at the University of Edinburgh, which he inaugurated with a ceilidh, an occasion for singing and dancing and general celebration, much to the astonishment of his Edinburgh hosts. The occasion played well back in Cape Breton. MacEachen in retirement caught the memoir itch, and composed one, but illness prevented him from carrying it through to publication before his death. MacEachen's successor, the Newfoundlander Don Jamieson, died before memoir writing, but he did leave behind a diary, subsequently published in two volumes, *No Place for Fools* and *A World Unto Itself*.[65]

Mark MacGuigan, Trudeau's foreign minister from 1980 to 1982, was another former university professor, in this case of the law. He could be acerbic when it came to his prime minister and skeptical about some of the international fauna he encountered. He might well have been. He had waited twelve long years on the Liberal backbench for his opportunity, which, when it came, surprised him and many others. The suspicion was that Trudeau wanted to be his own foreign minister and chose someone obscure enough to control. If that is true, it was a bad bet. MacGuigan was not without ego. He thought of himself as more dispassionate than Trudeau and less likely to allow his intellect to be overtaken by lesser instincts – an irony, given Trudeau's claim that he above all valued reason over passion. The two men were companions on many voyages, for example to the G7 summits, where the minister tried to rein in his leader's contempt for the American president, Ronald Reagan. "Grade two, grade two," Trudeau snarled of Reagan after a meeting in Bonn.[66] MacGuigan's memoir[67] should be read in conjunction with a very frank interview with him carried out by Robert Bothwell and J.L. Granatstein, as well as their exchanges with Ed Ritchie, J.H. Warren, Basil Robinson, and Allan Gotlieb, deputy ministers all, and other senior diplomats, officials, and politicians, including Michael Pitfield, the most important of Trudeau's clerks of the Privy Council, and Ivan Head, the prime minister's in-house foreign policy adviser. These documents are published in the Bothwell-Granatstein book *Trudeau's World*,[68] and are available in their original form in the Bothwell Papers at the University of Toronto. Interviews, entered into constructively by the parties on both sides, are an undervalued species of autobiography.

Trudeau and Head lived long enough to read the first assessments of their foreign policy, notably *Pirouette*, another Granatstein-Bothwell collaboration.[69] Though neither complained directly, Trudeau and Head did subsequently publish a whole book, *The Canadian Way*, that recasts events and materials from their standpoint. Head-Trudeau (written almost entirely by the former) is smart and soberly argued.[70] *The Canadian Way* and *Pirouette* can be consumed in tandem for a more complete insight into the shape and substance of Canadian foreign policy from 1968 to 1984. *The Canadian Way* asserts that Trudeau was a Pearsonian, but if so, he did not begin that way. The second chapter of the second volume of Pearson's memoirs, written by the former prime minister as he became very ill, is an angry attack at the Trudeau government's assertion that its predecessor had paid insufficient attention to sovereignty and the national interest in its headlong pursuit of internationalist enterprises. Pearson never mentions Trudeau's name in his defiant argument that an enlightened multilateralism goes hand in hand with a spirited nationalism, but the target is unmistakable.[71]

Allan Gotlieb's *Washington Diaries* canvass his remarkable tenure as Canadian ambassador to the United States from 1981 to 1989.[72] Appointed by Trudeau, he was kept in the job by Prime Minister Brian Mulroney. Gotlieb's diary resides in the National Archives in Ottawa, where the complete manuscript awaits eventual excavation by historians. The comparison to Paul Martin's London journal is obvious, but one very striking difference is that Great Britain was a fading power. Martin was reliving or recreating the world that he had known in the 1930s and 1940s, while Washington, in the last stages of the Cold War, was enjoying a political gilded age under Ronald Reagan. Better than any other diarist we know, including American ones, Gotlieb captures the spirit of the era. As an insider on Trudeau's peace mission of 1983–84, and in free trade negotiations with the United States, Gotlieb's chronicle is vivid and essential.

Wives can be the forgotten partners of ambassadors, but not Sondra Gotlieb, whose *Washington Post* columns poked fun at capital life in the

United States and her "pseudo-official" role as the "wife of" Canada's most important diplomat – "I say pseudo-official because I have no job description and I don't fit into any bureaucratic hierarchy. You might say that I'm the unpaid manager of a small hotel."[73] In her Washington memoir, Gotlieb recalls how she rebelled against "becoming that creature so despised by serious women, a full-time hostess," but also how she embraced "putting Canada on the map."[74] Gotlieb and her husband made their embassy a focus of social life – perhaps society more generally – by running an amply endowed salon at their residence. She won praise and profile, and raised hackles along the way, not least when it became widely known that she had slapped her social secretary at the start of one of the Gotliebs' much-noticed dinner parties. We also note two other ambassadorial wives who published their memories: the poet P.K. Page, in her lyrical *Brazilian Journal*, and Landon Pearson, in a collection of letters home from an early 1980s Soviet Union that she concludes was not one-dimensional, but "extraordinary, tormented, complicated, soulful."[75]

Canadian women ambassadors were rarities before the mid-1980s, and none wrote memoirs. Pamela McDougall glimpses at autobiography in her unusually personal 1981 Royal Commission Report on the challenges facing diplomats and their families, where she writes feelingly about the predicaments of women serving their country abroad and her own time as an unmarried ambassador to Poland, without a spouse to support her.[76] Joining the Department of External Affairs in 1949 as a clerk in spite of academic credentials from the University of Toronto and the Sorbonne, McDougall entered the foreign service by competitive examination in 1952, very early days for diplomatic women. She served in Bonn, Saigon, and New Delhi. When she presented her credentials as head of post in Warsaw, in 1968, McDougall became only the second Canadian woman to reach ambassadorial rank. What stories her memoirs could have told.

Canada's diplomatic autobiographers for the period from the 1920s to the 1980s are many, if not varied.[77] Francophones and women are often all but invisible in these works, and the perspective bends hard toward the Eurocentric,[78] but the writers we discuss weave texture, furnish detail, suggest nuance, clarify relationships, and capture body language – the mouths open, the jaws dropping, the unexpected turning point or illogical denouement. Our autobiographers have their limitations, but they take up the burden of history with serious intent. At their best, they write their own words, do their own research, and present themselves and their circumstances in terms that illustrate the human and even the humane. They personalize history. They achieve empathy, what R.G. Collingwood defined as the essence of the historian's art. Yet it is uncertain that the torch has been passed to later generations. Who among us, in our time of ghostwriters and talking points, bloodless bureaucratic prose, and the short attention spans of social media, are the keepers of diaries and the makers of memoirs?

NOTES

1 Alan Bennett, *Keeping On Keeping On* (London: Faber and Faber; Profile Books, 2016), 3.

2 Norman Hillmer, ed., *O.D. Skelton: The Work of the World, 1923–1941* (Montreal/Kingston: McGill-Queen's University Press; Toronto: The Champlain Society, 2013). The originals of the Skelton diaries are located in his papers at Library and Archives Canada (hereafter LAC).

3 "Diaries of Prime Minister William Lyon Mackenzie King," LAC, http://www.bac-lac.gc.ca/eng/discover/politics-government/prime-ministers/william-lyon-mackenzie-king/pages/search.aspx. On the diary's long history, see Christopher Dummitt, *Unbuttoned: A History of Mackenzie King's Secret Life* (Montreal/Kingston: McGill-Queen's University Press, 2017).

4 Skelton, quoted in Hillmer, *O.D. Skelton: A Portrait of Canadian Ambition* (Toronto: University of Toronto Press, 2015), 93, 294.

5 Dandurand, quoted in Marcel Hamelin, ed., *Les Mémoires du Sénateur Raoul Dandurand (1861–1942)* (Quebec: Les Presses de l'Université Laval, 1965), 265, 365.

6 Dandurand, quoted in Hillmer, *Skelton: A Portrait of Canadian Ambition*, 125.

7 Hamelin, *Mémoires du Sénateur Raoul Dandurand*, chaps. 20–22, and 24–26. See also Lorna Lloyd, "Le Sénateur Dandurand, pionnier du règlement pacifique des différends," *Études internationales* 23, 3 (1992): 581–606.

8 Charles Ritchie, *The Siren Years: A Canadian Diplomat Abroad, 1937–1945* (Toronto: Macmillan of Canada, 1974), 100–1. Some of the "truth" that Ritchie sought about the Second World War and the Anglo-Canadian military relationship can be found in Charles G. Power, *A Party Politician: The Memoirs of Chubby Power*, ed. Norman Ward (Toronto: Macmillan of Canada, 1966); and the excellent Maurice A. Pope, *Soldiers and Politicians: The Memoirs of Lt.-Gen. Maurice A. Pope* (Toronto: University of Toronto Press, 1962).

9 Ritchie, *Siren Years*, 101.

10 Vincent Massey, *What's Past Is Prologue: The Memoirs of the Right Honourable Vincent Massey, C.H.* (Toronto: Macmillan of Canada, 1963).

11 Claude Bissell, *The Imperial Canadian: Vincent Massey in Office* (Toronto: University of Toronto Press, 1986), 292. The title was an unfortunate choice for a biographer who wanted his subject to be viewed sympathetically. "Dried up" comes from a review of the book by Robert Fulford, "A Man Blessed with but Little Gift," *Toronto Star*, 13 September 1986.
12 T.W. Keeble, "The Commonwealth at the Thirteenth Session of the General Assembly," January 1959, UN 73/2717, DO 35/10705, Records of the Commonwealth Relations Office, National Archives of the United Kingdom.
13 See, for example, Charles Ritchie, *Storm Signals: More Undiplomatic Diaries, 1962–1971* (Toronto: Macmillan of Canada, 1983), 166. The originals of the Ritchie diaries are preserved in the Thomas Fisher Rare Book Room at the University of Toronto.
14 Ritchie, *Storm Signals*, 1.
15 The characterization is Bissell's, *Imperial Canadian*, xi.
16 Charles Ritchie, *My Grandfather's House: Scenes of Childhood and Youth* (Toronto: Macmillan of Canada, 1987), 11. Ritchie's family made the distinction between "British" and "English" and identified as the former, not the latter.
17 Ritchie, *Siren Years*, 7.
18 Ritchie, *Siren Years*, 96.
19 L.B. Pearson, *Mike: The Memoirs of the Rt. Hon. Lester B. Pearson*, vol. 1, *1897–1948* (Toronto: University of Toronto Press, 1972); H.L. Keenleyside, *Memoirs of Hugh L. Keenleyside*, 2 vols. (Toronto: McClelland and Stewart, 1981–1982).
20 J.L. Granatstein, *The Ottawa Men: The Civil Service Mandarins, 1935–1957* (Toronto: Oxford University Press, 1982).
21 Keenleyside, *Memoirs*, 2, 115–25.
22 Arnold Heeney, *The Things That Are Caesar's: Memoirs of a Canadian Public Servant*, ed. Brian Heeney (Toronto: University of Toronto Press, 1972), 137n.
23 John English, *Shadow of Heaven: The Life of Lester Pearson*, vol. 1, *1897–1948* (Toronto: Lester and Orpen Dennys, 1989), 394.
24 English, *Shadow of Heaven*, 233–36; Pearson, *Mike*, 1, 192–94.
25 Hillmer, *Skelton: A Portrait of Canadian Ambition*, 335.
26 George Ignatieff, with Sonja Sinclair, *The Making of a Peacemonger: The Memoirs of George Ignatieff* (Toronto: University of Toronto Press, 1985), 109.
27 On this point, and in general on the dating of the "golden age," see Hector Mackenzie, "Golden Decade(s)? Reappraising Canada's International Relations in the 1940s and 1950s," *British Journal of Canadian Studies* 23, 2 (2010): 179–206.
28 Escott Reid, *Radical Mandarin: The Memoirs of Escott Reid* (Toronto: University of Toronto Press, 1989), 245, 267.
29 John W. Holmes, *Canada: A Middle-Aged Power* (Toronto: McClelland and Stewart, 1976), v.
30 Holmes, quoted in English, *The Worldly Years: The Life of Lester Pearson*, vol. 2, *1949–1972* (Toronto: Alfred A. Knopf, 1992), 138.
31 See, for example, the memoir-cum-rant by diplomat Arthur Andrew, *The Rise and Fall of a Middle Power: Canadian Diplomacy from King to Mulroney* (Toronto: James Lorimer, 1993). Andrew has Mackenzie King still as prime minister from 1950 to 1953, resisting to the last breath the golden age of activist diplomacy (33). King died in 1950.

32 Reid, *Radical Mandarin*. The four volumes by Escott Reid are *Time of Fear and Hope: The Making of the North Atlantic Treaty, 1947–1949* (Toronto: McClelland and Stewart, 1977); *Envoy to Nehru* (Delhi, India: Oxford University Press, 1981); *On Duty: A Canadian at the Making of the United Nations, 1945–1946* (Toronto: McClelland and Stewart, 1983); and *Hungary and Suez 1956: A View from New Delhi* (Oakville, ON: Mosaic Press, 1986). Reid notes that, among his 1952 heads of mission and foreign service officer colleagues, thirty-seven wrote books. He helpfully lists the authors (*Radical Mandarin*, 242).

33 L.B. Pearson, *Mike: The Memoirs of the Rt. Hon. Lester B. Pearson*, ed. John A. Munro and Alex I. Inglis, vol. 2, *1948–1957* (Toronto: University of Toronto Press, 1973), 59.

34 John W. Holmes, *The Shaping of Peace: Canada and the Search for World Order, 1943–1957*, 2 vols. (Toronto: University of Toronto Press, 1979–1982), 1, ix.

35 See Holmes, *The Shaping of Peace*, 2, 391.

36 English, *Pearson*, 2, 127–40.

37 John English, "'A Fine Romance': Canada and the United Nations, 1943–1957," in *Canada and the Early Cold War*, ed. Greg Donaghy (Ottawa: Department of Foreign Affairs and International Trade, 1998), 80.

38 Ritchie, quoted in English, "Fine Romance," 88.

39 English, "Fine Romance"; Greg Donaghy, "Coming Off the Gold Standard: Re-assessing the 'Golden Age' of Canadian Diplomacy," http://www.suezcrisis.ca/pdfs/Coming%20off%20the%20Gold%20Standard.pdf; Mackenzie, "Golden Decade(s)?"; Norman Hillmer and J.L. Granatstein, *Empire to Umpire: Canada and the World into the Twenty-First Century* (Toronto: Nelson, 2008), 206.

40 Dale C. Thomson, *Louis St. Laurent: Canadian* (Toronto: Macmillan of Canada, 1967).

41 Jimmy Gardiner fonds, Glenbow Museum Archives, Calgary.

42 A copy of Brooke Claxton's memoir is in the Brooke Claxton fonds at LAC.

43 Paul Hellyer, *Damn the Torpedoes: My Fight to Unify Canada's Armed Forces* (Toronto: McClelland and Stewart, 1990).

44 Robert Bothwell interview with Dale Thomson, August 1976.

45 Gordon Robertson, *Memoirs of a Very Civil Servant: Mackenzie King to Pierre Trudeau* (Toronto: University of Toronto Press, 2000), 39. Robertson served less than a decade in the Department of External Affairs, but in temperament and ways of doing public business, he never left External.

46 John G. Diefenbaker, *One Canada: Memoirs of the Right Honourable John G. Diefenbaker*, vol. 2, *The Years of Achievement, 1957–1962* (Toronto: Macmillan of Canada, 1976), 82.

47 *The Mackenzie King Record*, ed. J.W. Pickersgill, 4 vols. (Toronto: University of Toronto Press, 1960–70). Volumes 2 to 4 were coedited with D.F. Forster. "The record" was King's name for his diary.

48 Authors' personal recollections; Dummitt, *Unbuttoned*, 148–51, 178–79, 188, 194–201.

49 J.W. Pickersgill, *My Years with Louis St. Laurent: A Political Memoir* (Toronto: University of Toronto Press, 1975).

50 J.W. Pickersgill, *Seeing Canada Whole: A Memoir* (Markham, ON: Fitzhenry and Whiteside, 1994).

51 Diefenbaker, *One Canada,* 3 vols. (Toronto: Macmillan of Canada, 1975–1977).

52 H. Basil Robinson, *Diefenbaker's World: A Populist in Foreign Affairs* (Toronto: University of Toronto Press, 1989).

53 Donald M. Fleming, *So Very Near: The Political Memoirs of the Honourable Donald M. Fleming,* vol. 1, *The Rising Years*; vol. 2, *The Summit Years* (Toronto: McClelland and Stewart, 1985). "Compelling duty" is from 1, 9–10; the characterization of Diefenbaker's leadership is from 2, 441.

54 Paul Martin, *A Very Public Life,* 2 vols. (Ottawa: Deneau, 1983–1986).

55 *Paul Martin: The London Diaries, 1975–1979,* ed. William R. Young (Ottawa: University of Ottawa Press, 1988).

56 Marcel Cadieux, Journal intime, 20 October 1966, file 10, vol. 12, Cadieux fonds, LAC.

57 Points eloquently made by Brendan Kelly in *The Good Fight: Marcel Cadieux and Canadian Diplomacy* (Vancouver: UBC Press, 2019). Kelly makes ample use of the Cadieux diary. Diplomat Eldon Black's history-memoir is a further and able rumination on the French Fact in Canadian foreign policy: *Direct Intervention: Canada-France Relations, 1967–1974* (Ottawa: Carleton University Press, 1976).

58 A similar comment may be made about the Canadian military. See *Mémoires du Général Jean V. Allard,* avec la collaboration de Serge Bernier (Ottawa: Les Éditions Mortagne, 1985). The book was translated into English and published by UBC Press in 1988.

59 Claude Morin, *L'art de l'impossible: la diplomatie québécoise depuis 1960* (Montreal: Boréal, 1987); Morin, *Les choses comme elles étaient: une autobiographie politique* (Montreal: Boréal, 1994). Among Morin's roles was a stint in the 1970s in the pay of the Royal Canadian Mounted Police, a fact made public (not by him) in 1992. An early campaigner for "une présence internationale du Québec" was the province's education minister (1964–66), Paul Gérin-Lajoie. See his *Combats d'un révolutionnaire tranquille: Propos et confidences* (Montreal: Centre Éducatif et Culturel, 1989), 315–31.

60 Mitchell Sharp, *Which Reminds Me ... : A Memoir* (Toronto: University of Toronto Press, 1994). We can testify that Sharp's autobiography was entirely of his own devising.

61 Dana Wilgress, as a pioneer in international trade negotiation, was in a unique position to be helpful on the subject, but his autobiography is almost devoid of the ins and outs of tradecraft. *Dana Wilgress Memoirs* (Toronto: Ryerson Press, 1967). The best sources on the behaviour of Canadian trade negotiators are in the American Foreign Affairs Oral History series of the Association for Diplomatic Studies and Training, which can be accessed at https://adst.org/oral-history/. The interviews with Philip Trezise, Willis Armstrong, and Julius (Jules) Katz are particularly informative. US trade diplomats express respect as well as fellow feeling for their Canadian counterparts and report that the Canadian negotiators were very toughminded, a point that is never made disparagingly.

62 Sharp, *Which Reminds Me,* 115, 148.

63 *Walter L. Gordon: A Political Memoir* (Toronto: Macmillan of Canada, 1977).

64 Stephen Azzi, *Walter Gordon and the Rise of Canadian Nationalism* (Montreal/Kingston: McGill-Queen's University Press, 1999), 185–86.

65 Don Jamieson, *The Political Memoirs of Don Jamieson,* ed. Carmelita McGrath, 2 vols. (St. John's, NL: Breakwater, 1989–1991).
66 Robert Bothwell and J.L. Granatstein interview with Mark MacGuigan, 19 January 1988.
67 Mark MacGuigan, *An Inside Look at External Affairs during the Trudeau Years: The Memoirs of Mark MacGuigan,* ed. P. Whitney Lackenbauer (Calgary: University of Calgary Press, 2002).
68 Robert Bothwell and J.L. Granatstein, *Trudeau's World: Insiders Reflect on Foreign Policy, Trade, and Defence, 1968–84* (Vancouver: UBC Press, 2017).
69 J.L. Granatstein and Robert Bothwell, *Pirouette: Pierre Trudeau and Canadian Foreign Policy* (Toronto: University of Toronto Press, 1990).
70 Ivan L. Head and Pierre Elliott Trudeau, *The Canadian Way: Shaping Canada's Foreign Policy, 1968–1984* (Toronto: McClelland and Stewart, 1995). Trudeau's memoirs, written by acolytes, are anemic. Pierre Elliott Trudeau, *Memoirs* (Toronto: McClelland and Stewart, 1993).
71 Pearson, *Mike,* vol. 2, chap. 2; also Norman Hillmer interview with L.B. Pearson, September 1972.
72 Allan Gotlieb, *The Washington Diaries, 1981–1989* (Toronto: McClelland and Stewart, 2006).
73 Sondra Gotlieb, *Wife of ... : An Irreverent Account of Life in Washington* (Toronto: Macmillan of Canada, 1985), 10.
74 Sondra Gotlieb, *Washington Rollercoaster* (Toronto: Doubleday Canada, 1990), 47, 66.
75 Landon Pearson, *Letters from Moscow* (Newcastle, ON: Penumbra Press, 2003), 254; P.K. Page, *Brazilian Journal* (Toronto: Lester and Orpen Dennys, 1987).
76 *Royal Commission on Conditions of Foreign Service* (Ottawa: Minister of Supply and Services Canada, 1981), 28.
77 We have not included the memoirs of diplomats whose careers reached their peak after 1984. See, for example, Derek H. Burney, *Getting It Done: A Memoir* (Montreal/Kingston: McGill-Queen's University Press, 2005); and James Bartleman, *On Six Continents: A Life in Canada's Foreign Service, 1966–2002* (Toronto: McClelland and Stewart, 2004).
78 For exceptions, see Chester Ronning, *A Memoir of China in Revolution: From the Boxer Rebellion to the People's Republic* (New York: Pantheon Books, 1974); and, up to a point, Reid, *Hungary and Suez 1956;* and Geoffrey A.H. Pearson, *Anecdotage,* a reminiscence privately published for his family and friends.

CHAPTER 2

THAT BOUNCY MAN

Americans and Lester B. Pearson

Galen Roger Perras and Asa McKercher

Taking a break from his usual reports covering Canadian economic nationalism, Quebec separatism, and anti-Vietnam War protests in 1967, William Walton Butterworth, the American ambassador in Ottawa, apprised Secretary of State Dean Rusk of an error in a press release announcing the new Order of Canada honours system. While the awards were meant to bear a biblical passage from Hebrews 11:16, "they desire a better country …," the press release from the office of Canadian prime minister Lester B. "Mike" Pearson quoted Hebrews 12:16, "lest there be any fornicator, or profane person, as Esau, who for one morsel of meat sold his birthright." For Butterworth, this amusing blunder demonstrated "how remarkably accident-prone Mike Pearson's Government was in matters of considerable importance."[1] Stinging, this judgment typified what was then the prevailing view that Pearson, an able diplomat, made a poor prime minister. Nor was Butterworth – Pearson's friend since their mutual postings to London in the 1930s – the sole American to mock Canada's renowned diplomat-cum-politician.

Although he counted many American officials as friends, Lester Pearson's desire to fashion an independent path in foreign affairs often perturbed his US counterparts. This propensity achieved its apogee in April 1965 when President Lyndon Johnson harangued Pearson – "You don't come here and piss on my rug" – over his public suggestion, on US soil, of a pause in the American bombing of North Vietnam. Sharing Johnson's choler, former secretary of state Dean Acheson denounced Canada – but really Pearson – as the "Stern Daughter of the Voice of God," always hectoring Washington. Having dealt with Pearson for decades, Acheson complained to Canadian ambassador Charles Ritchie: "You will see that bouncy man come and do it again."[2]

Below, we examine Americans' views of Pearson during his transformation from professional diplomat to foreign minister to politician and then to prime minister. American observers had predicted, indeed welcomed, said transition for they judged that Pearson was firmly on the side of the United States. Indeed, Pearson's Canadian foes, to use John Warnock's phrase, denigrated him as Washington's "boy in Ottawa," a view that lingers still in some circles.[3] However, as John English noted in his biography of Mike, far from being an American chore boy, Pearson, through his long service in the United States and his interactions with Americans, had a keen sense of the factors motivating US policy and an ability to interpret American viewpoints. This outlook set him apart, for instance, from "his colleagues and political masters in Ottawa who had quaffed copious portions of the heady brew of nationalism and functionalism," as well as from those Canadians who embodied the anti-American currents prominent in Canadian life.[4] Pearson put Canada first, and some Americans grew disappointed, even angry, with Mike and his brand of Canadian foreign policy long before his fateful encounter with Johnson at Camp David. Reflecting John English's focus on the intersection of people and policy, we note that Americans' opinions of Pearson were entangled with the way they perceived Canada's shifting foreign policy during the roughly two decades that followed the Second World War. Discussing Kennedy administration officials' views of Prime Minister John Diefenbaker in a recent paper, Stephen Azzi recounts that they described Diefenbaker – and Canada too – as immature, unbalanced, and hysterical.[5] Similarly, while American officials and media figures saw Mike as the lead statesman of a helpful ally, mistrust of Canada's growing independence in foreign affairs was marked, an indication of the tensions percolating beneath the smooth veneer of the Canada-US relationship during the early Cold War.

Hired by Canada's Department of External Affairs (DEA) in 1928, Pearson's brief sojourn in Canada's Washington, DC, legation, in 1929, sparked friendships with State Department officials and journalists. These early ties proved valuable when he returned to Washington in 1942 amid wartime bustle, and they all occupied "senior and more respectable positions."[6] During the war, as his frustrated DEA colleagues demanded that small nations must influence strategy-making when their interests and expertise were involved, Pearson feared – as he would throughout his career – that Americans, seeing Canada as necessary but not necessary enough, would have little regard or respect for Canadian interests or independence. In 1944, when the US War Department disclosed its contingency plan to grab Canada's nickel mines, he joked about Canada's impregnable defences to John Hickerson, the State Department's Canadianist; privately, Pearson was disturbed that such a scheme existed when bilateral relations were "firm and friendly."[7] While Mike enjoyed his "free-swinging" verbal jousts with Hickerson,[8] when the American confessed in 1944 that his State Department colleagues resented Canada's privileged position among the Allies and its role as an information pipeline to Britain, Pearson carped to Norman Robertson that Hickerson's "frankness often merges into explosiveness."[9]

In November 1944, when Leighton McCarthy retired as minister of Canada's Washington legation, he told US officials that Pearson should succeed him.[10] Agreeing with this notion and certain that Pearson "had a great future" ahead of him, Prime Minister W.L.M. King appointed him as the legation's minister and then ambassador in 1945 when the legation became an embassy. Given the wartime high tide of bilateral relations, there was much praise for this appointment. When Pearson presented his credentials on 22 January 1945, President Franklin Roosevelt declared that he had "already won a place in our affection."[11] Highlighting Mike's past employment as a soldier, teacher, and sausage maker, the *Baltimore Sun* praised his informality. Not only did Mike's missives often induce "a chuckle," he worked with his shirtsleeves rolled up and his feet planted on his desk. Similarly, a social affairs columnist relayed how Pearson had declined to pull rank after an officious train conductor had demanded to see his ambassadorial credentials. Another reporter noted that not only was Pearson an agreeable dinner companion, he also spoke "English with almost no Canadian trace."[12] Britain's embassy recorded that given his merits and hard work, Pearson's appointment was universally welcomed in the American capital, adding that Mike offered "an essentially Canadian position" between Britain and the United States. Pearson was "immensely popular" in US official circles, Acting Secretary of State Dean Acheson later advised President Harry Truman.[13]

The connection between "Corporal Pearson and General Acheson" – Mike's own characterization – encapsulated the Canada-US relationship that emerged after 1945 as both countries pursued internationalist foreign policies in the ensuing Cold War. For Canadian journalist Bruce Hutchinson, "Acheson was a stoic realist," Pearson "a frustrated idealist."[14] In his memoirs, Pearson said that he knew well and admired Acheson. When the latter was formally appointed secretary of state, Mike professed to being "delighted personally, officially, internationally, alcoholically." For his part, Acheson opined in 1946 that few responsibilities had been more pleasant than "dealing with the Canadian Ambassador."[15] Still, no real friendship existed as Mike found Acheson distant, and the American much preferred Pearson's colleague Hume Wrong.[16] When Pearson was considered to lead the United Nations in 1945, Acheson averred that Mike's colleague Norman Robertson – a congenial trade negotiator with Hickerson in the 1930s – would better serve US interests as Robertson surpassed Pearson in character and ability.[17]

Pearson did possess some merits, and he was courted for higher office in Canada and abroad. In early 1946, Mike was being considered to serve as UN secretary-general. Warning him about serving many masters instead of one, nonetheless King okayed this plan. However, Moscow vetoed Mike's candidacy. US Ambassador Raymond Atherton soon buttonholed defence minister Douglas Abbott about Pearson's future. Though Pearson was focused on his diplomatic career, Abbott admitted that King wanted him to enter politics.[18] In September 1946, King appointed Pearson undersecretary of state for external affairs, a move that the prime minister saw as necessary preparation for politics, which, he speculated, "I think [Pearson] would like to do."[19] According to the *New York Times*'s James Reston, Pearson's humour, informality, and simple approach to problem-solving ensured that while "Washington was not happy to see him go," he had quit the American capital with enhanced prestige.[20]

When Pearson arrived in Ottawa, rumours swirled about who might replace the aging King. Many touted Louis St. Laurent, promoted to secretary of state for external affairs (SSEA) in 1946, after King had separated that post from the premiership earlier that year. There was some speculation among US diplomats that Pearson himself might enter the race to succeed King as Liberal leader, but by early 1947, Atherton had concluded that St. Laurent would emerge as party chief. What did that mean for Pearson, St. Laurent's deputy in the DEA, and for Canadian foreign policy?[21] Atherton dampened concerns that changes in Canada's foreign ministry might injure US interests as "Mike Pearson handles the important issues."[22] Indeed, Pearson earned the thanks of President Truman himself when, in 1947, Britain vacated its fractious Palestine mandate, and the Canadian convinced the UN to form separate Jewish and Arab states, a development that diplomat John Holmes later credited with initiating "Canada's role [and] reputation as a moderate middle power."[23]

Americans were much less chuffed when King opposed a Canadian role in the UN Temporary Commission on Korea (UNTCOK), a body meant to reunite Korea with a national election. Dreading embroilment in this Soviet-American flashpoint in a country of peripheral interest to Canada, King faced off with St. Laurent and Pearson, who reluctantly backed Canada's involvement to buttress the UN. When St. Laurent, pushed by Mike, threatened to quit cabinet, King accepted Canada's prescribed membership in UNTCOK. But before making that climb down, King had sent Pearson to make, unsuccessfully, King's case to a puzzled Truman in January. Pearson was forced to "walk a tight-rope" between presenting King's views and emphasizing his own position that UNTCOK was a worthwhile endeavour. For good reason, US officials judged Mike to be their friend in Ottawa.[24]

The UNTCOK standoff signified a passing of the torch between King and more globally minded officials. This transfer was completed in August 1948. Announcing his retirement for November, King told his successor, St. Laurent, to bring Pearson into politics.[25] With the US embassy reporting that St. Laurent had offered Pearson the SSEA post at the August Liberal convention, Minister Julian Harrington observed that the Canadian would find it difficult to decline as his "whole interest" was foreign affairs. On 10 September, Pearson, jesting that he had been a Liberal "since last evening at 5 o'clock," became SSEA.[26] Little would change for the United States, Harrington predicted, as Pearson, "a dominant figure," favoured close ties to the United States. The American embassy advised that his "capacity, youth, and attractive personality" made Pearson a valuable cabinet addition.[27]

The embassy analysis was deft, but the North Atlantic Treaty Organization's creation in 1948–49 revealed that Pearson and Canada did not always accept the dominant US viewpoint. Unwilling to be stuck between European and American "dumbbells" or to rely on unilateral US security guarantees, Mike wanted NATO to exhibit dynamic economic and cultural dimensions, to be embodied in Article 2 of the alliance covenant. While Hickerson posited that a purely military pact would be "unfortunate," Acheson differed.[28] A consummate cold warrior who had penned the 1947 Truman Doctrine's affirmation that the United States would aid free peoples resisting subjugation, he warned Mike shortly thereafter that "all the towns on the road over which we are traveling are named 'Munich.'"[29] Becoming secretary of state in 1949, Acheson ensured that there would be no appeasing Moscow, and he manifested no goodwill for Canada's Article 2, dismissing it as a pointless distraction that aimed to fulfill "every worthy aspiration that ever occurred to any human being." Telling Hickerson that the article was a dud, Acheson nevertheless acquiesced, only to later ridicule Pearson's inability to find a use for it. Acheson's wrath, Robert Bothwell avers, "never really cooled." When Pearson complained once about unilateral US decisions, Acheson "exploded" about "moralizing, interfering Canadians."[30]

Not all Americans held grudges. In April 1949, as NATO was finalized, the *Philadelphia Inquirer* averred that Pearson was a skilled negotiator who had brought the alliance to fruition. George Sokolsky, a conservative commentator for the Hearst chain who soon became one of Mike's harshest critics, argued that Pearson, having correctly appraised the Soviet threat, prudently had brought Canada into NATO. To Americans, the Canadian foreign minister had emerged as a key statesman and friend. By autumn 1949, with Pearson chairing the UN's political committee, the *Detroit Free Press* purred with "satisfaction" at his appointment. And although confused about the basic facts of Canadian governance, the *Pittsburgh Press* asserted that Pearson's rise demonstrated "our sister republic's increasing voice in global affairs."[31]

Pearson's questioning of US policy in Asia savaged his reputation in some American circles. When North Korea invaded South Korea in June 1950, Truman and Acheson demanded UN military intervention. Although Canada offered three destroyers and some transport planes, the Americans pressed Pearson for more. Ambassador Stanley Woodward appealed for more substantive aid from Washington's "closest friend," and Acheson "quite forcibly" told Mike that Canada must send ground forces as Korea was a touchstone for Western determination to meet global challenges.[32] With Pearson urging the need to meet this request, in early August St. Laurent announced that a brigade would go to Korea. Having gone out on a limb for the Americans, Pearson was shaken by the quick series of events that unfolded that autumn: the successful US counterattack and subsequent invasion of North Korea, then communist China's military intervention in November. Months earlier, Pearson had urged that American forces should stop at the 38th parallel and issue terms to North Korea.[33] That advice was ignored, and the war widened when China blunted the US advance and invaded South Korea.

Pearson's doubts about the war and US strategy to win it grew when General Douglas MacArthur threatened to drop multiple atomic bombs on China. Congressional assaults on Canadian diplomat E.H. Norman as a communist spy only compounded Pearson's frustration. So, in April 1951 he delivered a fateful public address in Toronto. Canada was not concerned "*whether*" the United States would discharge its international responsibilities, he stated. Rather, Canadians were worried "how she will do it, and whether the rest of us will be involved." In a notable turn of phrase, Pearson posited that the "relatively easy and automatic relations with our neighbour are, I think, over." Such comments, he explained privately, reflected "our feeling of dependence on the United States and the frustration over the fact that we can't escape this no matter how hard we try."[34] Whether about Korea or China, Canadian policy was heavily influenced by its relationship with America. A reaction to this situation involving the United States, Pearson's Toronto speech, much like his 1965 comments on Vietnam, had repercussions as some commentators credited Mike with prompting Truman's dismissal of MacArthur just days later. While the *Boston Globe* praised its "candid" nature, George Sokolsky, unsure if the timing of MacArthur's dismissal and Pearson's speech was coincidental, blamed Truman for damaging relations with Canada. Pearson's comments, Sokolsky affirmed, "should have been as startling as our defeat in Korea." Although a *Washington Post* editorial denied the merit of Pearson's criticisms, Robert Estabrook, a *Washington Post* journalist who followed Canada, agreed with Mike's remarks.[35]

Unsurprisingly, Acheson was displeased yet contrite. Informing Wrong that he had "never regarded Canada as the echo of anybody's voice," – a reference to another line in Pearson's speech – he added that Canadian policy was "forcibly and ably put forward by the present Foreign Minister of Canada, for whom I have the greatest respect." Wrong, meanwhile, confided to State Department officials that he deplored Mike's comments, while other members of Canada's "much embarrassed" embassy feared the repercussions.[36] Writing to Pearson, Wrong noted that US officials had found the timing of Pearson's speech – amid a domestic brouhaha over Korea – unfortunate. Mike maintained that the fuss confirmed his thesis that Canada was ignored "unless we say something critical, and then the attention becomes surprised, pained and irritated." Still, he regretted the phrase "relatively easy and automatic," admitting that he should have said that simpler bilateral relations had been supplanted by ties to America as a coalition leader whose policies determined war and peace.[37] In outlining its response to the speech, the State Department advised Woodward to "convey to Pearson, in a joshing manner, the impression that his viewpoint has received" the department's full attention.[38] Instead, dismissing Pearson's speech as "a rather disjointed exposition" of US-Canada relations, Woodward accused Mike of damaging Canada's standing in Washington. Pearson retorted that US opinion must recognize that Canada was "growing up as a nation."[39] Relations were uneasy indeed.

Worse was coming. Exhibiting the arch-conservative views of owner Robert McCormick, the *Chicago Tribune* assailed Truman's foreign policy, praised MacArthur, railed against US support for European colonialism and State Department "pantywaists," and harped on real and imagined spy rings.[40] When Pearson critiqued Washington's demand to have the UN name communist China as an aggressor in January 1951, the *Tribune* labelled him a "leading" appeaser. Then, in July, the paper decried the outsized influence that the Oxford-educated Pearson plus the "Rhodes wards" in Canada's DEA wielded in Washington's halls of power. Insinuating that Pearson's critique had led Truman to fire MacArthur, in a flight of truly remarkable fantasy, the *Tribune* linked the late Cecil Rhodes' ambition to reintegrate America into Britain's empire to Pearson's desire to make NATO into a political federation. When Mike ran to head the UN in 1953, the *Tribune* averred that communist states might back Pearson given his anti-Americanism. After the Soviets blocked Mike's candidacy, the *Tribune* claimed that Moscow desired "some stooge even more abject than Pearson."[41] Taking such criticism in stride, Mike replied, "I don't have to hide away, yet."[42] Still, he remained in the crosshairs of the American Right.

As for Pearson's rocky relationship with Acheson, it unravelled in 1952. With fighting in Korea continuing amid furtive negotiations, North Korea and China refused to agree to a ceasefire until all of their POWs in US/UN hands were returned; Washington would not repatriate any prisoners unwilling to return. Wanting the UN to settle the matter, India's foreign minister, Krishna Menon, backed Beijing's view that forcible repatriation accorded with Geneva Convention strictures. Desiring an armistice, Pearson reluctantly backed Menon's plan, as Chinese support suggested that it might succeed.[43] Acheson was irate. In November 1952, he flew to Ottawa to lobby against Menon. Pearson, slated initially to accompany Acheson, stayed in New York. After Canada's cabinet backed Pearson, Acheson convinced the UN to reject forced repatriation, and the Korean slaughter continued.[44] Fuming, Acheson stunned British foreign secretary Anthony Eden by calling Pearson an "empty glass of water" and threatening to bring Canada "to heel." Time did not heal this wound. Denouncing the Pearson-Menon cabal in his 1969 memoir, Acheson crowed that Mike's cancelled trip had left Pearson's "rear exposed to hostile action."[45]

If the Truman years had ended in American vituperation about Canada, the Eisenhower years were more productive. War hero Dwight Eisenhower was popular in Canada and a deft statesman thanks to his wartime command. While Acheson – a maternal descendant of Canadians – had proved a difficult partner for Pearson, John Foster Dulles, the Republican secretary of state who hailed from the bordertown of Watertown, NY, and owned a cabin on Lake Ontario's Canadian side, perhaps possessed a greater appreciation for Canada – not that there was perfect harmony between Pearson, the consummate diplomat, and Dulles, Manichean in outlook and personally blunt. Having a chance to chat alone with Eisenhower during the presidential visit to Ottawa in November 1953, Pearson responded to the president's complaint that Dulles rubbed foreign officials the wrong way by asserting that "Mr. Dulles's handicap in this regard was usually overcome when people got to know him better," adding that his opinion of his US counterpart "had gone up" since they had begun working together.[46]

Whatever disagreement they may have had, neither Mike nor Dulles, as John English remarks, "made their differences personal."[47] This diplomatic relationship – plus a good personal connection between Eisenhower and St. Laurent – saw productive bilateral cooperation to construct the St. Lawrence Seaway plus radar arrays placed across Canada to detect Soviet aircraft, and the creation of a cabinet-level joint committee to manage an increasingly continental economy. There was wrangling, but the trend was toward compromise, largely attributable to Canadian influence within American policy-making circles.[48] "It doesn't matter what area you were in," recalled US diplomat George Vest:

> For those who worked with them, this was one of the great periods of Canada. I mean, the prime minister was Louis St. Laurent; the foreign minister, external affairs minister, was Mike Pearson; the man in charge of the economy was a great old man named C.D. Howe. These people were tremendous leaders, very important, and they knew everybody in Washington and in New York and in Chicago. It was a very interesting time.[49]

Not all went well. While the US embassy in Ottawa noted approvingly that "Canada shares without reservation our basic opposition to Communism and all that it stands for," still, "the Canadian Government, influenced by Pearson," was soft on communist China. The Canadians mulled diplomatic relations with Mao Zedong's regime and fretted over the volatile Sino-American military standoff in the Taiwan Strait. When Pearson explored means to settle the Taiwanese crisis, Washington judged his intervention as out of line, and Mike backed off.[50] Independent Canadian views on international issues induced tensions in the relationship with Eisenhower's administration. Dulles once groused that

> you Canadians are always complaining that we never consult you about our policies, "Ike" as you know is a great golfer and, who knows, he may want [us] to play a few holes … If we do and the score is all square on the 18th green, I'll wager that you'll intervene just as I am about to make the deciding putt to demand that I consult you about it first.

"If I did, Foster," Pearson retorted, "it would be merely to tell you that you were using a No. 9 iron."[51]

From his first meeting with Dulles in February 1953, Pearson warned that US policies meant to produce "uneasiness in the Soviet Union" could also spark "uneasiness among" American allies. Still, his recounting of his USSR visit in 1955 – the first by a leading NATO official – was one of many issues on which Dulles enjoyed "helpful informal discussions" with Pearson.[52] He also condemned anti-American sentiment in Canada. "The times are too serious," Pearson warned in 1956, "and the problem too real for irresponsible exaggeration" of American foibles. Pleased by this defence of Washington's reputation and his diplomatic efforts generally, the *New York Times* labelled Pearson "a big man from a country that is a small power," and judged – perhaps correctly – that he was probably better known abroad than in Canada itself.[53]

The 1956 Suez crisis cemented Mike's international diplomatic reputation. The Anglo-French invasion of Egypt imperilled NATO, the Commonwealth, the UN, and British-US ties. Though the equally appalled St. Laurent and Eisenhower stridently opposed the attack, American and Canadian officials sought to "get the British and French 'off the hook.'"[54] Drawing on an American draft resolution, Pearson proposed creating a UN peacekeeping force – his aim since the late 1940s – to allow Britain and France to quit Egypt and save face. "I gave [Mike] the paper," American UN ambassador Henry Cabot Lodge recalled. "And he just looked at the paper and he said, 'Yes' just like that, adding 'Yes, I'll take it.'" While Lodge later groused that the Canadian foreign minister got all the credit, including a Nobel Peace Prize, writer Antony Anderson stresses that as Pearson had first proposed the peacekeeping force and as Canadian lobbying ensured the resolution's passage, Mike's accolades were well earned.[55] Eisenhower himself credited Pearson's "key proposal" with helping to resolve the crisis, telling St. Laurent, "never have I seen action on the part of a government that excited me more than the rapid way that you & your Government moved into the breech. You did a magnificent job & we admire it."[56] The apex of Pearsonian internationalism, the Suez crisis also marked a key moment in Canada-US cooperation.

When Pearson won the Nobel Peace Prize in October 1957, US newspapers lauded "Mr. United Nations." Though "we cannot claim him as an American diplomat," lamented the *New York Times*, "we would like to do so." The *Detroit Free Press*, pointing out that Pearson "has worked closely enough with United States diplomats and policymakers so that we can think of him almost as being one of us … we rejoice along with his fellow Canadians." To the *Washington Post*, Pearson was an outstanding leader who had "contributed rich resources of wit and good will to the tasks of diplomacy." "All Americans," the *Seattle Times* declared, "should rejoice that Lester B. Pearson, good friend and good neighbor," had won.[57] But conservative skepticism about liberal internationalism existed too. The *Dallas Morning News* pointed out that while the peacekeeping force had ended the Suez crisis, it had not brought peace to the Middle East nor the wider world. But maybe "the Canadian did his best to ease the tension." "Mr. Pearson seems to be admired in Norwegian circles which have $40,000 to spare," sneered the *Chicago Tribune*, "and he will be entitled to be regarded as a peacemaker in the Middle East until the next time the contentious inhabitants of that area start shooting one another full of holes."[58] Undoubtedly envious, Acheson later kvetched that his essay, "Canada: 'Stern daughter of the voice of God,'" should have read: "Or how to win a Nobel Peace Prize without trying."[59] Acheson aside, the conservative criticisms of Pearson and his liberal internationalist inclinations reflected wider doubts that existed in American right-wing circles thanks to allegations about Pearson's supposed communist leanings.

Although as secretary of state for external affairs Pearson would oversee investigations into potential national security breaches, he loathed the clumsy red-baiting characteristic of 1950s McCarthyism, dismissing Senator Joseph McCarthy as "one of the most horrible creatures of the twentieth century." He was concerned as some in Congress, the media, and the FBI had targeted him plus other diplomats. Convinced of Mike's communist bona fides, newspaper baron Robert McCormick, Pearson's fiercest conservative critic, dubbed him "the most dangerous man in the English-speaking world."[60] Allegations that Pearson was a closet communist derived from fanciful claims made by Elizabeth Bentley, a Soviet courier turned informant. In 1951, the FBI opened a file after Bentley stated that during the Second World War, Pearson had passed along information to a friend who had transmitted it to Bentley who then had given it to the Soviets. But asked to produce evidence, Bentley could recall only "gossip" and doubted that Pearson was "conscious of the fact that he was supplying information." As gregariousness was a poor foundation on which to construct a conspiracy case, the bureau closed Pearson's file in 1952, briefly reopened it in 1953 when Mike was up to head the UN, and revived it again in 1957 as Pearson readied to take over leadership of the Liberal Party. In both cases, agents merely regurgitated Bentley's tall tale. Pearson's file, once held by the US National Archives, mysteriously has been destroyed.[61]

Pearson upset red-hunters on two counts. First, though he had helped to create Canada's postwar foreign policy that plainly opposed Soviet expansionism, the smear against him reflected American doubts about Canada's more independent line. In 1957, as evidence of a supposed alignment with Moscow, FBI agents pointed to some of Mike's diplomatic initiatives: his support for nuclear disarmament, his 1955 USSR trip, his wish to recognize Mao's regime, and UN peacekeeping.[62] Second, Pearson condemned McCarthyism. "We have recently witnessed the spectacle of innocent and respectable people being prosecuted and almost destroyed by innuendo and unjustified suspicion," he had affirmed in 1950 as congressional hearings on the red menace ramped up.[63] The hearings ensnared Herbert Norman, a Canadian diplomat who had been a communist in his youth, prompting Norman's tragic suicide. Mike's denunciation of the Norman investigation prompted Sokolsky to declare, "Methinks Lester Pearson doth protest too much."[64] Arnold Heeney, serving as Canada's ambassador in Washington during the investigations, noted that the congressional hearings "cast real shadows on relations with the USA," as Ottawa resented the Eisenhower administration's failure to condemn red-baiters. In 1955, Mike had complained to Dulles about congressional "insinuations" made about his supposed communist sympathies and less serious but still unfounded press accusations that he was obstructing White House policy because he was "a well-known Democrat-lover." Contrite, Dulles assured Pearson that he "had been very happy about our co-operative and friendly relations … and had no complaint of any kind to make." Even so, Dulles and other senior American officials were mum when it came to publicly defending Pearson.[65]

Some Americans celebrated the collapse of St. Laurent's government in 1957, the formation of John Diefenbaker's Progressive Conservative minority government, and Diefenbaker's decisive trouncing of the Pearson-led

Liberals in a 1958 snap election. The *New York Daily Mirror* accused Pearson of "building an anti-American attitude in Canada" with his protests against anti-communist investigations. Canada-US relations, the paper contended, had grown "less pleasant during the past decade than they had been in a century." Sokolsky argued that Pearson was "most responsible for the disruption" of Canada-US relations as he had the temerity to seek "an unrealistic equality between the United States and Canada." He predicted that Diefenbaker was unlikely "to be as chauvinistic" as Pearson, nor would he "cut off his nose to spite his face."[66] Other American commentators lamented the Liberal defeat, "a loss to more than Canada" as Pearson, a "firm friend" of the United States, "no longer led" Canadian foreign policy. "His services," complained the liberal Republican *New York Herald Tribune*, "are no longer being used by the free world."[67]

Conservative American praise for the Canadian Tories seemed somewhat incongruous as Diefenbaker, a fiery Anglophile populist, had trashed the Liberals for aligning Canada too closely with the United States. Thus, his campaign rhetoric had carried more than a touch of anti-American nationalism.[68] Mindful of this rhetoric, after initial contacts with Canada's new government, US officials concluded that the Tories were "basically no less friendly to the United States than the Liberals." Rather, they would be "more vigorous in countering any reduction, or appearance of reduction, of Canadian sovereignty." Washington's goal, Dulles wrote in mid-1958, was to "establish the same mutual confidence and close working relationship with the new government that we enjoyed with the Liberal Government for 22 years."[69] But the St. Laurent era soon acquired an air of halcyon days gone by when, after Diefenbaker proved recalcitrant on several policy files, Eisenhower professed in 1960 to be "distressed ... that a Liberal government in Canada seems more desirable ... than a Conservative government."[70]

For US diplomats, the practical political realities of being in Opposition affected Mike's outlook on Canada-US relations. A 1960 report for Eisenhower's National Security Council judged that with Canadian "sensitivity" to the United States' importance in Canada's political life, the Liberal Party was "casting itself in the role of guardian of Canadian sovereignty," compelling Diefenbaker "to outdo the Opposition" on this nationalist score. The Liberals, a US diplomat noted in 1961, had adopted "a more pro-nationalist attitude because of the supposed importance of this Canadian sentiment."[71]

There had been wide support at the Liberals' January 1961 National Rally to quit the North American Air Defence Command (NORAD) and to reject tactical nuclear weapons for Canada's military. Pearson, favouring nuclear disarmament, stated that while a Liberal government would keep Canada in NORAD, Canada would shift from defending against threats to North American airspace to merely monitoring them. "Pearson's tactic is to rival Diefenbaker in using nationalism as a political device," a senior State Department official told the incoming secretary of state, Dean Rusk, another Washington friend of Pearson. Tory accusations that Liberals were in Uncle Sam's pocket had "so stung Liberal leaders that they have never forgotten it and have attempted to seize every specific opportunity to throw Diefenbaker's words back at him."[72] Clearly, the nationalist tenor of Canadian politics in the early 1960s proved bothersome for US officials.

The state of Canada-US relations concerned John F. Kennedy's new administration and other American observers. Not only did Canada's wavering on nuclear weapons and its ongoing trade with communist Cuba strain relations, US observers also recognized a rising Canadian nationalist sentiment, including a skein of neutralism exposed by James Minifie's *Peacemaker or Powder-Monkey?*, a 1960 bestseller. "Canadian-American relations are now the worst they have been in history," wrote consummate Washington reporter Stewart Alsop in February 1961. Citing Canadian politicians' anti-Americanism, Alsop blamed, in part, "Mike Pearson, once accounted a friend of the US … now a leading Yankee-baiter."[73] One State Department Canadianist recalled that Pearson "was all over the countryside in terms of most issues. A nice guy, but kind of a screwball." Meanwhile, a briefing note produced for President Kennedy conceded that while Pearson had amassed "an international reputation as a diplomat and conciliator" and thus secured "for Canada an important place in the councils of the West," as a politician he has "flirted with propositions which are disturbing from a United States point of view." In the formulation offered by the State Department briefers, Pearson was "a strong nationalist as well as internationalist," a duality reflecting Mike's willingness to see Canada shoulder international burdens while still asserting itself with its southern neighbour.[74]

Kennedy needed little introduction to Pearson. In 1959, reviewing a book of Mike's lectures, the then senator had named Pearson "the chief architect of the Canadian foreign service, probably the best in the world."[75] This admiration was genuine. As John English states, the Canadian "had the Nobel Prize that Kennedy coveted, was a close friend of *New York Times* columnist Scotty Reston, whose approval the administration craved, and expressed in a North American accent that British global sense he so admired."[76] While much is made of Kennedy's feud with Diefenbaker, no ill will existed between Kennedy and Pearson. Indeed, the latter warm relationship had an impact on the coolness of the former. During the president's May 1961 trip to Ottawa, US ambassador Livingston Merchant hosted a reception at his residence. Enjoying after-dinner cigars and brandy, Kennedy and Pearson, Merchant recalled, spent an inordinate amount of time chatting while ignoring Diefenbaker. Merchant feared that the president's "behavior, unconsciously, had been such to cause a very vain man, Mr. Diefenbaker, to feel that he had been slighted."[77]

Having little time for Diefenbaker, Kennedy made time for Pearson. In 1955, Mike had met Nikita Khrushchev and since Kennedy himself was due to meet the Soviet premier soon after his Ottawa visit, he was keen to get the Canadian's insights into his Soviet foe. Upon returning to Washington, Kennedy arranged for Pearson to meet with him in the US capital for a briefing.[78] The following April, Mike attended a White House gala celebrating Nobel Prize winners. While urging a tête-à-tête as Pearson was "making no public or private sense on defense matters particularly nuclear," Merchant wanted the matter handled quietly "lest Diefenbaker and company" conclude that "Pearson is receiving attention in Washington disproportionate to that shown them."[79] Mike met with Rusk, his former Oxford University classmate, and chatted with Kennedy in the White House residence before the Nobel dinner, with Pearson later emphasizing that he and the president had been "very very correct" in their chat. Although Merchant had cleared the visit with Diefenbaker, Pearson's presence was misconstrued given Canada's impending election. Nor did Kennedy help matters by showering Pearson with attention.[80] As photos of Mike and Jack warmly conversing splashed across Canadian papers, Pearson, one columnist wrote, could return to the hustings with "a sprinkling of new frontier political gold-dust."[81]

Pearson's meeting with Kennedy sent Diefenbaker into a rage. Summoning Merchant to his office, he proceeded to harangue him, in the process revealing that he had in his possession a briefing note for Kennedy that the president had left in Diefenbaker's office in May 1961. If the White House continued to intervene in Canadian affairs, Diefenbaker would give the document to the press and tout himself as the leader able to oppose Washington. This blackmail attempt was bizarre, for the "Rostow memorandum" was an innocuous list of talking points which, contrary to later speculation, did not mention nuclear weapons. Though the prime minister did not share the document, Kennedy vowed that he had "no intention of seeking a meeting with Diefenbaker in the near future."[82]

The poor Kennedy-Diefenbaker relationship was one factor that contributed to the fall of Diefenbaker's government in early 1963. A series of events connected to the question of Canada's adoption of nuclear weapons brought about Diefenbaker's downfall, sparking accusations that the Kennedy administration had intervened to benefit Pearson's Liberals.[83] Certainly, US officials wanted a Liberal win. Recalled one diplomat, as the president was "extremely anxious" for Diefenbaker's defeat, "one of our chief problems was keeping Mr. Kennedy out of the Canadian election, because he just wanted to get in there and campaign for Pearson."[84] Favouring the Liberal, American observers were disappointed with his campaigning, contrasting Diefenbaker's fiery populism with Mike, "already a two-time loser," whose campaign was "sober and responsible if uninspired."[85] After a bitter federal election marked by charges of American interference to aid the Liberals, Pearson eked out a narrow win. Although condemning Diefenbaker's "whistle-stop demagogic" campaign, Butterworth predicted that Pearson's government would be stocked with talented and tough negotiating ministers as they were "none the less Canadians and their relative sophistication does not mean they do not suffer from familiar national compulsion to demonstrate to themselves and others that they are not Americans." Unlike Diefenbaker, Butterworth added, Pearson at least lacked the "same ignorance and mistrust of us."[86] Expecting Pearson's government to be "much less petty" and "more efficient" than its predecessor, White House officials thought it "would want and work for cordial relations" but would seek to avoid, "especially initially, any implication or image of being a US pawn." Thus, one must not "expect automatic solutions" to outstanding problems "simply because the Liberals are in power."[87]

Seeking to better US-Canada relations, Kennedy invited Pearson to his family compound in Hyannisport. "The meeting," Canadian ambassador Charles Ritchie reflected, "was tinged with euphoria" as the men and their advisors shared friendly banter and agreed that Canada would take nuclear weapons. Kennedy reported to several aides that Pearson had impressed him, and years later Butterworth reflected that the meeting was akin to "a new page being turned in Canadian-American relations." The warm optics, symbolized by photos of the leaders chatting in repose, were noted. "Mr. Pearson has reversed the basically isolationist and anti-American stance of the Diefenbaker regime," trumpeted the *New York Times*. Eminent columnist Walter Lippmann likened the Pearson-Kennedy honeymoon to "a good scrubbing and cool shower after a muddy brawl." To *The Atlantic Monthly*, Pearson's visit was a goodwill mission "in purest simplest form" that would "clear away the doubt and suspicion and irritability which have bedeviled Canada's external relationships in recent years." Still, Liberals would defend national sovereignty as Canadians of all political stripes "naturally" wished to differentiate their country from its overbearing neighbour.[88] Indeed, the summer of 1963 was marred by Canadian-American disputes over economic questions, notably attempts by Walter Gordon, the Liberal finance minister, to limit US investment in Canada.[89] Alarmed by such contretemps, in one of his last acts as president, Kennedy ordered officials to create a bureaucratic machinery in the White House to handle relations with his country's restive northern ally.

After Kennedy's 1963 murder, Rusk told President Lyndon Johnson that "our relations with Canada have grown increasingly sticky." Despite needing US capital and markets, Canadians, concerned by the "overwhelming size and power" of the United States, preferred "highly nationalistic policies – fearing that otherwise Canada would become, if not the 51st State, at least a neighbor heavily dependent on the US Colossus." Diefenbaker had pursued such policies vigorously but had lost power. The Liberals, Rusk observed, "in spirit, friendly to us and, in principle, much more sympathetic with U.S. objectives," also "felt compelled to take a series of measures that have kept our relations on the edge of tension."[90] Such tensions exploded in April 1965 with Pearson's public appeal to Johnson to pause the bombing of North Vietnam. As Greg Donaghy and Brendan Kelly each note, Mike chose to speak out about Vietnam after an American friend and journalist,

Marquis Childs, visited Pearson in March 1965. Contending that an isolated President Johnson, surrounded by war hawks, badly needed an outside opinion about Vietnam, Childs assured Mike that his intervention "would not be resented in Washington."[91] Childs was wrong. Probably compounding the president's anger at the Temple speech was the fact that Pearson had convinced Johnson to sign the lucrative Auto Pact in January 1965 over the objections of some US officials who had complained that the deal favoured Canada. The signing ceremony at Johnson's beautiful ranch in the Texas hill country, though, was marred when Johnson referred to Pearson as Harold Wilson, Britain's prime minister.[92] The Temple speech ensured that the president never forgot Mike's name. To use Bothwell's phrase, Canada found itself in the "presidential doghouse."[93] Pearson did not remain there for long.

Johnson, as a consummate politician, may not have welcomed the Canadian's advice on Vietnam but he recognized Mike's position. Two months after Pearson's outburst, the president complained that the war's opponents were winning over public opinion: "They have Harold Wilson on the ropes and they have the Prime Minister of Canada dodging and ducking."[94] "I like Mr Pearson," the president stated a year later. Reminding Canada's incoming ambassador that he did "not like speeches … 'in his own yard' telling him what to do," nonetheless, Johnson admired Mike, stating that "when the Canadians were asked to help they did so," as with the peacekeeping mission in Cyprus, where Canada's prime minister "had been as good as his word."[95] Pearson also followed through on renewing NORAD and maintaining military forces deployed in Europe as part of Canada's NATO commitment, moves taken over opposition in Canada and within the Liberal Party. More acrimonious was wrangling over recognition of communist China, with Pearson ultimately agreeing to continue toeing the American line despite his own personal conviction that Ottawa should recognize Beijing. There were even sharper differences on several economic files driven by nationalist elements within the Liberal Party. Interestingly, some of the sharpest criticism of Pearson came from Butterworth, his friend of many decades. US diplomatic files produced during the Pearson government are filled with Butterworth's acid reporting on Canada's "second-rate leaders" and his full-throated denunciations of what he saw as the Liberals' efforts to pursue "policies at variance with US views and harmful to US interests, which spell a general outlook which, if not anti-American in inspiration, is certainly anti-American in result."[96] There was little sympathy for Mike from a man who knew him well, even if Butterworth should have known better in regard to Pearson's supposed anti-Americanism.

That Johnson looked past the Temple speech to work cooperatively with Pearson should not surprise. After all, Canada and the United States were "tolerant allies" during the Cold War, capable of disagreement while still committed to containing Sino-Soviet power and building a mutually beneficial continental economic relationship.[97] Mike's career had showcased the tolerant alliance in action, and he very much personified this characterization of the Canada-US relationship. Having lived and worked in the United States, especially amid that country's wartime emergence as a superpower, Pearson had a keen appreciation for and understanding of Americans, their domestic politics, and the drivers of their country's foreign policy. Moreover, he was familiar with many important Americans, a key consideration in an era in which bilateral diplomacy was carried out by a small network of elites who largely shared the same worldview. This situation began to change markedly when Pearson left political office in 1968.[98] Yet, evidently, familiarity bred contempt. In explaining why Butterworth or Acheson often felt so angered with Mike, one is tempted to conclude that the reason lay partly in the fact these men had well-established social relationships, meaning that sharp differences over important policy matters – frequently Canada's hesitancy to follow the US line – provoked deep personal resentments. It is important, though, not to overstate the differences. During this period, Canadian and American officials were largely sympatico on the fundamental issues of containment and continentalism. Though Mike often had disagreed with Americans and had earned the opprobrium of Acheson et al., as Ritchie advised Johnson aide McGeorge Bundy, the United States "would never have a better or more understanding friend" than Pearson.[99] Sometimes friends have to piss on someone's rug.

NOTES

1 Butterworth to Rusk, 24 April 1967, Files of Dean Rusk, Miscellaneous Correspondence, RG 59, National Archives and Records Administration (NARA).

2 John English, *The Worldly Years: The Life of Lester Pearson*, vol. 2, *1949–1972* (Toronto: Knopf, 1992), 364; Dean Acheson, "Canada: 'Stern Daughter of the Voice of God,'" in *Neighbors*

Taken for Granted: Canada and the United States, ed. Livingston Merchant (New York: Praeger, 1966); Acheson cited in Charles Ritchie, *Storm Signals: More Undiplomatic Diaries, 1962–1971* (Toronto: Macmillan, 1983), 83.

3 J.W. Warnock, "Canadian Policy in Vietnam: Ready Aye Ready," *Canadian Dimension* 3 (May–June 1965), 3; Ian McKay and Jamie Swift, *Warrior Nation: Rebranding Canada in an Age of Anxiety* (Toronto: Between the Lines, 2012), 134; Linda McQuaig, *Holding the Bully's Coat: Canada and the US Empire* (Toronto: Doubleday, 2007), 159, 148; and Yves Engler, *Lester Pearson's Peacekeeping: The Truth May Hurt* (Vancouver: Fernwood, 2012).

4 John English, *Shadow of Heaven: The Life of Lester Pearson,* vol. 1, *1897–1948* (Toronto: Lester and Orpen Denys, 1989), 282.

5 Stephen Azzi, "The Problem Child: Diefenbaker and Canada in the Language of the Kennedy Administration," in *Reassessing the Rogue Tory: Canadian Foreign Policy in the Diefenbaker Era,* ed. Janice Cavell and Ryan Touhey (Vancouver: UBC Press, 2018), 103–20.

6 Lester B. Pearson, *Mike: The Memoirs of the Rt. Hon. Lester B. Pearson,* vol. 1, *1897–1948* (Toronto: University of Toronto Press, 1972), 73.

7 Pearson to Hickerson, 6 May 1944, reel 6, Matthews-Hickerson Papers, NARA; Gordon Stewart, *The American Response to Canada since 1776* (East Lansing: Michigan State University Press, 1992), 177–78; Galen Roger Perras, *Franklin Roosevelt and the Origins of the Canadian-American Security Alliance, 1933–1945: Necessary but Not Necessary Enough* (Westport, CT: Greenwood Press, 1998).

8 Pearson, *Mike,* 1, 268–69.

9 Pearson to Robertson, 3 November 1944, file Robertson N.A. to Dec 1945, vol. 13, Lester Pearson Papers, Library and Archives Canada (hereafter LAC); English, *Shadow of Heaven,* 296.

10 Edward Stettinius, memorandum, 14 November 1944, file 701.4111/11–144, State Department Records, Decimal File 1940–44, RG 59, NARA.

11 Entries, 13 June, 29 September, and 13 November 1944, W.L.M. King Diary, LAC; "The President's Reply to the Remarks of the Newly Appointed Ambassador of Canada Mr. L.B. Pearson," 22 January 1945, file Pearson LB – Appointment Ambassador to US, vol. 48, Pearson Papers, LAC.

12 "Canada's Envoy – A Man Called Mike," *Baltimore Sun,* 23 December 1944; Charles Driscoll, "New York Day by Day," *Williamsport Sun-Gazette,* 19 June 1946; Jean Eads, "Washington Letter," Hagerstown *Daily Mail,* 9 August 1946.

13 Balfour to Bevin, 6 August 1945, file T15944, vol. 4114, FO372, The National Archives of the United Kingdom; Acheson to Truman, "Joint Defense Measures with Canada," 1 October 1946, file State: Foreign Countries, box 138, President's Secretary's Files, Harry Truman Papers, Harry S. Truman Presidential Library (HSTL).

14 L.B. Pearson, *Mike: The Memoirs of the Rt. Hon. Lester B. Pearson,* vol. 2, *1948–1957,* ed. John A. Munro and Alex I. Inglis (Toronto: University of Toronto Press, 1973), 184; Bruce Hutchison, *The Far Side of the Street* (Toronto: Macmillan, 1976), 285.

15 Pearson, *Mike,* 2:56; English, *The Worldly Years,* 10; and Acheson to Pearson, 16 October 1946, file 27–5, box 27, Dean Acheson Papers, HSTL.

16 English, *Shadow of Heaven,* 296, 385n.

17 J.L. Granatstein, *A Man of Influence: Norman A. Robertson and Canadian Statecraft, 1929–1968* (Ottawa: Deneau, 1981), 69.

18 Entry, 11 January 1946, King Diary, LAC; English, *Shadow of Heaven,* 296–97; Atherton to Parsons, 2 February 1946, file 842.022/2–246, State Department Records, Decimal File 1945–49 (hereafter DF45–49), RG 59, NARA.

19 Entries, 21 February, 25 March, and 4 September 1946, King Diary, LAC.

20 James Reston, "Canadian Envoy Departs with Enhanced Prestige," *New York Times,* 4 October 1946.

21 Clark to Parsons, 5 September 1946, file 842.021/9–546, DF45–49, RG 59, NARA; Lewis Clark, *Diplomacy as a Career: Hard Work, Hardship, and Happy Times* (Washington, DC: Association for Diplomatic Studies and Training Collection, 2012), np, https://adst.org/OH%20TOCs/Clark-Lewis-memoir.pdf; Atherton to Foster, 18 April 1947, file 842.00/4–1847, DF45–49, RG 59, NARA.

22 Harrington, "Probable Early Resignation of External Affairs Secretary St. Laurent – Predicted Retirement of Prime Minister King," 23 July 1947, file 842.002/7–2347, DF45–49, RG 59, NARA; Atherton to Foster, 10 July 1947, file 842.021/7–1047, DF45–49, RG 59, NARA.

23 English, *Shadow of Heaven,* 324–25; John Holmes, *The Shaping of Peace: Canada and the Search for World Order, 1943–1957,* vol. 2 (Toronto: University of Toronto Press, 1982), 63; "Tactics for Passing, in Security Council, Palestine Resolution under Article VII," 28 May 1948, file Palestine-Miscellaneous Memos 3 of 3, box 13, Clark Clifford Papers, HSTL.

24 Wailes to Lovett, 9 January 1948, in *Foreign Relations of the United States [FRUS], 1948,* vol. 6 (Washington, DC: Government Printing Office, 1948), 1084.

25 English, *Shadow of Heaven,* 331; entry, 11 August 1948, King Diary, LAC.

26 Harrington to Snow, 9 September 1948, file 842.00PR/9–948, DF45–49, RG 59, NARA; Pearson, *Mike,* 2:4.

27 Harrington to Marshall, 13 September 1948, file 842.002/9–1348, DF45–49, RG 59, NARA; Fox to Marshall, 9 September 1948, file 842.00OR/9–948, DF45–49, RG 59, NARA.

28 Robert Bothwell, *Canada and the United States: The Politics of Partnership* (New York: Twayne, 1992), 41, 44.

29 Pearson to Robertson, 12 February 1946, file Robertson NA Canada External Affairs 1942–1946, vol. 13, Pearson Papers, LAC.

30 Robert Beisner, *Dean Acheson: A Life in the Cold War* (Oxford: Oxford University Press, 2006), 130; Dean Acheson, *Present at the Creation: My Years in the State Department* (New York: W.W. Norton, 1969), 277; Bothwell, *Canada and the United States,* 45, 39; Pearson, *Mike,* 2:68.

31 "Sketches of Diplomats Who Will Sign Pact," *Philadelphia Inquirer,* 4 April 1949; George Sokolsky, "These Days," New Philadelphia *Daily Times,* 28 April 1949; "As We See It," *Detroit Free Press,* 22 September 1949; "Canada to the Front," *Pittsburgh Press,* 3 October 1949.

32 Pearson to St. Laurent, 26 July 1950, file Korean Canadian Policy 1950–1951, vol. 35, Pearson Papers, LAC; Acheson, "Formosa: Contribution of Troops by Canada," 29

July 1950, in Dennis Merrill, ed., *Documentary History of the Truman Presidency: Volume 18* (Bethesda, MD: University Publications of America, 1995), 319–20.

33 Jessup, "Canadian UN Forces," 21 September 1950, file 310 Defense, box 1, Entry UD2195C, RG 84, NARA; English, *The Worldly Years,* 52.

34 DEA, *Statements and Speeches* 51/14, 10 April 1951 (Ottawa: DEA, 1951); Pearson to Wrong, 16 April 1951, file Korea: Canadian Policy 1950–1951, vol. 35, Pearson Papers, LAC.

35 "Uneasy Canada," *Boston Globe,* 12 April 1951; Sokolsky, "These Days," *Bridgeport Telegram,* 19 April 1951; Sokolsky, "These Days," *Washington Times-Herald,* 23 April 1951; "Canadian Plaint," *Washington Post,* 29 April 1951; Estabrook cited in minute sheet to Wrong, 19 April 1951, file Pearson LB Personnel File 1952–1954, vol. 48, Pearson Papers, LAC.

36 Wrong to DEA, 25 April 1951, file 1415–40, vol. 6184, RG 25, LAC; Wade, "Conversations at Canadian Embassy May 1, 1951," 14 May 1951, file 320 Canada-United States, box 8, Entry 2195C, RG 84, NARA.

37 Wrong to Pearson, 26 April 1951, file USA-Canada Relations 1945–1953, vol. 65, Pearson Papers, LAC; Pearson to Wrong, 16 April and 2 May 1951, file USA-Canada Relations 1945–1953, vol. 65, Pearson Papers, LAC.

38 Bliss to Woodward, 17 April 1951, *FRUS 1951, Volume 2,* 883–84.

39 Woodward to Acheson, 10 April 1951, *FRUS 1951, Volume 2,* 882–83; Woodward memorandum, 18 April 1951, *FRUS 1951, Volume 2,* 884–85; Minute sheet, 18 April 1951, file Pearson LB Personnel File 1952–1954, vol. 48, Pearson Papers, LAC.

40 Joseph Gies, *The Colonel of Chicago: A Biography of the* Chicago Tribune*'s Legendary Publisher, Colonel Robert McCormick* (New York: E.P. Dutton, 1979), 232–33.

41 "Peiping Named as Aggressor in Korean War," *Chicago Tribune,* 31 January 1951; "Canada Offers Fine Field to Rhodes' Wards," *Chicago Tribune,* 23 July 1951; "Pearson Steps Up His Race for UN's Top Post," *Chicago Tribune,* 18 February 1953; "Suckers," *Chicago Tribune,* 20 March 1953.

42 "Broadway Roundup," *New York Daily News,* 27 November 1953.

43 Greg Donaghy, "Blessed Are the Peacemakers: Canada, the United Nations, and the Search for a Korean Armistice, 1952–53," *War and Society* 30 (August 2011): 138.

44 Robert Bothwell, *Alliance and Illusion: Canada and the World, 1945–1984* (Vancouver: UBC Press, 2007), 102–3.

45 Evelyn Shuckburgh, *Descent to Suez: Foreign Office Diaries, 1951–1956* (New York: Norton, 1987), 54; Acheson, *Present at the Creation,* 700–3.

46 Lester B. Pearson to St. Laurent, 16 November 1953, vol. 65, MG 26 N1, LAC.

47 English, *The Worldly Years,* 121.

48 Daniel Macfarlane, "Caught between Two Fires: The St. Lawrence Seaway and Power Project, Canadian-American relations, and Linkage," *International Journal* 67 (2012): 465–82; Alexander W.G. Herd, "A 'Common Appreciation': Eisenhower, Canada, and Continental Air Defense," *Journal of Cold War Studies* 13 (2011): 4–26.

49 George Vest Oral History, 1998, ADST, https://adst.org/OH%20TOCs/Vest,%20George%20S.toc.pdf.

50 US Embassy Canada to State Department, no. 108, 30 July 1953, *FRUS 1952–1954, Volume 6*, document 975; Greg Donaghy, "Canadian Diplomacy and the Offshore Islands Crisis, 1954–1955: A Limited National Interest," *International Journal* 68 (2013): 242–54.
51 Pearson, *Mike*, 2:69.
52 Memorandum of Conversation between John Foster Dulles and L.B. Pearson, 15 February 1953, file 1415–40, pt. 12, vol. 4170, RG 25, LAC; Dulles to Pearson, 12 December 1955, file 1415–40, pt. 4.1, vol. 6786, RG 25, LAC.
53 Pearson, "Some Aspects of Canadian-American Relations," 27 March 1956, vol. 11, Pearson Papers, LAC; "He Doesn't Pontificate," *New York Times*, 31 May 1956.
54 Memorandum of Conversation, 2 November 1956, *FRUS 1955–1957, Volume 16*, document 941. See Marc J. O'Reilly, "Following Ike? Explaining Canadian-US Co-operation during the 1956 Suez Crisis," *Commonwealth and Comparative Politics* 35 (1997): 75–107.
55 Peter Stursberg, *Lester Pearson and the American Dilemma* (Toronto: Doubleday, 1980), 143–44; Antony Anderson, *The Diplomat: Lester Pearson and the Suez Crisis* (Fredericton, NB: Goose Lane Editions, 2015), 285–87.
56 Dwight Eisenhower, *The White House Years: Waging Peace, 1956–1961* (Garden City, NY: Doubleday, 1965), 84; Phone call, 6 November 1956, box 6, folder Canada (8), Whitman, File, Dwight David Eisenhower Library [DDEL].
57 "Mr. United Nations," *The Oregonian*, 16 October 1957; "A Well-Earned Peace Prize," *The New York Times*, 15 October 1957; "A Truly Deserved Prize for Pearson," *Detroit Free Press*, 15 October 1957; "Peacemaker," *Washington Post*, 15 October 1957; "High Honor for a Good Friend of US," *Seattle Times*, 16 October 1957.
58 "Irony of Peace," *Dallas Morning News*, 16 October 1957; "It Ain't Hay, but, It Isn't Peace," *Chicago Tribune*, 16 October 1957.
59 Acheson to Eden, 29 June 1966, in David McLellan and David Acheson, eds., *Among Friends: Personal Letters of Dean Acheson* (New York: Dodd, Mead, 1980), 278–79.
60 Pearson, *Mike*, 3, 166; English, *The Worldly Years*, 88.
61 Hoover to Nicholson, "Lester B. Pearson," 3 October 1951, Ladd to Hoover, "Lester B. Pearson," 23 October 1951, Schweppe to Branigan, "Lester B. Pearson," 8 February 1952, FBI file 65–6–356 Lester Bowles Pearson. We thank Antony Anderson for the FBI file.
62 Belmont to Boardman, "Lester Bowles Pearson," 16 April 1957, FBI file 65–6–356 Lester Bowles Pearson.
63 "Happenings in US Cited by Pearson," *Ottawa Citizen*, 3 May 1950.
64 George Sokolsky, "Pearson of Canada Protests Too Much," Montgomery *Journal*, 25 April 1957.
65 Diary, 16 April 1957, vol. 2, A.D.P. Heeney Papers, LAC; Pearson, "Memorandum of Conversation with Mr. Dulles, Paris, December 15, 1955," 20 December 1955, vol. 65, MG 26 N1, LAC.
66 "Victory for Reason," *New York Daily Mirror*, 2 April 1958; George Sokolsky, "Conservative Victory in Canada Should Help Relations with US," Appleton *Post-Crescent*, 8 April 1958.
67 "Canada's Modest Man of Peace," *Milwaukee Journal*, 17 October 1957; Philip Cook, "Liberals Pin Hopes on Pearson," *New York Herald Tribune*, 15 October 1957; "Mr. Pearson's Nobel Prize," *New York Herald Tribune*, 15 October 1957.

68 Janice Cavell, "The Spirit of '56: The Suez Crisis, Anti-Americanism, and Diefenbaker's 1957 and 1958 Election Victories," in *Rethinking the Rogue Tory*, 67–84.

69 "United States Objectives," July 1958, folder Canada Visit, July 1958, box 3, Ann Whitman File, International Meetings, Briefing Paper, DDEL; Dulles to Eisenhower, "Your Visit to Ottawa, July 8–11, 1958," *FRUS, 1958–1960, Volume 7*, 686.

70 A.J. Goodpaster, memorandum of conference with the president, 3 June 1960, folder June-July 1960, box 4, State Department Subseries, Office of the Staff Secretary, WHO, DDEL.

71 James Lay, "Memorandum for the National Security Council," 24 May 1960, folder NSC 5822, box 26, White House, Office of the NSA, NSC Series, Policy Papers, DDEL; Delmar Carlson to Rufus Smith, 27 February 1961, folder 320 Canada 1959–61, box 2, Entry US2195C, RG 84, NARA.

72 Kohler to Rusk, "Statements by Canadian Liberal Leader Lester Pearson Bearing on US-Canadian Relations," 11 January 1961, box 4, folder Canada, NORAD – Press Releases and Press Articles 1956–61, RG 59, NARA.

73 Alsop to Sommers, 2 February 1961, folder 5, box 30, Stewart Alsop Papers, Library of Congress Manuscript Division.

74 Willis Armstrong Oral History, 1988, np, ADST, https://adst.org/OH%20TOCs/Armstrong,%20Willis%20C.%201988.toc.pdf; Briefing note, "Pearson, Lester Bowles (Mike)," May 1961, box 113, folder Canada-Kennedy Trip to Ottawa, 5/61, President's Office File, John F. Kennedy Presidential Library (JFKL).

75 John F. Kennedy, "Review," *Saturday Review*, 1 August 1959.

76 English, *The Worldly Years*, 269.

77 Livingston Merchant, Livingston Merchant Oral History, Spring 1965, folder Kennedy, John F. Library, Oral History Project, box 13, MC095, Mudd Manuscript Library, Princeton University.

78 Pearson, *Mike*, 3, 100. Liberal MP John Matheson placed this meeting in Boston, as Kennedy had arranged for Pearson to get an honorary degree from Boston University (BU) so that he could pick his brain about Khrushchev. Pearson received an honorary doctorate from BU in June 1961, but Mike's meeting with Kennedy was in Washington. Stursberg, *Lester Pearson and the American Dilemma*, 181.

79 Merchant to State Department, no. 1030, 11 April 1962, folder Canada, General 4/62–5/16/61, box 18, National Security File (NSF), JFKL.

80 Knowlton Nash, *Kennedy and Diefenbaker: The Feud That Helped Topple a Government* (Toronto: McClelland and Stewart, 1991), 157; "49 Nobel Guests at Notable Evening," *Washington Post*, 1 May 1962.

81 Creery, "Political Benefits in Visit to Kennedy," *Ottawa Citizen*, 30 April 1962; "A Chat before Dinner," *Globe and Mail*, 30 April 1962.

82 Merchant to Ball, 5 May 1962, and Bundy to Ball, 8 May 1962, folder Canada, General, 4/62–5/16/61, box 18, NSF, JFKL.

83 Asa McKercher, *Camelot and Canada: Canadian-American Relations in the Kennedy Era* (Toronto: Oxford University Press, 2016), 176–206; Michael Stevenson, "'Tossing a Match into Dry Hay': Nuclear Weapons and the Crisis in U.S.-Canadian Relations, 1962–1963," *Journal of Cold War Studies* 16 (2014): 5–34.

84 Armstrong oral history, 1988, ADST, https://adst.org/OH%20TOCs/Armstrong,%20 Willis%20C.%201988.toc.pdf.
85 Ottawa to State, A-808, 11 March 1963 and Ottawa to State, no. 1196, 20 March 1963, folder Canada, General 3/16/63–3/31/63, box 18, NSF, JFKL.
86 Butterworth, quoted in McKercher, *Camelot and Canada,* 203.
87 Butterworth to State Department, no. 1328, 15 April 1963, folder Canada, General 4/11/63–5/3/63, box 18, NSF, JFKL; Brubeck to Bundy, "Outlook for New Canadian Government and Possible U.S. Tactics," 11 April 1963, folder Canada, General 4/11/63–5/3/63, box 18, NSF, JFKL.
88 Ritchie, *Storm Signals,* 48; Bundy to Rusk, 13 May 1963, folder 5/4/63–5/31/63, box 18a, NSF, JFKL; Butterworth Oral History Interview, JFKL; "Canada's New Course," *New York Times,* 7 May 1963; Walter Lippmann, "Today and Tomorrow," *Washington Post,* 16 May 1963; "Report on Canada," *Atlantic Monthly* (July 1963).
89 Stephen Azzi, *Walter Gordon and the Rise of Canadian Nationalism* (Montreal/Kingston: McGill-Queen's University Press, 1999).
90 Rusk to Johnson, "U.S.-Canadian Problems," 12 December 1963, folder Canada 12/63–7/64, box 165, National Security File, Lyndon Baines Johnson Presidential Library (LBJL).
91 Childs quoted in Greg Donaghy, *Tolerant Allies: Canada and the United States, 1963–1968* (Montreal/Kingston: McGill-Queen's University Press, 2002), 129; See also Brendan Kelly, "Lester B. Pearson's Temple University Speech Revisited: The Origins and Evolution of the Proposal for a Bombing Pause," *American Review of Canadian Studies* 47 (2017): 376.
92 Norman Hillmer and J.L. Granatstein, *For Better or For Worse: Canada and the United States into the Twenty-First Century* (Toronto: Thomson Nelson, 2007), 221; Robert Bothwell, *Your Country, My Country: A Unified History of the United States and Canada* (Toronto: Oxford University Press, 2015), 260.
93 Bothwell, *Canada and the United States,* 96.
94 Johnson-Bayh Telcon, 15 June 1965, 1:20 p.m., Recordings and Transcripts of Telephone Conversations and Meetings, White House Series, June 1965, box 7, LBJL.
95 Washington to DEA, tel. 2163, 23 July 1966, file Presentation of Credentials to President L.B. Johnson, vol. 9, A.E. Ritchie Papers, LAC.
96 Ottawa to State, 504, 23 October 1967 attached to Rostow to Johnson, 26 October 1967, folder Canada, Cables, box 166, NSF Country Files, LBJL.
97 Donaghy, *Tolerant Allies.*
98 Brian Bow, *The Politics of Linkage: Power, Interdependence, and Ideas in Canada-US Relations* (Vancouver: UBC Press, 2009).
99 Ritchie, *Storm Signals,* 82–83.

CHAPTER 3

THE LUMBERJACK WARS, 1943–44

Canadian-American Relations at the Border and the Lives of Ordinary People

Angelika Sauer

The Canadian ambassador in Washington was not happy. He had been called into the office of Secretary of State Cordell Hull and had been told that the unresolved tensions in Canadian-American relations were approaching a "combustible state," with Capitol Hill about to unleash a barrage of hostile criticism on Canada. While Allied armies were planning the invasion of the Nazi-dominated European continent, diplomats in Washington and Ottawa had to work overtime. Sharp words were exchanged. The Canadian government felt badgered and blackmailed, the American press howled, and a congressional committee sent a secret spy into Quebec. The issue at stake: Canadian lumberjacks. For over a year at the height of the Second World War, a harmonious North American relationship, supposedly infused with the spirit of neighbourly cooperation, was noisily disrupted over the issue of seasonal woodworkers.

How did this happen? Just a few years earlier, on 20 April 1941, US president Franklin D. Roosevelt and Canadian prime minister W.L. Mackenzie King had signed the Hyde Park Declaration as an economic measure to shore up the defence of the northern part of the western hemisphere. Designed to solve foreign exchange problems and eliminate production bottlenecks, Hyde Park signalled not only an acceleration of wartime economic integration but, according to King, also laid the foundation of a new world order "based on international understanding, on mutual aid, on friendship and goodwill."[1] None of these traits were in evidence two years later when a war of words broke out over how many Canadian woodworkers should be made available for seasonal work in the forests of Maine and Vermont.

How could an issue as seemingly insignificant as temporary labour migration reach the highest echelons of both governments? Lumberjacks – those rough-and-tumble individuals celebrated in Walt Whitman's poetry – seemed to exist in a different universe from the nations' capitals. Yet one does not have to look too far to find that the northern borderlands held a special place in the hearts and minds of politicians and diplomats escaping steamy Washington, DC, in the summertime for a few weeks in Bar Harbor, Maine, or in the case of Franklin Roosevelt, Campobello Island. Roosevelt's emotional affinity for the issue went much further. Having grown up in the Hudson Valley, he had developed a lifelong passion for forests, which he viewed through the lens of conservation as well as recreation. His New Deal Civilian Conservation Corps (CCC) was responsible for planting millions of trees even as the Works Progress Administration's Federal Art project murals celebrated cutting the trees down in commercial lumbering. Forest management, rather than a celebration of untouched wilderness, defined New Deal environmentalism. This meant, for example, that Roosevelt could jokingly suggest to his visitor from Canada, William Lyon Mackenzie King, in April 1941, that he was planting trees around Hyde Park to make the place self-sustaining through the sale of Christmas trees. Mackenzie King, himself the owner of a sizable estate in the Gatineau Hills, could relate to the recreational value of a secluded cottage but preferred the ambiance of the gentle English countryside and classical ruins for his own hideaway. However, they both agreed that decisions were sometimes best made away from their respective capitals, in the serenity of their nature retreats. This serenity could be a *leitmotif* of Canadian-American wartime relations. Then what explains the temporary tempest?

Political biographies tell the histories of turning points in broad strokes, allowing readers to see a complex world through the eyes of a protagonist whose actions are based on rational thought processes and an understanding of a developing trend. At their best, these biographies layer dense context around the causes and effects of individual actions. Individual agency is embedded in, and sometimes constrained by, impersonal structures. The broader social and cultural milieu of the era shapes what is plausible and possible for the main character to conceive and understand.

Other points of view come into play in the form of other political actors. The biographer's primary sources are a deft mix of public and private records to produce a multidimensional character who moves readers through events of historical significance, providing clarity and meaning.

In some respects, this chapter does not depart significantly from the mould of political biography. It presents well-known figures of Canadian political and diplomatic history wrestling with a problem that needed to be solved for more important things to happen. It shows Mackenzie King and Franklin Roosevelt, Norman Robertson and Lester Pearson, and American diplomats Cordell Hull and John D. Hickerson managing a minor crisis in the midst of world conflict. Yet the chapter also hints at different interests being swept to the surface by players who were not at the centre of events. And by introducing the wider framework, by showing how a minor political crisis was possibly a major crisis in the lives of ordinary people, this chapter, like Penny Bryden's, somewhat decentres traditional political biographies and surrounds Canadian-American relations with a context defined by social, cultural, and transnational migration history.

"DISREGARDING THE BOUNDARY": SEASONAL WORKERS AT THE BORDER TO LATE 1941

For most of the early twentieth century, casual wage labour constituted a substantial part of the North American workforce in resource-extracting industries, such as mining and logging, as well as in the agricultural work force in general, where seasonal workers made up 25 percent of the work force. Who were these workers? An American study conducted at the end of the Second World War, when the presence of foreign guest workers had become a politically charged topic, concluded that under normal peacetime conditions, the seasonal agricultural work force was native-born.[2]

However, historians of the North American borderlands have demonstrated how little international land borders (both in the south and in the north) mattered to itinerant workers. In the North American Upper West, historian Evelyne Stitt Pickett has argued, workers "moved freely across the boundary because the industries that employed itinerant workers were the same whether north or south of the border."[3] American historian Marcus

Lee Hansen's study from the 1930s on the mingling of the North American peoples also observed that industrialization led to the development of international industrial areas "where workers developed the habit of disregarding the boundary in their choice of employment," especially in the forest, mining, and milling industries.[4] Challenging migration models that postulate permanent unilateral movement from less developed agricultural regions or countries to industrializing or fully industrialized regions or countries, seasonal workers remind us of the comfortable coexistence of traditional forms of agriculture with industrialization, where one, in fact, maintains the other. For example, in many areas in the Midwest, small family farming and casual wage labour in industrial or semi-industrial sectors formed a symbiotic relationship.[5] Similarly, in the border region between Quebec, New Brunswick, and Maine, Montreal-based immigration historian Bruno Ramirez has shown, winter jobs in the lumber camps on either side of the border had long been a supplement to subsistence agriculture, as "the industry offered winter jobs to farmers who would have otherwise remained idle during their dead season."[6] York University's Yukari Takai also describes the mutually dependent relationship of lumber companies and rural families in the Quebec-Maine borderlands, both as a phenomenon that explains the workings of the family economy, in which young male family members were sent out to work from October to April to supplement the family farm income, and as a rite of passage and cultural initiation into the company of adult men.[7]

In these patterns of seasonal migration related to logging, proximity of home and work was a determining factor. A contemporaneous Canadian memorandum exploring the history of seasonal lumber worker cross-border migrations described lumbermen as farmers living "in parishes along the United States border and [being] employed within a few miles of their farms to which they return from time to time from their working in the United States."[8] This partially explains why seasonal work in the lumber industry was identified by contemporary observers as having the particular problem of high transience. One study done in 1912 showed that lumber camp workers stayed on the job an average of only fifteen to thirty days.[9] Woodworkers were farmers first, and the demands of their farms determined their availability. No doubt, the extremely harsh conditions in most lumber camps also contributed to men leaving the job frequently and early,[10] but, again, the close proximity of the family farm or other camps on either side of the border encouraged and facilitated higher mobility. This made recruitment of workers for the lumber camps a difficult exercise during which the employer had to create a much larger pool of potential supply than was actually required.

There were other historic patterns related to Canadian-American trade and economic relations that further complicated, but did not prevent, the free movement of lumberjacks. First, forest resources fell under radically different patterns of ownership in both countries. Whereas in Canada, 90 percent of forest areas were owned by the Crown and administered by provincial governments that leased woodland areas to pulp and paper mills, in the United States forest areas were largely privately owned. Second, the development of Canadian pulp and paper manufacturing, Canada's leading industry by the mid-twentieth century, was entirely dependent on the expanding American market, yet entry into that market was highly contested by mutually exclusive interests.[11] As American trade negotiators confessed to their British and Canadian counterparts in the late 1930s, they had to satisfy the interests of the American lumber industry "of whose log-rolling activities they were very much afraid."[12]

If trade in lumber and wood products had long been a slight but steady irritant in Canadian-American relations, the movement of woodworkers also became complicated in the 1930s. During the 1920s, the Canadian-American border had remained relatively open for workers despite calls by Canadian employers to stop the exodus of their own labour supply and lobbying by American unions, combined with a sympathetic attitude toward protecting American workers by the American immigration authorities.[13] In nonindustrial border regions, such as the Maine-Quebec borderlands, where the flow of labour was largely one of seasonal and agricultural workers without union protection, "population and the local products went to and fro with a freedom that would have appalled the officials of stricter regions."[14]

All of this changed with the onset of the Great Depression. American immigration officials at all border points were instructed to apply the "likely to become a public charge" clause of the immigration act and contract labour laws broadly, and the number of visas issued to Canadian workers declined precipitously. "[L]ife along the Canadian-U.S. border had become quiet,"[15] and the 1930s presented "a picture of an immobility among North Americans which contrasts sharply with that of any other time in the continent's history."[16] The sudden shift in the administration and application of US immigration regulations left a bitter memory in Canadian official circles.[17] Whether old patterns of seasonal employment were really disrupted as drastically as official figures indicate is questionable. Canadian officials and industry spokespeople repeatedly hinted that throughout the 1930s Canadians continued to work in the woods of Maine after having "skipped across the border illegally."[18]

The outbreak of war in Europe in September 1939 once again changed the parameters of the lumberjack issue. With timber supplies from the Scandinavian countries drying up and new uses for pulp in explosives and surgical dressings sending demand soaring, Canada's role in the Allied softwood lumber trade became central.[19] Reflecting the new importance of this sector of the wartime economy, the Canadian government assigned control of production and supply to a federal timber controller, H.R. MacMillan, of British Columbia.[20]

Other types of economic regulation also structured Canada's war effort and the timber trade. In June 1940, the House of Commons passed the National Resources Mobilization Act, which set up a system of national registration and mobilization of "manpower" for the war effort administered by the new Department of National War Services. In October 1941, Prime Minister Mackenzie King announced a policy of price and wage controls.[21] These regulations would soon demand mechanisms that prevented Canadians from leaving the country without an exit permit – a complication for cross-border migration patterns.

In contrast, the United States was relaxing its border controls. The first signs of labour shortages in sectors of the Eastern Canadian economy coincided with reports that American immigration authorities had started to waive passport and visa requirements for Canadian workers and had admitted over three thousand workers under bond for the 1941–42 lumber-cutting season in Maine and New Hampshire. New Brunswick and Quebec politicians and the Canadian media did not react kindly to this development and demanded government action: The "stable door is about to be locked" to prevent the "unchecked exodus" of thousands of Canadian lumbermen, proclaimed the *Montreal Gazette* rather prematurely, while the *Winnipeg Free Press* deplored the "leak in border regulations" that allowed US interests to "borrow" Canadian workers with impunity.[22] When the State Department showed some alarm over the possibility of Canada imposing exit controls on lumberjacks, Undersecretary Robertson admitted that a new form of "arbitrary stoppage of the movement of men or materials back and forth across the international boundary line" made little sense from an efficiency perspective.[23] It was time for both governments to sit down and plan ahead.

COMPLEMENTARY, NOT COMPETITIVE: THE WOODWORKER ISSUE IN 1942

With the entry of the United States into the war in December 1941, attention turned more urgently to efforts to coordinate the war production of the two countries. Economic experts on both sides of the border, delighted at the prospect of creating a more efficient and integrated economic unit, found themselves part of a bilateral body called the Joint Economic Committees. Historian Jack Granatstein has dismissed the committees as an "abortive Canadian effort at co-ordination and integration."[24] This may be true for most of their work, but the committees did, in fact, introduce a mechanism for the migration of seasonal labour between the two countries that lasted well into the postwar period. It is worth emphasizing that of all the features of transnational economic integration, the movement of human resources across borders is often the trickiest issue to address. So, it is perhaps not surprising that, even in an emergency situation, national economic mobilization and international economic cooperation were destined to collide.

In January 1942, the Joint Economic Committees passed Resolution 7, stipulating that the most efficient use of continental economic resources "*should logically include labour* [emphasis mine]." The resolution reminded the two governments that the "economic development of border areas has depended upon a relatively free flow of labour across the border," and especially of seasonal workers; their free movement was marked as essential to continental efficiency.[25] National and international war needs and historic regional relationships found a place in this reasoning. The committees followed up with Resolutions 8 and 9 in late February. These resolutions proposed that the two countries find a more effective way of using their respective resources in agricultural production, using the war as an "opportunity of recognizing complementary, rather than competitive aspects" of both farming economies. As one component of agricultural integration, the committees suggested a mechanism to facilitate the movement of seasonal farm labour across the international boundary.[26] The Canadian cabinet approved these recommendations on 19 March 1942; Roosevelt announced parallel US arrangements on 10 April. Throughout the early summer of 1942, bureaucracies in both capitals worked out the details for waiving passport requirements and contract labour laws and for posting departure bonds. The arguments of the "economic efficiency" experts, who saw the movement of labour as essential to continental integration and considered the border an obstacle to rational economic practices, seemed to have won the day. However, as we shall see, sectional economic interests and national and patriotic arguments in both countries would soon complicate matters. The lumberjack issue was a test case of things to come.

Early in January 1942, while the joint economic committees were working on their recommendations, a request came from the United States for an additional 470 woodcutters to be allowed to cross the border. "The movement of these workers at this time," Robertson worried, "might have political consequences in Canada out of relation to its economic importance." He suggested that a policy statement on the wartime pooling of resources would "make it clear that there was nothing necessarily unpatriotic in a Canadian working in an American industry."[27] This was not a popular position in the cabinet war committee, where a majority of ministers favoured "exit control in order to keep Canadian labour in Canada."[28] The political difficulties generated by this issue in Canada seemed to outweigh economic arguments for finding anything beyond temporary and administrative solutions instead of a policy solution. For the next several weeks, the issue was passed around like a hot potato among several departments in Ottawa. In May, Robertson called another meeting with the American minister in Ottawa to repeat the government's concern "that owing to the wage differential between the two countries vital Canadian labour was being siphoned away from the Dominion to the United States." Canadian industry spokespeople had accused US authorities of turning a blind eye to illegal entries and visa overstays. Moreover, they alleged that several American companies recruiting Canadian workers were not actually doing war work and that Canadian operators with leases south of the border were blocked from obtaining a share of the Canadian workers admitted to the United States.[29]

What started as a temporary problem involving a few hundred workers increasingly looked like a larger and longer-lasting issue, inspiring bitterness and jealousies that defied the spirit of economic cooperation. In order to create a technical allocation mechanism, representatives of the American and Canadian pulp and newsprint industries met several times throughout the summer of 1942 and came up with a quota of 3,700 workers for the 1942–43 winter seasons. Both sides remained far apart on how these numbers would be enforced and distributed.[30] During this timeframe, the movement of other seasonal agricultural labour was discussed as well, and Congress authorized the War Manpower Commission to import western hemisphere residents for war-essential industries, including the lumber industry.[31] The woodworker issue might have been punted further down the road, as no doubt many of those involved were hoping, had it not been for a Canadian order-in-council instituting a strict individual exit permit system. This restricted American recruiting for workers to a designated time period and closed the border when a negotiated quota was filled. Canada reasoned that to enforce the wage ceiling in Canada and motivate underemployed workers in the border region to find seasonal employment in other Canadian regions, there could not be a permanent prospect of employment in the better-paid American labour market. The informal and illegal flow that had hitherto quietly trickled around attempts to regulate what people and businesses of the borderlands could do was about to meet the new and formidable obstacle. And the diplomats, who had up to this point only played a peripheral role, were about to get a lot busier.

ILLEGALS AND LOAFERS: THE LUMBERJACK WARS HEAT UP

The ingredients for a larger conflict came together by the fall of 1943. A quota of 3,500 workers had been designated for the period 15 June to 31 October, 1943, but individual exit permits were contingent on a release from military duty and, for Quebeckers, a certificate by the province's *agronomes* that the worker's absence would not negatively affect agricultural production in their district.[32] Initially, woodworkers tried to pursue their accustomed patterns of work, not swayed by either patriotic or efficiency arguments and employing creative means to dodge regulations. For instance, since exit permits featured neither photographs nor fingerprints, young men of military age tried to use permits made out to men in their late thirties or forties, as did the teenager who presented himself to the American Immigration and Naturalization inspector at St. Albans, in Vermont, with an exit permit that identified him as Aime Gilbert, age thirty-eight. In another case, thirty-one men were apprehended by American authorities, identified as draft evaders, and allowed to self-deport back to Canada.[33] Yet workers who legally obtained exit permits and went to Maine proved to be as transient as all woodworkers. They left camp and returned home to the farm whenever needed there, even if that meant they could not return to work. American operators complained bitterly that the quota was never filled because the Canadian government did not issue replacement permits for workers who left. An American company acerbically noted that "in years past the Canadians have gladly permitted ... French Canadians to freely cross the border to work in our wood camps," but now the Canadian government was using arbitrary rules to give the Canadian pulp and paper industry an edge for the postwar period.[34]

Canadian operators fiercely disagreed that they unfairly benefited from the situation. Borderland workers without access to work in the United States, they explained, did not behave patriotically and accept Canadian jobs further away from home, no matter how essential the industry or how desperate the pleas of Canadian pulp and paper producers. Instead, they simply stayed home on the farm.[35] This left Quebec and New Brunswick politicians especially cranky and uncooperative. The only political leader still backing American demands for a quota for the 1943–44 winter months was labour minister Humphrey Mitchell, who reminded his colleagues that prior to the war an annual average of fifteen thousand workers from the region found employment in Maine and that just as many might expect access to the same opportunities in the postwar period.[36]

When the Labour Department took its arguments to the cabinet war committee on 22 September, deputy labour minister Thomas MacNamara received an earful. Neither historical nostalgia nor tactical planning for the postwar period, he was told, mattered when Canadian employers lacked the necessary workers to fulfill war orders. Instead, the ministers wanted a report on the impact of recalling all lumberjacks from the United States and closing the border. MacNamara had the disagreeable task of relaying this message to the US War Manpower Commission.[37] A lower-level administrative meeting on 28 September, to which the Department of External Affairs and the State Department sent observers, began hopefully but quickly descended into unpleasantness. "Everyone, of course," noted a Canadian participant, "said that they believed in the principle that the manpower involved should be used where it would most effectively serve the common war effort." Yet tempers flared when the American representative suggested that Canadian workers "would sit around in Canada doing nothing" if the border were closed. In his view, echoing American public opinion, Canada was already wasting plenty of its workforce in nonessential jobs, such as porters at Canadian railway stations. One imagines that MacNamara found it much easier at this point to firmly reply that there was "no chance" of the United States getting the 7,500 workers it had requested. Moreover, "disregarding domestic and international political considerations," it was more likely that current workers would be recalled and the border closed to allow Canadian employers in the lumber and base metal industries to fill open positions.[38]

The dispute now moved from the administrative to the intergovernmental level.[39] A meeting with the US minister was set up for the next day at the Department of External Affairs to find common ground and return to the spirit of the Hyde Park Declaration, which demanded that shortages be shared equitably. The meeting's participants defined the points of disagreement. The American side alleged underemployment by Canadian workers who were forced to stay in Canada; not unreasonably they pointed out that geographic isolation made the movement of Canadian workers to Maine rather than to more remote areas of Canada a "natural one owing to close proximity and habit." MacNamara, on the Canadian side, responded with hints that American authorities were aiding and abetting a steady drain of Canadian labour, if only by turning a blind eye to illegal entries. The Canadians also questioned whether American firms truly used Canadian labour for operations essential to the war effort rather than, say, for the production of newsprint.[40] Both sides agreed to provide data to clarify these points of friction. In the meantime, the Department of External Affairs got to work on a recommendation to the cabinet war committee that took all relevant factors into account. Economist John Deutsch made the case that "an overall

North American planning of forest production" done "on the basis of war needs and historical relationships" called for a reasonable quota to avoid waste. The broader context was acknowledged in that "failure to meet the American contentions would give opportunity for serious mischief in Canadian-American relations."[41] Canadian bureaucrats fully understood that letting men work in the woods of Maine "was not a popular proposition, and particularly so in the Province of Quebec."[42] But for the sake of the wartime relationship between the two neighbours, Canada had to be accommodating to a point. Prime Minister King agreed and personally intervened with his colleagues. On 25 October, cabinet approved a compromise, allowing current workers to stay in Maine and opening the border for a brief period in November to allow companies to recruit in specific regions close to the border. The number of Canadians allowed to work in the United States was capped at the prior quota of 3,500.

During this first skirmish, the Canadian side politicized the issue and brought historical grievances about capricious American border control enforcement into the discussions, giving the other side easy ammunition. It also became clear that the flow of information across the border had become quite decentralized, and unpopular points made by Canadian bureaucrats received wide circulation in Washington, where wartime appointees were working closely with industry representatives who did not hesitate to use the information to shore up their own political support. Consequently, discussions were no longer technical, and facts were interpreted very differently in both capitals. The return to the status quo ante by the end of 1943 may have appeared like a reasonable compromise to Canadian politicians but was seen as a capitulation in Washington. Just before Christmas, there were ominous rumblings that the problem would not go away in the new year: the representative of the US War Manpower Commission hinted that, bar a more favourable treatment of American demands, "the matter would become an open political issue in Congress."[43]

On 5 January 1944, Canada's ambassador in Washington, the aging Leighton McCarthy, received an unexpected summons to the State Department to meet with Secretary of State Cordell Hull. A future Nobel Peace Prize winner and one of the architects of the postwar liberal international order, Hull must have felt a little awkward lecturing the Canadian representative "that there was going to be on Capitol Hill adverse criticism of Canada of a combustible nature." McCarthy, who had been forewarned and briefed, explained that the quota numbers agreed on were "a great many more than we could or really ought to spare."[44] Both men parted with assurances of cooperation. Such was the veneer of diplomacy: Norman Robertson knew better. He forwarded the ambassador's report to the prime minister with a warning that the lumberjack question "has again become active and troublesome."[45]

A meeting in Ottawa on 11 January further hardened national positions. Ray Atherton, the American ambassador in Ottawa, insisted on the "premise that woods labour is a commodity to be shared in the best interest of our joint war effort." A short supply situation should never be an excuse to ban the export of any commodity. But was labour really a commodity like any other, to be shared under the principles of the Hyde Park agreement? Quietly, within the Canadian wartime bureaucracy, this fundamental question was now being articulated.[46]

Meanwhile, the two sides began to tally their data. Through a concerted effort by the Department of Labour, the Canadian woods labour force in eastern Canada had already doubled in size from 20,000 to 40,000 over just a few months. Moreover, Canadian operators were asking for another 20,000 workers. For their part, American operators in the far northeast complained that they were down to a fraction of the number of Canadians they would normally have working in their winter camps. They needed 12,500 workers but had only 2,500 local Americans available, leaving them short 10,000 Canadians. Where were the missing 30,000 Canadian woodworkers to be found, one wonders? Even the official American position seemed to acknowledge the basic absurdity of the debate about numbers of available workers that may or may not have existed. The official request that went to the cabinet war committee was for a survey of the border regions to address persistent rumours of idle available workers, as well as for an additional modest quota and a mechanism for replacements to keep the existing quotas filled.[47]

The only Canadian concession in mid-January 1944 was the commissioning of a survey of ten border counties in Quebec. There was no sense of urgency in Ottawa, when perhaps there should have been. Atherton did not receive a response to his communication following the 11 January meeting, and therefore the State Department could not run interference in Washington, where rumours swirled that Canadians were failing to do their part in the joint war effort. At the beginning of February, for instance, the *New York Times* and the *Boston Herald* both reported at length that "hundreds of able-bodied young men" in the Quebec towns adjacent to the border were seen "loafing in the streets, in garages and in stores." The reports accused the Canadian government of preventing these men from leaving, despite critical shortages in the Maine woods. The American Newspaper Publishers Association, clearly a party with a horse in the race, reprinted the story in its bulletin, blanketing the United States. Domestic critics of the governing Liberal Party in Ottawa proclaimed this, not unreasonably, a public relations disaster that was likely to undo much of the work of the Wartime Information Board. Americans, "having accepted conscription for service anywhere in the world, cannot be expected to understand … the weaknesses and bungling of our manpower policy," crowed the conservative *Globe and Mail*. The stereotype of the idle Quebecker, already circulating in English Canada, was now amplified for an international audience.[48]

The reality, as presented in the unscientific but nevertheless revealing survey, was different from the inflammatory picture presented in American papers. The survey presented a borderlands area that had been "thoroughly and efficiently checked over for manpower." Over twenty-two hundred men had been recruited into farms' winter woods operations, leaving behind only women, children, and old men to take care of farming operations. For example, in L'Islet County, a two hundred–acre farm with nineteen dairy cows, ten other cattle, and horses, pigs and poultry was looked after by a woman and a young boy, instead of the three men who usually did the work. Some of the men were now returning to the farms to do the necessary preparations for the spring. Mayors reported that it was very common for farmers to return every four to five days to do essential work. For this reason, they would not accept work 125 miles north. The expensive railway fare was another disincentive to accepting Canadian jobs, even when the border was closed. There were, in these anecdotes, plenty of rational reasons for able-bodied men in the surveyed area (108 out of 201, to be precise) to be found "idle," lending some credibility to the

American argument that the same men would have been contributing to the war effort if allowed to cross the border. As it was, food production in the borderlands was being affected and "idle" men were needed on neighbouring farms. As one mayor put it, the fact that he himself could not find needed help proved "that there are not many loafers in this village."[49]

The negative press coverage seemed to require a public statement by the government, and on 7 February, labour minister Mitchell explained the Canadian position in a speech to the House of Commons. He could not leave well enough alone, however, and he accused the Americans of not returning Canadian workers home once their time was up and of not providing accurate information about policing the borders. Atherton reacted with a very sharp note to Canada's Undersecretary of State for External Affairs, Norman Robertson, claiming that Ottawa's failure to provide data and valid arguments for its position had turned a small issue into an urgent and serious political problem in Washington, with congressional pressure on the State Department increasing.[50]

Robertson scrambled to draft the reply he had owed Ambassador Atherton, but the diplomatic damage was done. John D. Hickerson, the blunt Texas diplomat responsible for Canada in the State Department, declared the reply "pretty curt in form and unimpressive in content." Robertson had to agree. "I am afraid we are in for further public controversy," he sighed in a memo to King, admitting that the Canadian position was weak both in substance and in the way it had been conveyed publicly. His own communication, he added, was not "a very impressive statement of our position." To Robertson, the lumberjack question "ha[d] a nuisance value out of all relation to its economic importance either to us or to the Americans."[51]

At this point, heavy political pressure by pulp and paper representatives and newspapers on both sides of the border turned up the heat. On 18 February, the Canadian ambassador was once again called in for a formal interview, this time with Acting Secretary of State Edward Stettinius.[52] The next day the ambassador's deputy, Lester Pearson, received even rougher treatment and was lectured in no uncertain terms about American unhappiness at Canada's cavalier treatment of US requests for additional workers. The United States was especially upset with Canada's unwillingness to make a concession for the larger principle of friendly bilateral relations, if only to give the State Department ammunition to deal with congressional pressure. Pearson concluded that "we would very definitely hear more of this matter. I hope I am wrong, as it certainly would be a great misfortune if this issue, unimportant in itself, were permitted to develop serious irritations."[53] Indeed, by late February, the entire Hyde Park agreement was in trouble as cabinet began to wonder whether it applied to workers at all. Indeed, Canadian arguments assumed the priority of Canada's own national "manpower" mobilization policy over continental considerations.[54]

The next diplomatic black eye went to Washington. By the beginning of March, it had become obvious that an American, Haven Sawyer, of Bangor, Maine, was travelling around southern Quebec interviewing mayors about the labour situation. He seemed to have been sent by the Special Committee of the Senate to Investigate the National Defense Program, but nothing had been cleared through official channels.[55] It was insulting that a congressional committee saw fit to question and check on a report made by the Canadian government. Now it was up to the Canadian officials to read their counterparts the riot act and ask them to remove the "roving prober."[56] The State Department, with egg on its face, talked to the committee's chair, Missouri senator Harry S. Truman, who claimed that Sawyer was in Canada at the behest of an individual congressman rather than the committee itself. Still, when Truman's committee reported in March, it was scathing in its indictment of the attitude of the Canadian government toward the woodworker question, fuelling another round of inflammatory press reports in the United States focused on the Quebec or "nationalities" angle of the issue.[57]

DENOUEMENT: THE SPIRIT OF HYDE PARK

It took a surprisingly long time for diplomats to resume control of the form and content of the discussion. By 21 March, the State Department had received a detailed explanation, drafted by Robertson and verbally transmitted by Pearson, of the practical problems faced by the Canadian government in enforcing its wage control and labour force mobilization policies. In return, Hickerson apologized to Pearson for the Sawyer incident, admitting that he had no business crossing the border without prior clearance. "Relations, both official and unofficial, between our two countries," he reminded Pearson, "were so informal that the border is often overlooked."[58] The kiss-and-make-up exchange between the two foreign offices was followed by one last stand at the cabinet war committee on 12 April, when ministers expressed their outrage over being "badgered and blackmailed" by the flood of adverse publicity as a result of the "impertinent" American investigations. Not surprisingly, they decided to stand firm on their policy of not making concessions under public American pressure.[59]

And just as quickly as the storm had arisen, it ended. Quietly, at the administrative level, deputy minister of labour MacNamara assured the US War Manpower Commission that toning down the newspaper coverage would be enough to persuade Canadian ministers to allow farmers, who had gone home for the seeding season, to return to Maine when the spring work was done. Soon there was a joint announcement, on 21 April 1944, that 3,500 exit permits for Canadian lumberjacks had been renewed, and the newspapers moved on to different issues. The Department of Labour provided a pointed final rebuttal to the barrage of American accusations: "If one considers the fact that Canada has made an honest effort to provide labour for the Maine woods in the face of persistent domestic labour shortages it can be fairly stated that the spirit of the Hyde Park Agreement has been carried out."[60] Officials on both sides of the border went back to conducting the real war and planning global peace. Lessons learned, no further flare ups were permitted; by September of 1944, the beginning of lumberjack season, the State Department inquired quietly whether it would be smart to ask officially for a higher quota. In other words, no request would be made if the Canadians would reject it for political reasons. In fact, though, the employment situation in Canada was turning, and with unemployment on the rise in Quebec City and Montreal, men were now available for work in Maine. It would not be long before Canadian authorities would ask the Americans to guarantee a minimum number of admissions for woodworkers, rather than fight off an increase in exit permits. Normalcy had been restored.

CONCLUSIONS

The lumberjack wars of 1943–44 were a mere blip on the radar screen of Canadian-American relations during the Second World War, but they displayed several of the basic characteristics that were to define the postwar relationship. Lester Pearson saw the issue as one of many examples of the "disposition of Americans to ignore Canadian interests." Pearson complained, "The American authorities often tend to consider us not as a foreign nation at all, but as one of themselves." Obviously, this was not a good thing for Canada, or so his biographer John English implies.[61] Pearson's colleague Norman Robertson, undersecretary of state for external affairs in Ottawa, had similar concerns. His biographer, Jack Granatstein, quotes a memorandum penned in late December 1941 which diagnosed Washington's growing inclination "to take Canadian concurrence and support entirely for granted." The Roosevelt administration, Robertson complained, viewed Canada in a "more merely domestic perspective."[62] Both biographers suggest that Canadian officials sensed a seismic shift in the relationship with their southern neighbour and viewed the potential outcomes with some trepidation.

The lumberjack wars were a public relations disaster and a minor diplomatic crisis that vexed foreign policy experts and riled newspaper readers on both sides of the border. There were multiple positions that constituted the parameters of the debate. As Granatstein has pointed out, economic experts on both sides of the border were elated at the chance to integrate the two economies and make them more efficient, utilizing continental resources in more rational ways. These experts argued that labour had to be included in the liberalization of cross-border traffic. The diplomats and foreign offices in Ottawa and Washington worked within the larger context of cooperation for victory and the cementing of a friendly relationship. As historian Robert Bothwell has suggested, it would be an exaggeration to say that every exchange between the two countries was fruitful and friendly, but considering the volume of contact and the economic importance of the transborder trade, "it is surprising how few problems had to be resolved at the diplomatic or political level."[63] As long as things could be kept out of the public eye and in proper channels, diplomats could respect the other country's legitimate problems and be cooperative in their approaches.

The core factor of the lumberjack issue was that due to the heavy self-interest of the newspaper industry, these rules were broken, and the diplomats failed to control the message. Much mischief ensued. Politicians under public pressure had to be much pricklier and more nationalistic than the continentalist Hyde Park model demanded. The American public seemed to feel that some Canadians were not working hard enough and that Canadians should simply do what was asked of them by their neighbour. After all, under peacetime conditions, Canadian politicians seemed to be happy to have an outlet for their surplus workers in the American labour market. Canadians thought that Americans oversimplified the problem by making it all about French Canada and that Canada had a right to keep its own workers to maximize the Canadian war effort. They were the first to question that economic integration included people.

But what about the workers themselves? The lumberjack wars strongly suggest that Canadian-American international relations, in the end, are co-determined by individuals and their own relationship to the border. The interests of seasonal workers were not properly represented in the cross-border discussions. Only the Canadian Department of Labour seemed to be aware of the historical benefits for borderlands workers of a relatively open border and to be willing to extend cooperation for the sake of future American concessions to the Canadian workers. The other parties to the discussion constructed workers as pawns that could be moved on the chessboard of national or continental mobilization. However, workers had their own ways of resisting – in Pearson's words, they remained "immobilized." They simply did what was best for the family economy: higher wages made work in the Maine woods attractive even if they faced poor conditions in work camps and social discrimination.[64] Workers were patient to wait for the next opening of the border. Therefore, they simply sat tight and refused to take jobs elsewhere in Canada. Similarly, they left work camps without hesitation to return to farms across the border when they were needed. If necessary, they crossed the border illegally. If this was a way to evade the draft, they did this, too. Economic self-interest trumped patriotism.

What does this story tell us about the value, and the shortcomings, of political biography? If we are looking for the big themes of the era, such as Canadian-American wartime cooperation and North American economic integration, political biography illuminates how this particular crisis was handled and how it was eventually resolved. Overall, this case study confirms that while diplomats did not control all factors in the relationship, such as the actions of individuals, newspaper editors, or industry lobbyists, they were doing their best to keep a calm surface of partnership and cooperation on the roiling waters underneath. The Bothwell-Donaghy thesis of Canadian-American relations asserts that cooperation tends to prevail in the face of daily irritants is thus reinforced by this example.[65] And yet, by turning the perspective around, by adding to the inside-out view of traditional biographies the outside-in view of borderlands and migration studies, we obtain a more complex and nuanced picture of the dynamics of this time period that includes the daily lives of ordinary people.

NOTES

1 *Canada and the War: The Hyde Park Declaration; Cooperation in Economic Defence,* Statement by Right Hon. W.L. Mackenzie King in the House of Commons, 28 April 1941 (Ottawa: Ministry of National War Services, 1941), http://wartimecanada.ca/sites/default/files/documents/WLMK.HydePark.1941.pdf.

2 Harry Schwartz, *Seasonal Farm Labor in the United States: With Special Reference to Hired Workers in Fruit and Vegetable and Sugar-Beet Production* (New York: Columbia University Press, 1945), 14–15.

3 Evelyne Stitt Pickett, "Hoboes across the Border: Itinerant Cross-Border Laborers between Montana and Western Canada," in *The Borderlands of the American and Canadian Wests: Essays on the Regional History of the Forty-Ninth Parallel,* ed. Sterling Evans (Lincoln: University of Nebraska Press, 2006), 204.

4 Marcus Lee Hansen, *The Mingling of the Canadian and American Peoples,* vol. 1, *Historical* (New Haven, CT: Yale University Press, 1940), 252.

5 Frank Tobias Higbie, *Indispensable Outcasts: Hobo Workers and Community in the American Midwest, 1880–1930* (Chicago: University of Illinois Press, 2003), 52–53.

6 Bruno Ramirez, *Crossing the 49th Parallel: Migration from Canada to the United States, 1900–1930* (Ithaca, NY: Cornell University Press, 2001), 12.

7 Yukari Takai, *Gendered Passages: French-Canadian Migration to Lowell, Massachusetts, 1900–1920* (New York: Peter Lang, 2008), 27–28; J.J. Deutsch, Memorandum, October 1943, Records of the Department of External Affairs, file 2717-40 pt. II, RG 25, Library and Archives Canada (hereafter LAC).

8 Draft Memorandum to Prime Minister, 7 November 1941, file 2717-40, RG 25, LAC.

9 Pickett, "Hoboes across the Border," 204.

10 Higbie, *Indispensable Outcasts,* 40–41.

11 W.T. Easterbrook and Hugh G.J. Aitken, *Canadian Economic History* (Toronto: Macmillan of Canada, 1956), 543–54.

12 Ian M. Drummond and Norman Hillmer, *Negotiating Freer Trade: The United Kingdom, the United States, Canada, and the Trade Agreements of 1938* (Waterloo, ON: Wilfrid Laurier University Press, 1989), 136.

13 Donald H. Avery, "Canadian Workers and American Immigration Restriction: A Case of the Windsor Commuters, 1924–1931," *Mid-America: An Historical Review* 80, 3 (Fall 1998): 235–63; Thomas A. Klug, "The Detroit Labor Movement and the United States-Canada Border, 1885–1930," *Mid-America: An Historical Review* 80, 3 (Fall 1998): 209–34.

14 Hansen, *The Mingling of the Canadian and American Peoples*, 252.

15 Ramirez, *Crossing the 49th Parallel*, 137.

16 Hansen, *The Mingling of the Canadian and American Peoples*, 263.

17 Draft Memorandum to Prime Minister, 7 November 1941, file 2717–40 pt. I, RG 25, LAC.

18 Escott Reid to Robertson, 28 September 1943, reprinted in John Hilliker, ed., *Documents on Canadian External Relations [DCER]*, vol. 9, *1942–43* (Ottawa: Minister of Supply and Services Canada, 1980), 1338–39. Wartime estimates spoke of fifteen thousand Canadian woodworkers per year finding seasonal employment in Maine before the war. Heeney to Cabinet War Committee, 21 September 1943, reprinted in Hilliker, *DCER*, 9:1336–37.

19 Canadian pulp production surged from 4.2 million tons in 1939 to 5.6 million tons in 1945, and the export of pulp doubled. Over 90 percent of the exports went to the US, without tariff restrictions.

20 Easterbrook and Aitken, *Canadian Economic History*, 543–45.

21 J.L. Granatstein, *Canada's War: The Politics of the Mackenzie King Government, 1939–1945* (Toronto: Oxford University Press, 1975), 99–101, 180; Robertson, Memorandum, 23 March 1942, file 2717–40, RG 25, LAC.

22 "Lumbermen Exodus to Stop," *Montreal Gazette*, 8 November 1941; "Lumber Jobs in U.S. Raise Passport Points," *Winnipeg Free Press*, 19 November 1941.

23 Robertson, Memoranda to Prime Minister, 7 and 19 November 1943, file 2717–40, RG 25, LAC. In the 1941–42 logging season, 7,400 Canadians were employed in the New England woods. "Employment of Canadians in the Maine Woods," 14 January 1944, file 2717–40, RG 25, LAC.

24 Granatstein, *Canada's War*, 147.

25 Resolution N. 7, Joint Economic Committees of the United States and Canada, 16/17 January 1942, file 2717–40, RG 25, LAC.

26 Mackintosh, Chairman of the Canadian Committee of the Joint Economic Committees, Memorandum to Prime Minister, 3 March 1942, reprinted in Hilliker, *DCER*, 9:1434–37.

27 Robertson, Memorandum to Prime Minister, 3 January 1942, file 2717–40, RG 25, LAC.

28 US Minister in Ottawa, Memorandum, 30 January 1942, file 2717–40, RG 25, LAC.

29 American Representative in Ottawa, Memorandum, 4 May 1942, file 2717–40, RG 25, LAC. A draft of a cable from the Canadian embassy in Washington to External Affairs was blunt in describing the actions of US authorities as a "method of raiding our Canadian manpower."

30 H.F. Angus to Robertson, 8 July 1942, file 2717–40, RG 25, LAC.

31 Julia Henderson, "Foreign Labour in the United States during the War," *International Labour Review* 52 (1945): 611–13.

32 A.D.P. Heeney to Cabinet War Committee, 21 September 1943, reprinted in Hilliker, *DCER*, 9:1336–37.

33 INS District Director St. Albans, Memorandum, 4 October 1943, file 2717–40, RG 25, LAC.

34 Letter to State Department, 15 September 1943, file 2717–40, RG 25, LAC.

35 These points were brought up in a memorandum prepared by the US Legation in Ottawa, "The Need for Canadian Workers," 11 October 1943, file 2717–40, RG 25, LAC. J.J. Deutsch anecdotally confirmed this with the mayor of Saint-Zacharie, near the border with Maine: about 90 percent of regular cross-border lumberjacks would stay home if the border were closed rather than go to work in northern Quebec or New Brunswick.

36 Heeney to Cabinet War Committee, 21 September 1943, reprinted in Hilliker, *DCER*, 9:1336–37.

37 Minutes of Cabinet War Committee, 22 September 1943, reprinted in Hilliker, *DCER*, 9:1337–38; Deputy Minister of Labour, Memorandum to Chairman of War Manpower Commission, 24 September 1943, file 2717–40, RG 25, LAC.

38 Reid to Robertson, 28 September 1943, reprinted in Hilliker, *DCER*, 9:1338–39.

39 "Employment of Canadians in the Maine Woods," 14 January 1944, file 2717–40, RG 25, LAC.

40 Minutes of Meeting, 29 September 1943, reprinted in Hilliker, *DCER*, 9:1339–42; Minister of the US, Memorandum, 29 September 1943, reprinted in Hilliker, *DCER*, 9:1342–43; J.J. Deutsch, Notes on Meeting, 29 September 1943, file 2717–40, RG 25, LAC.

41 John Deutsch, Memorandum, "Canadian Workers for the New England Woods," 22 October 1943, file 2717–40, RG 25, LAC; Minutes of Meeting of Cabinet War Committee, 12 October 1943, reprinted in Hilliker, *DCER*, 9:1343–44.

42 Ambassador in the United States to SSEA, 7 January 1944, reprinted in Hilliker, *DCER*, 9:1623–24. "Quebec" here refers to employers rather than workers, an interesting conflation.

43 "Employment of Canadians in the Maine Woods," 14 January 1944, file 2717–40, RG 25, LAC.

44 Ambassador in the United States to SSEA, 7 January 1944. One wonders if the repeated use of the word "combustible" was a pun, given that the discussion was about alpha pulp for explosives.

45 Robertson to Prime Minister, 11 January 1944, file 2717–40, RG 25, LAC.

46 Fowler, Wartime Prices and Trade Board, to Robertson, 24 January 1944, file 2717–40, RG 25, LAC.

47 Atherton to Robertson, 12 January 1944, reprinted in Hilliker, *DCER*, 9:1624–25; SSEA to Ambassador in the United States, 14 January 1944, reprinted in Hilliker, *DCER*, 9:1626–29.

48 "Canada Bars Men from Maine Work: Low Cross-Border Quota Keeps Hundreds Idle While Pulpwood Cutters Cry for Help," *New York Times*, 1 February 1944; "Idle Manpower in Quebec," *Globe and Mail*, 4 February 1944. For the long history of the bitter internal divisions over conscription, see J.L. Granatstein, *Canada at War: Conscription, Diplomacy, and Politics* (Toronto: University of Toronto Press, 2020).

49 Department of Labour to Heeney, "Canadian Woods Labour for the New England States," 2 February 1944, file 2717–40, RG 25, LAC.

50 Atherton to Robertson, 8 February 1944, reprinted in Hilliker, *DCER*, 9:1629–31.

51 Robertson to Prime Minister, 19 February 1944, reprinted in Hilliker, *DCER*, 9:1633–34; Pearson to Robertson, 19 February 1944, reprinted in Hilliker, *DCER*, 9:1634–35.

52 Ambassador to SSEA, 18 February 1944, reprinted in Hilliker, *DCER*, 9:1632.

53 Pearson to Robertson, 19 February 1944, reprinted in Hilliker, *DCER*, 9:1634–35.

54 Minutes of Cabinet War Committee, 22 February 1944, reprinted in Hilliker, *DCER*, 9:1635–36.

55 Robertson to Pearson, 2 March 1944, reprinted in Hilliker, *DCER*, 9:1637; Pearson to Robertson, 6 March 1944, reprinted in Hilliker, *DCER*, 9:1639.

56 Wershof to Robertson, 15 March 1944, file 2717–40, RG 25, LAC.

57 Pearson to Robertson, 8 March 1944, file 2717–40, RG 25, LAC; Wershof to Robertson, 15 March 1944, file 2717–40, RG 25, LAC; "Mike" Pearson to "Norman" Robertson, 21 March 1944, file 2717–40, RG 25, LAC.

58 Robertson to Pearson, 17 March 1944, reprinted in Hilliker, *DCER*, 9:1640–41; Pearson to Hickerson, 21 March 1944, file 2717–40, RG 25, LAC; Pearson to Robertson, 8 April 1944, file 2717–40, RG 25, LAC.

59 Robertson, Memorandum, 15 April 1944, file 2717–40, RG 25, LAC; Robertson to Prime Minister, 19 April 1944, reprinted in Hilliker, *DCER*, 9:1642–43.

60 Department of Labour, Memorandum, 13 April 1944, file 2717–40, RG 25, LAC.

61 Pearson, quoted in John English, *Shadow of Heaven: The Life of Lester Pearson*, vol. 1, *1897–1948* (Toronto: Lester and Orpen Dennys, 1989), 256.

62 Robertson, quoted in J.L. Granatstein, *A Man of Influence: Norman A. Robertson and Canadian Statecraft, 1929–68* (Ottawa: Deneau, 1981), 118.

63 Robert Bothwell, *Canada and the United States: The Politics of Partnership* (Toronto: University of Toronto Press, 1992), 21–22.

64 Henderson, "Foreign Labour," 619, 627.

65 Bothwell, *Canada and the United States*; Greg Donaghy, *Tolerant Allies: Canada and the United States, 1963–1968* (Montreal/Kingston: McGill-Queen's University Press, 2002).

CHAPTER 4

COMPETING BIOGRAPHIES

How James Gladstone Became Canada's First Indigenous Senator

P. Whitney Lackenbauer

In early January 1958, Prime Minister John Diefenbaker called James Gladstone to inform him that he would be appointed to the Senate. "I was having a cup of tea at the home of my son-in-law in Calgary when the phone rang," Gladstone recounted. "I recognized the prime minister's voice and I just about dropped. He told me, 'I want to appoint you a senator.'"[1] There were a few preconditions that needed to be met, including property requirements, and Diefenbaker suggested that Gladstone buy some property off reserve. The next day, Gladstone purchased a five-room modern house on four-and-a-half acres in the east end of Cardston, Alberta. On 30 January 1958, he notified the prime minister by telegram that he had fulfilled the requirements.[2] Gladstone returned to his daughter Pauline Dempsey's house in Calgary to wait for a return call (because he did not want to speak with the prime minister using the party line on the reserve) but retreated to bed when the call did not come that evening. The next morning, a reporter from the *Lethbridge Herald* broke the official news. "I then received the official phone call from the prime minister," Gladstone recounted.[3] His wife Jane later laughed that when the news arrived, she "just about had heart failure."[4]

On 31 January 1958, Order-in-Council P.C. 1958–184 made Jim Gladstone Canada's first Indigenous senator. When a *Calgary Herald* reporter and photographer showed up at Hugh and Pauline Dempsey's house, Gladstone changed out of his usual attire and donned the improvised "Indian" outfit of a borrowed buckskin shirt, leggings, moccasins, and headdress that he had pulled together the previous summer for an event at the Calgary Stampede. Jane wrapped an Indian blanket from the chesterfield around her shoulders, thus ensuring that she also conformed sufficiently to Canadian stereotypes. Photographs of the proud couple, looking suitably "Indian," appeared in newspapers across the country.[5]

* * *

"A Canadian member of Parliament has proposed that the 160,000 Indian people in Canada have a direct representative in the Senate," *The Native Voice*, the official organ of the Native Brotherhood of British Columbia, informed its readers in mid-1955. "He is John Diefenbaker, Progressive-Conservative member for Prince Albert, Saskatchewan." On 25 March, Diefenbaker had risen in the House of Commons and suggested that the government appoint a "full-blooded Indian" to a seat in the Senate.[6] Although the vast majority of status Indians[7] did not have the right to vote for members of Parliament (never mind run for office) until 1960, their domestic plight and demands that the government recognize their Indigenous and treaty rights elicited increasing attention after the Second World War. Diefenbaker was a dedicated ally who tried to influence the government agenda.

Diefenbaker had limited leverage until he became prime minister two years later. An unpublished article by Chief Rising Sun, penned for *The Native Voice* in June 1957, summarized the situation:

> Among the election promises of our new Premier, John Diefenbaker, was to appoint an Indian to the Senate at Ottawa. We think this is an excellent idea and a sound one. The appointment of Senator is for life. The choice therefore must be carefully made … While the function of the Senate seems to be more of approval of legislation … rather than of its suggestion or creation, nonetheless most of these individuals get around and exercise great influence. The Indian selected, once he is appointed, should make it his business to be close to Ottawa at all times, and ready to act on behalf of Indians. He should possess a thorough knowledge of Indian affairs and [be] ready to deal with any official of that department. In other words our Indian Senator should really work at it – for life![8]

In January 1958, after months of internal debate and public speculation, Diefenbaker announced the appointment of James Gladstone, a member of the Blood Tribe, or Kainai Nation, to the Senate. The prime minister heralded the selection of Gladstone as a significant step forward in dealing with the "treatment and living conditions of Canada's first citizens, the Indians," which was "a matter of major concern to the Conservative Government."[9] Although the socioeconomic impact of Gladstone's appointment is difficult to gauge, its political symbolism was unmistakable. Historians, political scientists, and media commentators frequently point to this event as a step on the path toward formal recognition of Indigenous political rights in Canada.

Yet the story of why and how Gladstone was selected as senator has been subjected to remarkably little analysis. "The most important reason why James Gladstone of Alberta is our first Indian senator is that Alberta was the only province with both a first-rate candidate and a Senate vacancy," *Maclean's* magazine noted in March 1958. "Gladstone, a Blackfoot chief, was a surprise choice. More highly favored were Ontario mining executive G.C. (Slim) Monture and BC's Andy Paull. But Ontario's only Senate vacancy had been ticketed for Ottawa lawyer Lionel Choquette; and BC didn't have one. Alberta did, so Gladstone got the nod."[10] Even if geography was the prime reason why Gladstone became the first Indian senator over the other candidates, the process that led to his nomination and subsequent appointment to the Senate is revealing in terms of how supporters and detractors described the three shortlisted nominees. Correspondence between Diefenbaker and various political allies in his personal papers, coupled with other archival material and newspaper coverage, reveal how competing biographies of the three candidates highlighted desired traits that proponents believed would be most attractive to the prime minister. Reflecting on these various sources reinforces the inherently constructed and contested nature not only of political appointments, but also of biography and history itself.

* * *

Through the first half of the twentieth century, the Canadian government held out hope that what it conceptualized as the "Indian problem" would disappear through assimilation. "Our objective is to continue until there is not a single Indian in Canada that has not been absorbed into the body politic and there is no Indian question," Duncan Campbell Scott, the deputy superintendent general of Indian Affairs, 1913–32, infamously told a House of Commons committee in 1920.[11] This goal was never backed by commensurate resources, and by the mid-1940s popular Canadian attitudes about First Nations became increasingly sympathetic and sought to reduce the government's "paternalistic role and give the responsibility to the Indians themselves."[12]

To those who knew Diefenbaker, his proposal to support increased Indigenous political representation in Ottawa came as no surprise. Although his interest in working with Indians has been portrayed as simply a product of his desire to advance his business and professional interests, Diefenbaker had publicly displayed his admiration for Indians while expressing a genuine concern for their well-being.[13] Born in Neustadt, Ontario, he moved at the age of eight to the Tiefengrund Public School District, near Fort Carlton, Saskatchewan, where his father soon befriended the Métis leader Gabriel Dumont. The Diefenbaker household became the site of regular visits from both regional Métis and Cree for discussions over tea, and John eventually came to know Dumont, whom he would later describe as a military genius. These encounters sparked a lifelong interest in Indians and their affairs, an interest that carried over into his professional career.[14]

Following his graduation from law school and the establishment of a small law practice in Prince Albert, Saskatchewan, in 1920, Diefenbaker was one of a handful of lawyers willing to take on Indian clients. He proudly claimed to have never charged an Indian or Métis individual for legal advice because he was "distressed by their conditions, the unbelievable poverty and the injustice done to them."[15] Writing in the early 1970s, renowned Métis author Maria Campbell confirmed that Diefenbaker "would represent anyone rich or poor, red or white. If they had a case and no money he would help," adding that he had helped out her family in a time of need when "no one else would."[16]

Diefenbaker's political aspirations also opened other forums through which he sought reforms. As a member of Parliament beginning in 1940, he called for a Canadian bill of rights and "an unhyphenated nation" with all citizens enjoying equal treatment. By 1950, he was challenging changes to the *Indian Act* recommended by the joint parliamentary committee on the grounds that they left the Indian in a subjugated position and the Department of Indian Affairs "with near-to-tyrannical powers."[17] The committee was initially struck to investigate the Act and to consider treaty rights, band membership, Indian schools, enfranchisement, and other key issues. Its final report contained twelve major recommendations "designed to make possible the gradual transition of Indians from wardship to citizenship and to help them to advance themselves."[18] This approach, formally codified in the revised *Indian Act,* which Parliament passed in 1951, removed a couple of the most egregious prohibitions on Indians (such as the ban on dances and ceremonies, as well as on the pursuit of land claims) and added more powers to chiefs and band councils but left the essential elements of wardship status intact and Indians without the federal vote or representatives in Parliament.[19]

To address the parliamentary representation deficit, Diefenbaker began touting the idea of appointing a Canadian Indian to the Senate as early as 1944. When the MP for Prince Albert again floated the idea in Ottawa in 1954, the *Ottawa Journal* argued that "dignity demands that Indians not only have the right but the opportunity to speak," and that it was attracted by the prospect of an Indian senator "to give his people a voice in Canadian affairs. If the white man's education has not killed it, Indian oratory would be an asset to Parliament Hill."[20] Two years later, Diefenbaker promoted "an expansion of the rights of Indians to their own self-government" and administration. Quoting Lieutenant Governor Alexander Morris during the numbered treaty negotiations of the 1870s, Diefenbaker reminded his colleagues that the Crown had promised that "the ear of the Queen's government will always be open to hear the complaints of her Indian people and she will deal with her servants that do their duty in a proper manner."[21] This access was not available.

Diefenbaker's rise to power is well documented. With visionary language, he captured the Conservative leadership on the first ballot at the party convention in December 1956. During the ensuing federal election campaign, he proclaimed in speeches in Calgary and Prince Albert that "the time has come for the investigation of all Indian rights. The Indians should be given the right to speak in Parliament and to bring their views before Parliament."[22] Once his government was elected, he reiterated his earlier promise to appoint an Indian to the Senate. The national news media was enthusiastic. "How about a Good Indian in the Senate?," the *Financial Times* asked in early 1957. In recommending such an appointment, it reminded the Canadian public

> that the Indian has for a long time been a second class citizen, and has been disenfranchised in his own land for a long time. But the big argument is that he was and is and always will be the first Canadian. That is one thing you cannot take from an Indian. He is the true Canadian. You could have come out with Jacques Cartier and your families could have been here ever since, but the Indian still deserves recognition as the first Canadian.

The paper suggested G.C. (Slim) Monture, a highly educated Mohawk who had recently retired from the Department of Mines.[23]

Assuming office as the leader of a minority government, on 17 June 1957, Prime Minister Diefenbaker had sixteen vacant Senate seats at his disposition in the 102-seat chamber.[24] Exactly one month later, a Canadian Press story began to shape the public debate about his promise to appoint an Indian to the Red Chamber. "Prime Minister Diefenbaker is reported to be giving serious consideration to the selection of Mr. Monture to fulfill his election promise to put a representative of Canada's 150,000 native Indians in the Senate," it noted. Jim Gladstone, of the Blood Tribe, was another possible choice, although sources close to the prime minister intimated that Monture – an internationally recognized mining engineer – was a more likely choice than the farmer and rancher from Alberta. The third possible candidate was Andy Paull, the president of the Native Brotherhood of British Columbia.[25]

According to coverage in newspapers and the letters that Diefenbaker received, most Canadians seemed to support the move. "The general feeling about that appointment amongst the general Public is that a lot more people are for it than against it," Joe Hilderman, a citizen of Winnipeg, reassured the prime minister. It would be "fair and just," Mrs. Marjorie Bond of Calgary applauded. "Many of us feel that this would be a very commendable act," she gushed, "in keeping with the high principles and democratic spirit which we associate with you and your new government."[26] Editorial opinion across most of Canada was similarly supportive, but the reception was not universally positive. Simply selecting a senator on racial grounds rubbed some commentators the wrong way, smacking of tokenism or of a threat to convert the upper chamber into a collection of advocates of individual racial groups. A *Lethbridge Herald* editorial published in July 1957, for example, opposed the appointment of an Indian senator on purely racial grounds. "We are not in the least against having Indian senators, any more than we are opposed to French-Canadian senators or Scottish-Canadian senators," it noted. "We are opposed to senators for Indians – that is, senators named primarily because they have Indian blood in their veins and with the idea that they will officially represent their race. Such appointments, it seems to us, would be bad for the senate, threatening to turn it into a communal institution."[27]

Diefenbaker's private papers record fourteen Indian nominees submitted to the prime minister for the Senate position.[28] Several of the suggestions came through Progressive Conservative Party networks, with the prime minister and his staff reaching out to regional party associations for nominations. Unsolicited nominations came from church officials, non-Indigenous allies who worked with Indigenous organizations, the general public, and even from interested individuals themselves. The Rev. Peter Kelly, "a Haida aristocrat and Methodist missionary"[29] who had long advocated for Indigenous rights in British Columbia, was a natural candidate – but, as one correspondent emphasized, he was a Liberal, and "the Senate is overloaded with Liberals."[30] Reginald Hill, a Seneca born on the Six Nations Reserve, seemed a good choice to Conservative supporter Jack Cauley, who touted him as "an exceptionally good mixer, a very able speaker and debater. He more than radiates personality and can and does mix with people in all walks of life."[31] James Emann, a Toronto resident, wrote repeatedly to Diefenbaker (and Mrs. Diefenbaker) asking that he be appointed senator. The PM's Office politely promised that his file would be considered alongside the others, but it was never taken seriously.[32]

GILBERT MONTURE: "UNQUESTIONABLY THE ABLEST CANADIAN INDIAN OF HIS GENERATION"

The front-runner was Gilbert Clarence Monture, a Mohawk from the Six Nations Reserve in Ontario with an exemplary record of civil service.

Progressive Conservative M.R. Jack, who prepared Monture's nomination dossier for the Senate post in July 1957, described him as "the Indian of this generation, who has contributed more to his country than perhaps any other person of Indian birth." He carefully explained that Monture, who still had "his roots with his people and is not enfranchised but a voter by virtue of active military service," had "gained world recognition as a mining engineer and mining economist."[33] That same month, the *Lethbridge Herald* echoed many newspapers in asserting that "the strongest chances for the appointment of the first Indian to the upper chamber of Parliament are believed to be held by Gilbert C. Monture, 60, a Canadian Indian who has gained world recognition as a mining engineer."[34]

Born in 1896 on the Six Nations Reserve near Hagersville, Ontario, Monture was a descendant of the famous chief Joseph Brant and one of the "Feathered Loyalists" who fled the American Revolution to maintain their connection to the British Crown. Monture grew up in a farming family on the Mississaugas of the New Credit settlement, attended the Methodist church (and quoted scripture as well as Greek mythology freely throughout his life), and matriculated from Hagersville High School in 1912. Monture taught school on the reserve for a year to save money to enrol in the Queen's University School of Mining, in 1914. In the summer of 1917, "Slim" (as he was nicknamed in college because of his tall, lithe figure) assisted a field surveyor from the federal Department of Mines in northwestern Ontario before enlisting for military service. After several months on the Western Front with the 3rd Royal Canadian Engineers, he was invalidated to Britain with a leg wound and a severe lung infection. After convalescing, he was commissioned as a lieutenant. When the war ended, Monture returned to Queen's to continue his studies. He graduated with his Bachelor of Science degree in mining and metallurgy in 1921, and then spent another year taking business, finance, accounting, economics, and commercial law courses. During his studies, he set up a university employment service and a cooperative bookstore, and married Elva Leona Penwarden from Kingston. When he finished, they moved to Ottawa.[35]

"In his prime, Gilbert Monture was a forceful but kindly figure," his biographer and cousin Enos Montour wrote. Handsome and charismatic, Monture stood six feet, two inches tall, with a "permanently bronzed" face that "showed the predominance of his Mohawk blood" and a "slowness of speech, accentuated by a slight drawl, [that] added to his personal charm."[36] An avid reader of poetry and prose, Monture had a great sense of humour, which he used to defuse tense situations at meetings and conferences. "We had a poor immigration policy," he once quipped to the Canadian Club when speaking of the way Europeans had overwhelmed the Indigenous Peoples of Canada.[37] Despite his rise to prominence in his professional career, Monture observed discrimination first-hand. He had no tolerance for anti-Indigenous racism that continued to permeate Canadian society.[38]

Rather than working to achieve reform from outside the machinery of state, like Paull and Gladstone, Monture's career situated him firmly within the Canadian bureaucracy. His record of government service was exemplary, revealing "a talent for diplomacy at the technical level."[39] In 1923, he became editor of publications for the Dominion Department of Mines and six years later became chief of the Division of Mineral Economics of the Mines Branch in Ottawa. During the Second World War, he worked in the Department of Munitions and Supply and served as a key advisor to Canadian and international war service production boards and commissions, earning him the Order of the British Empire in 1946, and the University of Western Ontario awarded him an honorary Doctor of Sciences degree in recognition of his outstanding contributions to the fields of mineral resources and economics in 1948.

During the 1950s, he added an international dimension to his work, frequently serving as a mining and mineral expert on government delegations to the United Nations, the North Atlantic Treaty Organization, and the British Commonwealth. When he retired from public service as the chief of the Mineral Resources Division of the Mines Branch of the federal Department of Mines and Technical Surveys in 1956, he joined the private sector and became the vice-president of Stratmat, a Canadian mineral exploration company primarily interested in metallurgical processes.[40]

Monture's leadership was rooted in his expertise in mining and economics rather than in his advocacy of Indigenous rights. "Experts in the Mining Industry have told me that he has prepared more technical papers on mining research and development and delivered more speeches on the potential of this industry in the economy of Canada than perhaps any other person," Jack noted in his brief to the prime minister. Given Diefenbaker's interest in developing Northern Canadian resources, this expertise was particularly enticing.[41] Monture's nominator noted that "vision and sound practical policies will be required to make these vast resources available, not only to meet the requirements of an expanding industrial economy but to assure our survival as a free, democratic nation should that right ever be challenged." Jack's logic tied Monture and economic prosperity to democratic freedom in an era of Cold War anxieties. "As a representative of his people in the Senate of Canada, I am confident the appointment would be widely acclaimed by the Canadian people and the Indians," Jack concluded.[42]

Monture also received honours within the Indigenous community that validated his role as a potential Indian senator. He received the 1957 Indian Achievement Award of the Chicago-based Indian Council Fire – the first Canadian so honoured. The following year, he was appointed honorary chief of the Six Nations of the Grand River and received the name Ohs thoh se ra go wah, or "Big Feather" in English.[43]

As the emphasis in Indian policy shifted from land and treaty administration to addressing the socioeconomic challenges facing Indigenous Peoples in Canada, Monture promoted a more enlightened integration agenda.[44] "All of Canada seems for the minute concerned with the so-called problem of Indian integration," he noted in late 1957.[45] His declared goal was to restore a sense of pride and dignity for Canada's First Peoples.[46] In a July 1957 letter, Monture described himself as "one of the Indians who have broken away from the old mode of life but are still proud of their racial ancestry." He lamented that it would

> be a long and difficult task [for many Indians] to overcome the inferiority complex which has been instilled in the Indian through years of paternalism, discrimination and neglect. When one adds to this the intransigence of a great number of the Indians themselves, a great number of whom are still living in the past and resent any attempt to integrate them into the Canadian economy, the difficulties are added to.[47]

He emphasized the importance of education and having the Indigenous community "propose changes in their status which rightly or wrongly many of them jealously privilege." In response to enfranchisement discussions, for example, Monture noted that "until [Indians] are ready to accept the full responsibility of citizenship, I see no uplifting force in enfranchisement. Please let us stay neutral in this field and carry on our education program of both Indian and non-Indian in reconciling social, racial and cultural differences."[48]

Monture offered a message of inclusivity and shared ideals – the language of the "Feathered Loyalists" rather than of the sovereigntist Haudenosaunee traditional longhouse. In a national radio broadcast describing First Nations to other Canadians, he proclaimed that

> our numbers are increasing and soon our reserves will be too small to support us and our children. We must therefore forget the old traditions and take our place among the whites. We have contributed much to your culture. We are capable of contributing more. To do that, however, we must merge our identity with yours. You must accept us, not as Indians, but as Canadians whose ideals are the same as yours – the building up of a united Canada free from sectionalism and the prejudices of race and creed – a Canada founded on the British principles of justice, truth and loyalty.[49]

While scholars might find Monture's message discordant with today's dominant Indigenous rights discourse,[50] his creed was one that most newspaper reporters and political advisors found palatable in the 1950s. "No one was prouder of his Indian heritage, of the fact that he was born in a log cabin, a poor boy who by brains and work and some luck rose to the top of his field and to a place of esteem in the white-man's world," one story noted.[51]

Letters to Diefenbaker reveal the way Monture's credentials could be read two ways. Mrs. Susan Purcell from Mission City, BC, had read in her local newspapers that Monture, Gladstone, and Paull were being considered and wrote the prime minister that "to us it appears that Mr. Monture is the logical choice in that he has had considerable experience in governmental business as well as being a successful businessman and therefore could fill the post admirably, [while] the other two are little known outside of their reserves but may have worked hard for their people in some respects."[52] In short, Monture's expertise and worldliness made him an excellent candidate – a view shared by Ontario Progressive Conservatives, particularly MP Ellen Fairclough, for whom he was the preferred candidate for Senate.[53] An unsigned letter to the prime minister in October 1957, however, suggested that not everyone shared Purcell's and Fairclough's enthusiasm about Monture's suitability. "I think that in the interests of the Party you should know that the candidature of one Gilbert Monture for Indian representative in the Senate is being promoted by a pressure group who knowing his unscrupulous nature want him there for purposes of their own which will not agree with the aims of the Party," it noted. This partisan critique, which offered no specifics, asserted that Diefenbaker "would not be honoring Indians by appointing Monture because he has had nothing to do with fellow Indians for many years."[54] By contrast, this critique could not be levelled at Paull or Gladstone.

ANDREW PAULL: "CANADA'S INDIAN CONSCIENCE" AND A LEADER "ON THE WARPATH"

Whereas Monture was the dedicated civil servant in Ottawa, Andrew Paull (or Chief Andy Paull, as Vancouver newspapers usually called him) was an outspoken advocate of Indigenous rights. "A relentless political force in his own right," historian Brendan Edwards summarized, "Paull was known as 'Canada's Indian conscience,' publicly fighting for improvements in the status of Aboriginal peoples in British Columbia, Canada, and the United States."[55] An ardent anti-assimilationist, Paull fought tirelessly for equal opportunity in employment and education, legal recognition of Aboriginal rights, and improved living conditions for Indigenous Peoples. As the long-time president of the North American Indian Brotherhood, which he co-founded in 1944, Paull used the organization as a "megaphone" to share complaints, broadcast his views, and rise to "national prominence" as a spokesperson for Canadian Indians in general.[56] Given this profile, Mi'kmaq chief Anthony Francis, of the Big Cove Band (Elsipogtog First Nation) in New Brunswick, recommended Paull for the Senate in 1957 because he alone of the candidates "understands the Indians from coast to coast, their culture and their way of life."[57]

Andrew Paull was born in February 1892 to Dan Paull and Theresa Paull (née Lacket-Joe) of a prominent Sḵwx̱wú7mesh (Squamish) family. Initially raised in the village of Stawamus, he enjoyed a close relationship with his maternal grandmother, who conferred on him the name Xwechtáal ("the Serpent Slayer"), passed down from a legendary ancestor.[58] At the age of seven, the Sḵwx̱wú7mesh chose him to be "the one to learn the ways of the white man and speak for the Indian," and he made a solemn oath "to be the eyes, ears and spokesman for the Indians and to serve them faithfully."[59] His family resettled in the village of Eslha7an, in North Vancouver, and he attended St. Paul's Indian Residential School from 1899 to 1906. He did not know a word of English at the onset but soon learned from the nuns and teachers, whom he would applaud for the rest of his life for giving him the tools to become a strong writer, speaker, and political organizer.[60] His purpose at the school, Oblate priest Herbert Francis Dunlop explained, "was not to learn how to become a white man. He went there to learn how to use the tools of the white man, and with these tools to speak for and fight for the rights of his people."[61] Despite the fervour with which he criticized the Canadian government and Indian Affairs for their failures to fulfill treaty promises and provide adequate schooling, he was strikingly positive about the work of missionaries, and he remained lifelong friends with two of the nuns who taught him, as well as a devout Roman Catholic throughout his life.[62]

Paull's expertise in the history, culture, and traditions of his people was honed during two years of Sḵwx̱wú7mesh education with local chiefs, which he considered vital to his development. "A knowledge of our history and legends was similar as an education is regarded among whitemen," he explained. "Those who possessed it were regarded as aristocrats. Those who were indifferent, whether adults or children, were rascals ... It was the responsible duty of responsible elders."[63] He did his duty as a young man to learn these stories, which gave him particular credibility as a speaker and activist.

He complemented this education with an informal apprenticeship at a local law firm during his teenage years, where he learned general legal procedures and developed an expertise in the law as it applied to Indigenous rights.[64] Although he could not become a lawyer without renouncing his Indian status (which he would not do), his friend and colleague Maisie

Hurley recalled that "he had a marvellous mind. He could recite cases chapter and verse. He was considered the greatest authority on this continent on Indian aspects of the law. He would have been one of the country's most brilliant criminal lawyers if he'd had a degree. He had dignity, drama. He was superb." From this point onward, he considered himself "a lawyer without a ticket."[65]

Paull proved an exceptionally resourceful labour and political organizer in the years ahead. Early in his career he served as the secretary of the Squamish band, became politically immersed in the Indian land question as a member of the Indian Rights Association beginning in 1907, and was active in the International Longshoremen's Association.[66] He quit his job as a longshoreman to work as an interpreter for the McKenna-McBride Royal Commission on Indian Affairs in the Salish-speaking areas of British Columbia, from 1913 to 1916. He and Haida leader Rev. Peter Kelly became key organizers within the Allied Tribes of British Columbia beginning in 1916,[67] and Paull assumed the leadership of the organization in 1922, which claimed to represent all British Columbia First Nations except the small portion with treaties (a contested claim, but one that justified his prominent voice). Under his leadership, the Allied Tribes successfully petitioned Parliament for an inquiry into the land question, and Paull travelled to Ottawa to present his views before the Special Joint Committee of the Senate and House of Commons established in 1927.[68] When the 1927 *Indian Act* made it illegal for status Indians to raise funds for land claims, however, the Allied Tribes dissolved, and Paull embraced a career as an active sports and entertainment promoter and journalist in the interwar period. His colourful character, eagerness to speak on a wide range of topics, and articulate and strident defence of Indigenous rights made him particularly newsworthy and attractive to reporters.[69]

Paull could not resist the lure of politics. In 1942, he emerged from a fifteen-year hiatus to become the business manager of the Native Brotherhood of British Columbia and orchestrated its amalgamation with the Kwakwaka'wakw-led Pacific Coast Native Fishermen's Association. Internal tensions between coastal and internal BC First Nations continued to fragment the organization, however, and when Paull was accused of financial mismanagement he left the Native Brotherhood to co-organize the North American Indian Brotherhood (NAIB) in 1944, a political organization he would guide until his death fifteen years later.[70] Although Paull reached out to fledgling Indian movements in the Prairie provinces and central Canada, he was unable to pull together "a national, united front for dealing with Ottawa."[71] Yet, his presidential title gave his statements *gravitas*, facilitating access to decision makers in Ottawa and allowing him to present himself as a national Indian leader.[72]

Paull's formidable presence was honed over the subsequent decade as he pounded out critiques of the government in newspaper articles, dissected court cases, and kept the First Nations population abreast of Indian policy developments. In 1956, the *Vancouver Province* described how Paull's "approach combines the eloquence of the zealot, the dialectic skill of the lawyer and the shrewdness of the politician." Another journalist observed that "tall, built like a prizefighter, [and] endowed with a magnificent courtroom manner, Andy Paull dedicated his life to improving the conditions of his people."[73] Under the NAIB banner, he stood (literally refusing to sit) before the Special Joint Committee of the Senate and House of Commons on 27 June 1946 to impress on parliamentarians how the government had violated treaties and how Indians would not be assimilated and needed proper education, and to make the case for greater Indigenous involvement in Indian Affairs. His ability to recite long portions of archival documents that he had memorized, coupled with his eloquence and knowledge of Western literature, showcased his skills as a spokesperson. What Paull presented to the committee "was not a consistent, water-tight program of alternatives to Indian policy," historian Palmer Patterson noted, "but a loud protest on specific grievances and an expression of general and vague distrust and discontent."[74]

Paull's advocacy efforts in Ottawa piqued his interest in a more direct role in parliamentary decision-making. In 1951, the NAIB called for Indian membership in the Senate. In *The Thunderbird* (the newspaper that he published), Paull explained that Indians had previously refused the possibility of Senate appointments because they feared that it would jeopardize their chances of securing representation in the House of Commons. They had changed their minds, he suggested, and "feel that the Senate would now be acceptable. A number of obstacles hindering members of our race from sitting in the House have been explained to us and we would be happy, at the present, if we could place Indians in the Senate."[75] Paull nominated himself as a possible candidate through his Oblate connections, using the Catholic Church as a conduit to lobby Louis St. Laurent's Liberal government. When Diefenbaker considered an Indian Senate appointment a few years later, these previous overtures and Paull's well-known leadership made him a credible candidate.

The archival record is silent on how seriously Diefenbaker's inner circle took Paull's candidacy. Despite national newspapers regularly listing him as a third leading contender, there is no extensive paper trail in the Diefenbaker archives affirming that he was a likely choice. His strident anti-assimilationist message and flair for the dramatic made him a potent political force, but it also would have deterred Progressive Conservative political advisors who sought a less belligerent voice to represent Indians in the Senate. After all, the national media frequently depicted Paull as an Indian leader "on the warpath" opposing government, which made him a risky fit for appointment to the upper chamber. "We'd be a bunch of fools to celebrate the centennial with a bunch of robbers who stole our country," he told reporters in early 1957, anticipating BC's centenary the following year. This date only marked "the biggest land steal" on record, not a commemoration worthy of celebration.[76]

JAMES GLADSTONE: "A SUCCESSFUL FARMER AND RANCHER"

"It is an excellent idea, to give Canadian Indians a voice in our Parliament, in the Upper House because they have no voice in the Commons," a *Calgary Herald* editorial commented on 20 July 1957. "Now comes the matter of choosing this first-time-in-history Indian senator." Its proposed candidate was James Gladstone, "an especially appropriate choice" for two primary reasons:

> Firstly, Mr. Gladstone has devoted the major part of his life to the development and betterment of his own people, has worked with them on the reserve and helped them to a better way of life while he made outstanding success of his own.
>
> Secondly, it is in Alberta where the most recent and victorious battles on behalf of Canada's treaty Indians have been fought. The

> eyes of the whole nation were focused on Alberta earlier this year during the notorious Hobbema case in which some of the iniquitous provisions of the revised Indian Act were exposed and brought to a dead standstill by the courts.

The life of James Gladstone is well known through the biography written by his son-in-law Hugh Dempsey. While predictably hagiographic, Dempsey draws on a wealth of written and oral sources to reveal the way Gladstone, a man of mixed racial ancestry, became an accepted member of the Blood Tribe (otherwise known as the Kainai Nation) as well as a leading member of the Indigenous rights movement in Alberta. Gladstone was not born a Blood. His maternal grandfather (William Gladstone) was a Scottish Canadian who, while serving with the Hudson's Bay Company in the Northwest, married Harriet Leblanc of part Cree, Santee Sioux, and French Canadian ancestry. Their daughter, Harriet, had formed a relationship with a white lumbermill foreman that broke down in the mid-1890s, leaving the elder Gladstones to raise their four grandchildren. James, or "Jimmy," born in 1887, spoke Cree until he attended the Anglican school on the Blood Reserve, where he learned Blackfoot. Eventually accepted by the Blood as one of their own, he was not legally recognized as a status Indian by the Department of Indian Affairs until 1920. Nevertheless, Dempsey emphasized the ways his father-in-law's life reflected the "Indian experience" in the early twentieth century: James attended church-run residential schools, experienced frustrations as a businessman who encountered deep-seated paternalism, and faced the bureaucratic inefficiency and obstructionism of federal officials who cast a "fatherly eye" over near all aspects of reserve life.[77]

For Diefenbaker, the background on Gladstone and the case for his suitability were furnished by Indian Association of Alberta (IAA) secretary John Laurie. Born in Oxford County, Ontario, Laurie moved to the Prairies after the First World War and taught high school in Calgary with fellow teacher Douglas Harkness. He soon became an ardent proponent of Indian rights, and as secretary to the IAA from 1944 to 1956 he had a strong hand in directing the association's lobbying activities.[78] He also forged a close relationship with Gladstone, who he championed as a potential senator. The short biographical sketch of Gladstone that Laurie prepared for the prime minister emphasized that this seventy-year-old member of the Blood Tribe had "devoted the greater part of his life to the development of the Indians of Canada."[79] Laurie saw no need to introduce ambiguity about Gladstone's Indigenous background, simply noting that he was born in 1887 and was one of the first boys enrolled at St. Paul's Anglican Mission on the Blood Reserve, in 1894. In 1903, Gladstone was transferred to Calgary Indian Industrial School where he learned the printer's trade, eventually training as a typesetter in the composing room of the *Calgary Herald*.

After leaving school in 1905, Jim returned to the Blood Reserve and worked for a time as interpreter at the mission. He took the Indian name of Akay-na-muka, or "Many Guns" in the Blackfoot language, and worked on various ranches in the Fort Macleod district, where he gained information on the "white man's methods" that he would later adopt on his own ranch. In 1909, Jim married Janie Healy (known to her people as Pok-otun, or "Small Woman"), the daughter of Joe Healy, a noted Kainai community member who was the first Blood to speak fluent English and who served for many years as the tribe's spokesperson.[80] This family connection secured Gladstone access to and status within the reserve community.

Gladstone's family and his work tied him to the Kainai Nation. In 1911, he was appointed chief scout and interpreter for the Royal North-West Mounted Police at Fort Macleod, and he carried mail for the Blood Agency over the next three years. During the First World War, when the *Indian Act* was amended so that "under-utilized" reserve lands could be conscripted to increase the production of meats and grains, Gladstone worked to put large areas of Blood lands into crop to help in the war effort.[81] In 1920, he started his own ranch about five miles north of Cardston, on the lower part of the Blood Reserve. "Over the years he built up one of the finest ranches on the reserve and now, in partnership with his two sons, he runs about 500 head of cattle and has some 800 acres under cultivation," Laurie's sketch noted. Newspapers trumpeted his success as a rancher, praising his initiative and use of modern farming techniques. His "large and progressive agricultural venture … set the example for many other Bloods to follow as farmers and cattle ranchers,"[82] one story noted in 1957. This reinforced the narrative of Gladstone as trailblazer, a progressive and modern Indian leader.[83]

Gladstone, who was active politically on the Blood Reserve since the First World War, became involved in broader Indian organizations in the 1930s and 1940s. The IAA, formed in 1944, provided him with a mechanism to elevate the fight for Indigenous rights to the national level. Gladstone served as IAA president from 1948 to 1954 and again in 1957, working with Laurie to craft political strategies to influence the federal government. "During his work with the association, Mr. Gladstone was a delegate to Ottawa on three occasions to discuss proposed changes in the Indian Act, and to voice the opinion of his people," Laurie wrote in extolling his qualifications for a Senate seat.[84] Through his participation in Indian-government conferences and his central role in the consultations leading up to the 1951 *Indian Act* revisions, Gladstone became well known in Ottawa circles.

Although Gladstone did not actively seek a Senate appointment, Laurie sought one for his IAA colleague[85] – and his relationship with Conservative minister Douglas Harkness ensured that his recommendation reached Diefenbaker's ear. Harkness had raised Indian issues in the House of Commons since his election as the MP for Calgary East in 1945. Backed by his former teaching colleague, Laurie, he noted the rampant poverty on Indian reserves and the importance of extending social benefits to status Indians on an equal basis with other Canadians.[86] When Laurie wrote to him in late June suggesting Gladstone, Harkness told him to send a copy directly to the prime minister and to pass along any additional information that he thought pertinent.[87] Gladstone had no knowledge of the nomination, or of the machinations by Laurie and Harkness, at this stage.[88] Laurie wrote to Diefenbaker on 3 July recommending Gladstone.

Laurie's biographical pitch to Diefenbaker trumpeted Gladstone's credentials as an Indian knowledgeable in the traditions of his people, a successful farmer, and a morally upstanding community member. The letter also provided an effective spin on Gladstone never having served as a local chief or councillor, stressing instead the democratic nature of the IAA in an effort to subtly differentiate it from Paull's NAIB. Laurie did not disclose that Gladstone had run for head chief of the Bloods in 1956, falling well behind Jim Shot Both Sides in the final vote. Nor did Laurie note that just a week after Diefenbaker was elected prime minister, Gladstone had been voted out as president of the IAA.

Laurie, however, made sure that Diefenbaker knew that Gladstone enjoyed "the support of the quite powerful Horn Society and that is really important in the complex and little-known social structure of the Blackfoot-speaking groups." He had never received a salary or monetary gift from the IAA or any other group in Alberta that would place him in a position to owe special favours, which Laurie considered "quite unusual" and perhaps even "unique among Indians." Furthermore, Gladstone's "home and family life are above reproach. His morals are better than those of most whites; an Anglican by religion, he has served in many parochial offices, as representative to Diocesan Synods etc." All of these references resonated in a Settler context. "No Indian to my knowledge," Laurie concluded, "could better represent his race."[89]

Gladstone himself seized the opportunity to make a direct impression on the prime minister soon after. When appointed honorary president of the IAA at its June 1957 conference, he shrewdly suggested that the association honour Diefenbaker during the forthcoming Calgary Stampede for his long advocacy of Indian rights. It approved a ceremony and commissioned a scroll and painting from a Blood artist for Gladstone to present. "This raised an unusual problem," Dempsey noted, "as protocol required that all ceremonies in the stampede village be done by Indians in full buckskin regalia." Gladstone, who had always worn business suits or work clothes, did not even own an "Indian" outfit so he "borrowed a beaded buckskin shirt, leggings, moccasins, and an eagle-feather headdress so that he could make the presentation properly attired." Thus fitting the stereotypical Indian image, he impressed the prime minister, who later told Gladstone "that as soon as he saw him and spoke to him, he knew he was the man for the job."[90]

For the moment, however, the outcome was still far from certain. Writing from a café in downtown Calgary, his son-in-law Hugh Dempsey recorded on 17 July: "I phoned Laurie and he said the matter had been discussed with the PM but he didn't have the slightest idea how your chances were." A few days later, Dempsey was even more uncertain. "Judging by the reports from Canadian Press," Dempsey wrote Gladstone, "Monture seems to be the favorite, but you can never tell. Anyway, with 150,000 Indians in Canada, it is quite an honor to be among the three 'possibles.'"[91] The Canadian Press article, which released the alleged short-list of Monture, Paull, and

Gladstone, had Canadians talking. "I have heard via the grapevine, and it may not be correct, that the news story in connection with Mr. Monture was put out by some of his friends in an effort to pressure the prime minister into appointing him," Harkness gossiped to Laurie on 30 July. "If indeed this was the case I am sure it will defeat its own purpose."[92]

Monture's front-runner status generated local Alberta testimonies in support of Gladstone. Marjorie Bond of Calgary wrote Diefenbaker to stress that a senator "should be more than just a spokesman with Indian blood in his veins" and had to be "thoroughly conversant with Indian problems and Indian conditions." She believed that Gladstone was the most suitable: "For Mr. Gladstone has spent all his life on a reserve as a treaty Indian and brought his children up on the reserve under the changing conditions brought about by revised legislation and government policy. He is thoroughly and intimately acquainted with every phase of Indian life."[93]

Gladstone's supporters emphasized his connection with and ability to navigate both the Indigenous and Settler worlds, a skill that differentiated him from other candidates. Muriel McCready of Lethbridge noted that, from what she read in the newspapers, Monture appeared to be "a splendid choice to represent ... a successful Indian in the white man's business world." She was quick, however, to identify Gladstone as "a most worthy representative" of another group, "a man who is highly respected among his own people, lives on the Reserve and has made a success of such a life in a business way."[94] Similarly, Isobel Toth, a graduate of St. Paul's Indian School and a nurse in the File Hills and Qu'Appelle Indian Hospitals, applauded Diefenbaker for his longstanding efforts as a "fighter for Indian rights" and hoped that he would appoint Gladstone to the Senate:

> Being a member of the largest band on the biggest Indian reserve in Canada it seems only right that the Blood Indians choice be selected. Mr. Gladstone has spent his life on the reserve and has always been in the forefront in trying out new methods of farming and bringing new ideas on to the reserve that will help his people. It is a fact that Indians from far and near seek him out for counsel and advice. As president of the Indian Association and living on a reserve he has never lost contact with the Indian, not only on his own reserve, but

> other bands as well. Mr. Gladstone's home and family life is exemplary and although he has no university education an example of his progressiveness is the fact that his children have been trained in farming business and nursing.[95]

The theme of the letter was clear: Gladstone was a model Indian who lived on the reserve *and* embodied all the virtues of modern Canadian citizenship. Letters of support for Gladstone trumpeted his "traditionalist" credentials alongside his Christian background and successes as a farmer and rancher. Laurie highlighted that Gladstone was a member of the Crazy Dog Society on the Blood Reserve "and has been a strong supporter of native traditions and religious practices."[96] Despite the assimilationist agenda that continued to dominate Indian Affairs in this period, it is striking how Gladstone's empathy for Indigenous spirituality and traditions were highlighted to prove his suitability as an Indian representative.

For his part, Gladstone did not see a potential appointment as token or ceremonial – he intended to use it as a pan-Canadian Indian voice. "The newspapers are giving my name as the one who will best represent and maintain the Indian rights as given them by Solemn [Treaty]," he wrote to Andy Paull in late July. "I know that whoever is chosen will have to get the wisest and principal men of each province and chiefs together in order that a united front be presented to the Government always." Aware that Paull was rumoured to be on a short-list, Gladstone's overture laid the groundwork for future cooperation on a national scale.[97]

The small biographical profile of Gladstone that appeared in the September 1957 issue of *The Native Voice* newsletter indicated his modest "credentials" compared to those of Paull and Monture.[98] Nevertheless, Gladstone's supporters – among them R.D. Burt, a Cardston department store owner and the president of the local PC Association, who wrote to Diefenbaker that month – continued to highlight his many virtues. "I have had a visit this morning in my office from Mr. James Gladstone, an old friend of mine from The Blood Indian Reserve," Burt wrote. The prime minister had called Jim to Ottawa for a meeting on 13 October, and "we have presumed that it is about the proposal to appoint an Indian as Senator." Burt did not personally favour the move, given his decades of business experience in dealing with the Blood Indians, and he "saw little to be gained from [appointing an Indian to the upper chamber], either for the Indians themselves, the Country as a whole, or the Party." He would squarely back the prime minister if he went ahead with the appointment, however, and noted that if he decided to appoint an Indian,

> you could not make a better choice than Mr. Gladstone. He is an honorable man, who has raised a good family here on the Blood Reserve. He and his family (they are all married now) are trusted by the business men of Cardston, which is the headquarters of the Bloods. They all pay their bills, and are well respected in this area. This perhaps does not sound like much to you, but Indians who are to be trusted, and who pay their bills[,] are very rare on this Reserve. Most do not enjoy a favorable credit rating.[99]

In the highly gendered context of 1950s Canada, family credentials mattered. "Mr. and Mrs. Gladstone have six children, all of whom have shown the results of an excellent upbringing," Laurie's biography explained to Diefenbaker. All of his four daughters were married – an obvious sign of heteronormative success in the 1950s – and their achievements (only identified through their birth order, not their names) indicated success in what were considered gender-appropriate jobs in that era. Gladstone's two sons also enjoyed successful careers, with Fred "primarily a rancher" who had "also gained national prominence in the rodeo field and was formerly calf roping champion of Canada," and Horace working as a farming instructor on the Blood Reserve.[100] Supporter Muriel McCready highlighted how Gladstone's bloodlines ran to the "great Gladstone of English history" on the one side and a prominent family on the Blood Reserve on the other. She shared friendships with the Gladstones through the Anglican Church and the Girl Guides – appropriate organizations for any Canadian family to belong to in the 1950s.[101]

Gladstone was a non-offensive candidate. A short précis that summarized Gladstone's suitability based on the letters and biographical information that the Prime Minister's Office had received is revealing about the attributes that made Gladstone an attractive appointee. Describing Gladstone in glowing terms, the author focused less on his political and cultural accomplishments and more on his appearance and business acumen, accentuating characteristics that conformed with traits considered desirable in Canadian Settler society. Gladstone was a Treaty Indian, although not believed to be full-blooded. He was "light skinned" and "of good appearance," "well mannered" and, in general, "superior looking." He was a "good farmer and cattleman," and quite "prosperous." Despite having "little formal education," he "served as church warden for many years at Anglican Mission Church on Reserve and was succeeded by his son in that position." Regarding his home life, he had a "shy but charming wife who is superior looking" and his home was "spotless and very hospitable." In the opinion of the memo writer, Gladstone also had "the respect and confidence of the Indians."[102] John Laurie's comments supporting Gladstone's nomination sealed the case:

> "If you have to have an Indian, he is the man."
> "I can't see any other one in Western Canada."
> "He could fit into his surroundings – he might make some contribution."
> "I admire his wife greatly – she is a lady."
> "He has a fine home."
> "He is even-tempered."[103]

In whole or in part, these considerations played into the final decision to appoint Gladstone as Canada's first Indian senator.

THE DECISION

When the news broke on 31 January 1958 that Gladstone had been appointed a senator, letters poured into Ottawa and Calgary from across Canada and the United States congratulating Gladstone, endorsing his suitability, and praising the prime minister for his wise choice.[104] The local reception was especially jubilant. Journalist Bill Gold of the *Calgary Herald* reported a deluge of telephone calls to the newspaper from "scores of persons, all white[,] who saw in his appointment the dawn of a new age for Indians."[105] Local civic and business leaders expressed their pleasure, with the Chamber of Commerce president applauding the "well known and highly respected rancher" who had "always been most co-operative, progressive and alert to the needs of this region."[106] In the weeks ahead, hundreds of people gathered to celebrate Gladstone's achievement at commemorative banquets and balls, where speeches highlighted the justice of Indians finally securing a parliamentary voice.[107] The *Lethbridge Herald*, which had earlier expressed distaste at having a token "Indian representative" appointed to the Senate, welcomed Gladstone's appointment on 3 February "because we think it is fully merited. By leadership and by personal example, Senator Gladstone has done a great deal for his reserve, his race, and his country."[108] The *Calgary Herald* was less reserved. "The Prime Minister's choice," an editorial proclaimed, "is a serious, thoughtful man who has spent his entire life on an Indian reservation. He enjoys the respect of red man and white alike wherever he is known." It was a clear sign of progress. "It is asking too much that this single appointment will at a stroke remove all the obstacles which stand in the way of Indians achieving full citizenship, but it does denote a significant step forward in the Indians' social status," the coverage suggested.[109]

REFLECTIONS

> *"Whether or not interpreted as symbolic, the diversification of Senate membership can have representative implications"*
>
> – DAVID SMITH[110]

Much recent literature on the Canadian Senate explores the consequences of its inability to meaningfully represent regional interests and aspirations, its failure to function as a check and balance on the executive, and its inability to serve as an effective intermediary between the federal and provincial governments. Nevertheless, the Senate has long served as a symbolic site of struggle for marginalized groups seeking political representation. The famous Person's Case of 1929, in which the Judicial Committee of the Privy Council in London decided that women were indeed persons and eligible to sit in that chamber, prompted Prime Minister W.L. Mackenzie King to appoint Cairine Wilson – a member of the Liberal establishment and dedicated party organizer – as the first female senator, in February 1930. Some Canadians were incensed that the appointee had "never raised a finger in the fight to win for women the right to sit in the red chamber in Ottawa," while Emily Murphy and the other members of the Famous Five, who spearheaded the "Persons Case," never became senators.[111] Wilson, however, fit with other criteria: Senators had to embody the right values (including partisan loyalty) and could not be overly radical.

James Gladstone's selection as Canada's first Indian senator fits the model. "My work in the Senate will be aimed at improving the position of Canada's Indians, obtaining gradually for them better conditions as they want them and are ready for them, and without changes being forced upon them," Senator Gladstone explained at the start of his thirteen-year tenure in the Red Chamber.[112] He delivered his maiden speech in the Senate not in buckskin regalia but in a casual grey sports jacket and flannel pants.[113] Nevertheless, "history was made in the Senate of Canada on the afternoon of August 13, 1958," reporter Arthur Blakely observed. When the "slightly-built man with grizzled grey-white hair and green eyes" rose to speak, "the eyes of all of his colleagues were fixed upon him. Suddenly, the mild voice switched from English to another tongue; one with different sounds, a different rhythm, and with a history buried as deep in the past as Canada's own."[114] Gladstone, offering "a few words in the language of my own people, the Blackfoot Indians, as a recognition of the first Canadians," said:

> Eekoh-kinay-tam-etakee-kunay-apee un-ohk-ohtayts-tseeh-pee mukiy-sitsip suko-moh-kee unok-see awk-aw-kee-tsee-maks. Nitowat-simoyee-nukohk-okomot-ayhpo-wat-omohsah-ow.
>
> My words, translated into English, were these:
>
> The Indians of Canada are very happy to know they have someone in Ottawa to represent them in the Government of Canada. I pray that I will be able to speak the right words for them.[115]

In a "soft voice trembling with mixed nervousness and emotion," Gladstone appealed for better education, economic development, and more Indigenous control over their own affairs.[116] He spoke of the suffocating rules and regulations imposed from Ottawa that left "little room for new ideas or personal initiative."[117] When he finished, his fellow senators gave him a tremendous ovation. So did the national media. His speech "was not full of the usual platitudes so common on occasions of this sort … but contained plenty of 'meat' and several suggestions which could well be studied by the government," the *Calgary Herald* applauded.[118] "Editorials praised the firm but moderate approach," Dempsey observed, "urging Canadians to examine the way that Indians had been treated in the past and to find ways of improving their lot for the future."[119]

Long-time senator Arthur Roebuck wrote in 1954 that the purpose of the Senate was to perform a unifying function, which could only be successful if its membership was not elected by a particular constituency.[120] In practice, however, Gladstone firmly believed that he represented one: the Indians of Canada. As an appointed representative, he served as a voice for Indigenous Peoples in Ottawa without fear of voter recrimination, and he could represent Indigenous interests that spanned the entire country rather than focus his energies on a geographically confined constituency.[121] Thus, even though unelected, he was a representative actor. Political scientist David Smith cautions that "rhetoric about the Senate and representation may be inflated or at least misplaced, for representation and election are not the same thing." Precisely because this national institution is appointed, "the Senate has a more diversified membership in terms of gender, language, and race than any comparable second chamber in the Anglo-American world or than the House of Commons," with "the individual voices of senators ... speaking on behalf of minority or sectional interests."[122] In the case of Gladstone, Prime Minister Diefenbaker expected him to symbolize a growing acceptance that Indigenous leaders would have a say in government decision-making. "I want to be their voice in Ottawa until they all choose to take the federal vote for themselves," Gladstone explained.[123] With the repeal of section 112 of the *Indian Act* in 1960, all status Indians in Canada finally secured the franchise without sacrificing their treaty rights – one of Gladstone's key priorities.[124]

Although Senator Gladstone undoubtedly had his detractors,[125] his legacy is overwhelmingly celebrated. Political operatives supported his nomination to Senate because they considered him "a moderate, sensible critic of Indian administration: a person who would not generate uncontrollable political waves."[126] He did not disappoint. Historians Jean Goodwill and Norma Sluman observed that

> Senator Gladstone, a twinkly leprechaun of a man, while getting on in years, had seemingly inexhaustible energy, sharp intelligence and

> flashing wit. He worked effectively on various committees, usually those associated in some ways with Indian issues. The Senator and his lovely wife, Jane, were often photographed in their impressive Indian dress while attending various formal functions in Ottawa. They both charmed the Ottawa community.[127]

He served as senator until 1971, passing away later that year. Neither of the other Indigenous contenders for the Senate in 1957 served in the Red Chamber. Andy Paull, the strident "lawyer without papers," had suffered bouts of ill health since 1954 and passed away in 1959. Gilbert Monture, who some commentators described as insufficiently in touch with "Indian" realities in his career as a civil servant, continued to provide technical assistance to projects in the developing world. After he retired, he dedicated his energies to the Indian-Eskimo Association of Canada, applying his overseas experience to helping Indigenous Peoples within Canada.[128] Thus, it is a bust of Gladstone in a headdress that sits outside of the Senate chambers in the Centre Block, unveiled in 2001 in a tribute noting that "he broke new ground, pushed back the boundaries of convention and helped ensure that native issues were placed on our nation's agenda and that they remain there as a priority."[129]

NOTES

Acknowledgment: This research was originally initiated with Dr. Yale Belanger, University of Lethbridge, who was instrumental in framing ideas and the context of First Nations politics in the mid-twentieth century. Thanks also to Ryan Dean, Karen Everett, and Thirstan Falconer for research assistance. A St. Jerome's University faculty research grant facilitated final research in Calgary and Peterborough.

1 Hugh A. Dempsey, *The Gentle Persuader: A Biography of James Gladstone, Indian Senator* (Saskatoon, SK: Western Producer Prairie Books, 1986), 163–64.

2 "First Indian Senator Determined to Improve State of His People in Canada," *Lethbridge Herald,* 6 February 1958; James Gladstone, Telegram to John Diefenbaker, 5:18 p.m., 30 January 1958, vol. 57, 227551, MG 01/III/688, John G. Diefenbaker Archives (JDA).

3 Mel Hinds, "First Indian Senator Honored By Fellow Bloods and Whites," *Lethbridge Herald,* 19 February 1958. See also Dempsey, *The Gentle Persuader,* 164.

4 Jane Gladstone, quoted in Bill Gold, "Dawn Of New Age Seen For Canadian Indians," *Calgary Herald,* 3 February 1958.

5 Dempsey, *The Gentle Persuader*, 164–65.
6 "Indian Proposed as Canadian Senator," *The Native Voice*, May 1955, 1.
7 While First Nations or individual national names are now preferred to the outdated term "Indians," the latter remains a legal category in Canada. Given that Indian was the term in use in the 1950s, I have retained its use in this chapter to preserve historical context when referencing government and media coverage.
8 Chief Rising Sun, "New Canadian Indian Senator," special to *The Native Voice*, 19 June 1957, 227605–06, MG 03/III/688, JDA.
9 The Progressive Conservative Party of Canada, *Two Years of Great Achievement: A Summary of Accomplishments of the Progressive Conservative Party, 1957–59* (Ottawa: Progressive Conservative Party of Canada, 1959), 22.
10 "How to Pick a Senator," *Maclean's*, 15 March 1958.
11 Quoted in Brian Titley, *A Narrow Vision: Duncan Campbell Scott and the Administration of Indian Affairs in Canada* (Vancouver: UBC Press, 1986), 55. See also Hearing Testimony, 1921–22, file 473 pt. 12, vol. 6810, Record Group (RG) 10, Library and Archives Canada (LAC).
12 Ronald Graham Haycock, *The Image of the Indian: The Canadian Indian as a Subject and a Concept in a Sampling of the Popular National Magazines Read in Canada, 1900–1970*, Waterloo Lutheran University Monograph Series No. 1 (Waterloo, ON: Waterloo Lutheran University, 1974), 30, 37.
13 Garrett Wilson and Kevin Wilson, *Diefenbaker for the Defence* (Toronto: James Lorimer, 1988), 156.
14 John Diefenbaker, *One Canada: Memoirs of the Right Honourable John G. Diefenbaker*, vol. 1, *The Crusading Years, 1895 to 1956* (Toronto: Macmillan of Canada, 1975); Denis Smith, *Rogue Tory: The Life and Legend of John G. Diefenbaker* (Toronto: Macfarlane, Walter and Ross, 1995).
15 Diefenbaker, *One Canada*, 1:117.
16 Maria Campbell, *Halfbreed* (Lincoln: University of Nebraska Press, 1973).
17 "New Indian Act Is Just Mirage, Says Diefenbaker," *Globe and Mail*, 25 October 1950.
18 Special Joint Committee of the Senate and the House of Commons on the Indian Act, *Fourth Report*, 22 June 1948, 186; "Indian Affairs State Revealed by Government Committee," *The Saskatchewan Prince Albert Herald*, 17 May 1947.
19 On federal Indian policy during this era, see John F. Leslie, "Assimilation, Integration or Termination? The Development of Canadian Indian Policy, 1943–1963" (PhD diss., Carleton University, 1999).
20 "Send an Indian to the Senate?," reprinted in *The Indian Record*, November 1954, M-7655-401 (Scrapbook. - 1957–1958), James Gladstone Fonds, Glenbow Archives.
21 House of Commons, *Debates*, 3rd sess., 22nd Parl., 2 July 1956, 5564–65.
22 "Better Deal for Indians Promised by Diefenbaker," *Mount Pleasant News*, 10 July 1957, vol. 438, 3419221–22, MG 01/VI/635 (1959–60), JDA.
23 "How about a Good Indian in the Senate?," extract from the *Financial Times*, 8 February 1957, box 1, folder 4, Gilbert C. Monture Papers, 97-017, Trent University Archives (TUA).

24 "Blood Indian Up for Senate," *Calgary Herald*, 17 July 1957.
25 "Gilbert C. Monture May Go to Senate," *Globe and Mail*, 18 July 1957.
26 J. Geo. Hilderman to John Diefenbaker, 2 November 1957, vol. 57, 227511, 227563, MG 01/III/688, JDA; Marjorie Bond to John Diefenbaker, 19 July 1957, vol. 57, 227511, 227563, MG 01/III/688, JDA.
27 Editorial, *Lethbridge Herald*, 19 July 1957.
28 According to Diefenbaker's files, the names submitted were Daniel Cole, James Emann, James Gladstone, Jasper Hill, Reginald Hill, Rev. Peter Kelly, Brigadier Martin, Gilbert Monture, Nelson Elliott Moses, Andrew Paull, Omer Peters, Aylmer Plain, William Scow, and Guy Williams.
29 Anthony J. Hall, *The American Empire and the Fourth World*, vol. 1, *The Bowl with One Spoon* (Montreal/Kingston: McGill-Queen's University Press, 2003), 250.
30 J.E.L. Muir to John Diefenbaker, 19 September 1957, vol. 57, 227580, MG 01/III/688, JDA. On Kelly, see A.P. Morley, *Roar of the Breakers: A Biography of Peter Kelly* (Toronto: Ryerson Press, 1967).
31 Jack Cauley to W. Willis, 31 December 1957, vol. 57, 227508, MG 01/III/688, JDA.
32 J. Emann to John Diefenbaker, 18 November 1957, 1 December 1957, 15 December 1957, 28 December 1957, 8 January 1958, and 15 January 1958; Emann to Olive Diefenbaker, 15 January 1958; D.R.C. Bedson to Emann, 20 January 1958; John Diefenbaker to Emann, 21 January 1958, vol. 57, 227515–35, MG 01/III/688, JDA.
33 M.R. Jack to John Diefenbaker, "Strictly Private and Confidential," 23 July 1957, vol. 57, 227609–10, MG 01/III/688, JDA.
34 Editorial, *Lethbridge Herald*, 19 July 1957.
35 Enos T. Montour, *The Rockhound of New Jerusalem: A Tribute: Being the Saga of Dr. Gilbert Clarence Monture* (St. Catharines, ON: Go Print, 1981), 2–6.
36 Montour, *The Rockhound of New Jerusalem*, 7–8.
37 "Gilbert Montour," undated newspaper obituary, 1973, box 1, folder 11, Monture Papers, 97–017, Trent Archives.
38 For a telling anecdote, see Montour, *The Rockhound of New Jerusalem*, 11–12.
39 "Mohawk Has Served World as Economist," *The Amerindian* (January–February 1957): 2.
40 "Gilbert C. Monture," vol. 57, 227614–15, MG 01/III/688, JDA; Montour, *The Rockhound of New Jerusalem*, 19, 24.
41 See Philip Isard, "Northern Vision: Northern Development during the Diefenbaker era" (master's thesis, University of Waterloo, 2010).
42 M.R. Jack to Diefenbaker, "Strictly Private and Confidential," JDA.
43 See "Gilbert C. Monture," JDA; Montour, *Rockhound of Jerusalem*, 24–25; "Dr. G. Monture Receives Award," undated newspaper clipping, 1957, box 1, folder 11, Monture Papers, 97–017, TUA; "Honored by Indian Council," undated clipping from a Chicago newspaper, 1957, box 1, folder 4, Monture Papers, 97–017, TUA; Henry Fishcarrier, Secretary, Six Nations Council, 11 August 1958, box 1, folder 4, Monture Papers, 97–017, TUA. Additional information for this paragraph was derived from Monture's biography on the Trent University Archives website located at Trent University Library and Archives, http://www.trentu.ca/library/archives/97–017.htm.
44 See Kerry Abel and John F. Leslie, "Native Policy since 1945" (Ottawa: Indian and Northern Affairs Canada, 2000), 6–7; Leslie, "Assimilation, Integration or

Termination?" See also Hugh Shewell, *"Enough to Keep Them Alive": Indian Welfare in Canada, 1873–1965* (Toronto: University of Toronto Press, 2004).

45 Monture to Marion Gridley, 11 December 1957, box 1, folder 4, Monture Papers, 97-017, TUA.

46 "Dr. Monture: Challenge to Women: 'Restore Dignity of Indians,'" *The Native Voice,* June 1958, 2.

47 Monture to Vivian Williams, Executive Secretary of National Commission on the Indian Canadian, Toronto, 23 July 1957, box 1, folder 4, Monture Papers, 97-017, TUA.

48 Monture to W.H. Clarke, Chairman, NCIC, 16 June 1958, box 1, folder 4, Monture Papers, 97-017, TUA. See also his speech on enfranchisement in box 1, folder 12, Monture Papers, 97-017, TUA.

49 M.R. Jack to John Diefenbaker, "Strictly Private and Confidential," 23 July 1957, vol. 57, 227609–10, MG 01/III/688, JDA.

50 See, for example, Alan C. Cairns, "Aboriginal Research in Troubled Times," in *Roots of Entanglement: Essays in the History of Native-Newcomer Relations,* ed. Myra Rutherdale, Kerry Abel, and P. Whitney Lackenbauer (Toronto: University of Toronto Press, 2018), 403–36.

51 "Gilbert Monture," *Ottawa Journal,* 25 June 1973.

52 Susan Purcell to Diefenbaker, 20 July 1957, vol. 57, 227620, MG 01/III/688, JDA.

53 Leslie, "Assimilation, Integration or Termination?," 311.

54 Unsigned Letter to "John [Diefenbaker]," 1 October 1957, vol. 57, 227618, MG 01/III/688, JDA.

55 Brendan F.R. Edwards, "'I Have Lots of Help behind Me, Lots of Books, to Convince You': Andrew Paull and the Value of Literacy in English," *BC Studies* 164 (Winter 2009/10): 7–30.

56 E. Palmer Patterson, "Andrew Paull and the Canadian Indian Resurgence" (PhD diss., University of Washington, 1962), 249.

57 Anthony Francis to John Diefenbaker, 11 December 1957, vol. 57, 227632–33, MG 01/III/688, JDA.

58 Patterson, "Andrew Paull and the Canadian Indian Resurgence," 39. Paull's maternal grandfather, "Hundred Dollar Charlie," reportedly gave the last potlatch on Burrard Inlet before it was banned by the Canadian government in 1885.

59 Quoted in Edwards, "I Have Lots of Help behind Me," 8.

60 Edwards, "I Have Lots of Help behind Me," 9.

61 Herbert Francis Dunlop, *Andy Paull: As I Knew Him and Understood His Times* (Vancouver: The Order of the O.M.I. of St. Paul's Province, 1989), 24.

62 Edwards, "I Have Lots of Help behind Me," 9; Dunlop, *Andy Paull.*

63 Paull, quoted in J.S. Matthews, *Conversations with Khahtsahlano, 1932–1954* (Vancouver: Vancouver City Archives, 1955), 183.

64 Patterson, "Andrew Paull and the Canadian Indian Resurgence," 46n37, notes that there is no record of his apprenticeship with Hugh Cayley in the BC Law Society archives.

65 Maisie Hurley, quoted in Edwards, "I Have Lots of Help behind Me," 8.

66 Andrew Parnaby, "'The Best Men That Ever Worked the Lumber': Aboriginal Longshoremen on Burrard Inlet, BC, 1863–1939," *Canadian Historical Review* 87, 1 (March 2006): 53–78.

67 Peter Campbell, "'Not as a White Man, Not as a Sojourner': James A. Teit and the Fight for Native Rights in British Columbia, 1884–1922," *Left History* 2, 2 (1994): 47. See also Patterson, "Andrew Paull and the Canadian Indian Resurgence"; and on the McKenna-McBride Commission, see Paul Tennant, *Aboriginal Peoples and Politics: The Indian Land Question in British Columbia, 1849–1989* (Vancouver: UBC Press, 1990).

68 See Tennant, *Aboriginal Peoples and Politics,* chap. 8. On the Allied Tribes of BC, see also Darcy Anne Mitchell, "The Allied Indian Tribes of British Columbia: A Study in Pressure Group Behaviour" (master's thesis, University of British Columbia, 1977); and Cole Harris, *Making Native Space: Colonialism, Resistance, and Reserves in British Columbia* (Vancouver: UBC Press, 2002).

69 Patterson, "Andrew Paull and the Canadian Indian Resurgence," 182. On Paull's work as a promoter, see Chris Roine, "The Squamish Aboriginal Economy, 1860–1940" (master's thesis, Simon Fraser University, 1996), 83–84.

70 Paull co-formed the NAIB with John Tootoosis, a Plains Cree from Saskatchewan, and Jules Sioui, a Huron from Quebec. Decades later, the NAIB evolved into the Assembly of First Nations. See Hugh Shewell, "Jules Sioui and Indian Political Radicalism in Canada, 1943–1944," *Journal of Canadian Studies* 34, 3 (Fall 1999): 211–42.

71 J.R. Miller, *Skyscrapers Hide the Heavens: A History of Native-Newcomer Relations in Canada,* 4th ed. (Toronto: University of Toronto Press, 2018), 262–63.

72 Patterson, "Andrew Paull and the Canadian Indian Resurgence," 249.

73 James Roe, "Canada's Indian Conscience," *Vancouver Province,* 27 December 1956; Reynolds, "None to Take His Place," *Vancouver Sun,* 29 July 1959, quoted in Edwards, "I Have Lots of Help behind Me," 8, 9–10.

74 Patterson, "Andrew Paull and the Canadian Indian Resurgence," 299.

75 Paull, *The Thunderbird,* March 1951, 6, quoted in Patterson, "Andrew Paull and the Canadian Indian Resurgence," 328–29.

76 Paull, quoted in Jack McCaugherty, "Indians on Warpath over Centennial," *Vancouver Province,* 23 February 1957.

77 Dempsey, *The Gentle Persuader.* On the "Indian" experience during this era, see also Michael Mountain Horse, *My People the Bloods* (Calgary, AB: Glenbow, 1979); Joseph F. Dion, *My Tribe, the Crees* (Calgary, AB: Glenbow, 1979); and Chief John Snow, *The Mountains Are Our Sacred Places: The Story of the Stoney Indians* (Toronto: Samuel Stevens, 1977). On the role of Indian Affairs and Indian agents, see, for example, Titley, *A Narrow Vision;* Robin Jarvis Brownlie, *A Fatherly Eye: Indian Agents, Government Power, and Aboriginal Resistance in Ontario, 1918–1939* (Toronto: University of Toronto Press, 2003); and Keith D. Smith, *Liberalism, Surveillance, and Resistance: Indigenous Communities in Western Canada, 1877–1927* (Edmonton: Athabasca University Press, 2009).

78 Laurie Meijer Drees, *The Indian Association of Alberta: A History of Political Action* (Vancouver: UBC Press, 2002), 47, 49, 52, 53; Ruth Gorman, *Behind the Man: John Laurie, Ruth Gorman, and the Indian Vote in Canada,* ed. Frits Pannekoek (Calgary, AB: University of Calgary Press, 2007).

79 John Laurie, "James Gladstone," biographical sketch, attached to Laurie to John Diefenbaker, 18 July 1957, vol. 57, 227567–70, MG 01/III/688, JDA.

80 Laurie, "James Gladstone," vol. 57, 227567–70, MG 01/III/688, JDA; "Jim Gladstone of Blood Reserve is Named to Senate," *Lethbridge Herald,* 1 February 1958.

81 See Bruce Dawson, "'Better Than a Few Squirrels': The Greater Production Campaign on the First Nations Reserves of the Canadian Prairies," in *Plain Speaking: Essays on Aboriginal Peoples and the Prairie,* ed. Patrick Douaud and Bruce Dawson (Regina, SK: Canadian Plains Research Center, 2002), 11–21.

82 "Gladstone Mentioned for Senate," *Lethbridge Herald,* 19 July 1957.

83 John Laurie, "James Gladstone," vol. 57, 227568, JDA.

84 John Laurie, "James Gladstone," vol. 57, 227569–70, JDA.

85 Ruth Gorman suggested that Laurie's "first choice had always been Ralph Steinhauer. But unfortunately Ralph had already chosen to run and been defeated as a Liberal candidate. And no way could the Conservative party accept not only an Indian but also a Liberal." Gorman, *Behind the Man,* 188.

86 Meijer Drees, *The Indian Association of Alberta,* 54–55.

87 Harkness to Laurie, 26 June 1957, M-7655/23 Senate appointment 1957, James Gladstone fonds, Glenbow Archives.

88 Dempsey, *The Gentle Persuader,* 161.

89 John Laurie to Diefenbaker, 3 July 1957, vol. 57, 227572, MG 01/III/688, JDA. All quotes in this paragraph are from this source.

90 Dempsey, *The Gentle Persuader,* 162.

91 Dempsey to Gladstone, 17 and 22 July 1957, Family Correspondence, 1944–1957, M-7655/1, Gladstone fonds, Glenbow Archives.

92 Harkness to Laurie, 30 July 1957, M-7655/23 Senate appointment 1957, Gladstone fonds, Glenbow Archives.

93 Marjorie Bond to John Diefenbaker, 19 July 1957, vol. 57, 227563, MG 01/III/688, JDA.

94 Muriel McCready to John Diefenbaker, 22 January 1958, vol. 57, 227544–45, MG 01/III/688, JDA.

95 Isobel Toth to Diefenbaker, 1 August 1957, M-7655/23 Senate appointment 1957, James Gladstone fonds, Glenbow Archives.

96 John Laurie, "James Gladstone," vol. 57, 227570, JDA.

97 Gladstone to Andy Paull, 26 July 1957, M-7655/23 Senate appointment 1957, James Gladstone fonds, Glenbow Archives.

98 "Indian Senator May Be Named," *The Native Voice,* September 1957, 1.

99 R.D. Burt to Diefenbacker [sic], 25 September 1957, vol. 57, 227556–58, MG 01/III/688, JDA. In this document, Burt also intimated that Gladstone was a solid Conservative, having come by "elated with our victory" the day after the federal election to wire a letter of congratulations.

100 John Laurie, "James Gladstone," vol. 57, 227568–69, JDA. On Fred Gladstone, see Ian Dyck, "Does Rodeo Have Roots in Ancient Indian Traditions?," *Plains Anthropologist* 41, 157 (August 1996): 205–19.

101 Muriel McCready to John Diefenbaker, 22 January 1958, vol. 57, 227544–45, MG 01/III/688, JDA.

102 "Re: Jim Gladstone," vol. 57, 227573–77, MG 01/III/688, JDA.

103 "Re: Jim Gladstone."

104 Lillian Green to James Gladstone, 10 February 1958; Alice Basile to James Gladstone, 6 July 1958; Hamilton to John Diefenbaker, 10 February 1958; J.C. Johnston to Diefenbaker, 4 February 1958; Nolet to Diefenbaker, 5 February 1958, M-7655-24, Gladstone fonds, Glenbow Archives.

105 Bill Gold, "Dawn of New Age Seen for Canadian Indians," *Calgary Herald*, 3 February 1958.

106 "Appointment Jim Gladstone Pleases Cardston Leaders," *Lethbridge Herald*, 3 February 1958.

107 For examples, see M-7655-401 (Scrapbook. – 1957–1958), Gladstone fonds, Glenbow Archives.

108 Editorial, "Senate Gladstone," *Lethbridge Herald*, 5 February 1958.

109 Editorial, "A Voice to Speak for the Indians," *Calgary Herald*, 4 February 1958.

110 David E. Smith, *The Canadian Senate in Bicameral Perspective* (Toronto: University of Toronto Press, 2003), 81. Ironically, James Gladstone is never mentioned in Smith's book.

111 Valerie Knowles, *First Person: A Biography of Cairine Wilson, Canada's First Woman Senator* (Toronto: Dundurn Press, 1988), 83.

112 "First Indian Senator Determined to Improve State of His People in Canada," *Lethbridge Herald*, 6 February 1958.

113 Dempsey, *The Gentle Persuader*, 170. When rumours circulated about Gladstone's alleged plans to appear in Parliament in an Indian ceremonial outfit that would have conformed with stereotypical expectations of Indigenous leadership, Gladstone insisted that "I don't intend, nor did I ever plan, to appear in full Indian regalia with head-feathers." Arthur Blakely, "Canada's Indians Acquire a New Voice," newspaper clipping, circa 1958, file 384: News clippings 1954 to 1958, M-7655, Gladstone fonds, Glenbow Archives. Nevertheless, newspaper stories loved to depict him in Indian "costume," his wife clad accordingly at his side. For examples, see M-7655-401 (Scrapbook. – 1957–1958), Gladstone fonds, Glenbow Archives.

114 Arthur Blakely, "Canada's Indians Acquire a New Voice."

115 Canada, *Senate of Canada Debates* (13 August 1958), 514.

116 *Ottawa Citizen*, 15 August 1958.

117 Canada, *Senate of Canada Debates* (13 August 1958), 517.

118 Editorial, *Calgary Herald*, 15 August 1958.

119 Dempsey, *The Gentle Persuader*, 171.

120 A.W. Roebuck, "Tinkering with the Senate of Doubtful Value," *Saturday Night*, 27 February 1954, 7–8.

121 On the concept of an interest-based constituency and the ability of individual senators to "knit together national constituencies of people who might otherwise have an inadequate voice in Parliament," see Mark Audcent, *The Senate Veto: Opinion of the Law Clerk and Parliamentary Counsel* (Ottawa: Senate of Canada, 1999), 11.

122 Smith, *The Canadian Senate in Bicameral Perspective*, 21, 88, 172.

123 Canada, *Senate of Canada Debates* (13 August 1958), 518; Also quoted in "Senator Gladstone Ask for Equality Canadian Indians," *Lethbridge Herald*, 14 August 1958.

124 Gladstone often noted that if Indians were given the vote, it had to be "with no strings attached" and "without the Indian losing any of his rights on the reservation." Bill

Gold, "Dawn of New Age Seen for Canadian Indians," *Calgary Herald,* 3 February 1958.

125 Gorman suggested that Laurie came to regret his choice to recommend Gladstone to Diefenbaker because the senator supported liquor on reserves, believing that prohibition was a source of ongoing discrimination. See, for example, Canadian Press, "Indian Drinking Advocated," *Lethbridge Herald,* 1 March 1958; Canadian Press, "Sen. Gladstone Advocates Drinking Rights for Indians," *Calgary Albertan,* 3 March 1958.

126 Leslie, "Assimilation, Integration or Termination?," 311.

127 Jean Goodwill and Norma Sluman, *John Tootoosis* (Winnipeg, MB: Pemmican, 1984), 205. Senator Gladstone co-chaired the Special Joint Parliamentary Committee to examine the *Indian Act* from 1959 to 1961. Meijer Drees, *The Indian Association of Alberta,* 158.

128 David Webster, "Canadians and the 'First Wave' of United Nations Technical Assistance," in *Canada and the United Nations: Legacies, Limits, Prospects,* ed. Colin McCullough and Robert Teigrob (Montreal/Kingston: McGill-Queen's University Press, 2016), 97.

129 Dan Hays, "Bust of Senator James Gladstone Unveiled," 25 October 2001, The Honourable Dan Hays: Web Site Archive of the Former Speaker of the Senate, Jan. 26, 2001 – Feb. 7, 2006.

CHAPTER 5

PRIME MINISTER LESTER PEARSON

A Leadership Biography

Stephen Azzi

"Leadership is a rare topic among historians," John English once wrote.[1] It was not always so. From at least the time of Plutarch, historians were concerned with leadership, often using biography to explore the topic. By the mid-twentieth century, biography was the preferred form for studying leadership. In 1978, James MacGregor Burns, biographer of Franklin Roosevelt, wrote the pivotal work that helped create the interdisciplinary field of leadership studies.[2] But by then biography was already under attack in the academic community. Scholars came to eschew the study of powerful individuals – almost inevitably white and male – whose experience was far removed from the great majority of people. For political scientists, what mattered were the larger forces at play. For historians, society was much more important than leaders. Political biography came to be seen as the "shallow end of history," to use the words of literary biographer Michael Holroyd.[3]

Yet Burns showed that powerful individuals can and do shape history. As with national leaders elsewhere, Canadian prime ministers often change the course of events, making decisions with far-reaching consequences. After half a decade of constitutional stalemate, Pierre Trudeau forced the patriation issue, enshrining an amending formula and a Charter of Rights in the constitution over the objections of the Quebec government, a risky move that none of his predecessors had been willing to take. Brian Mulroney proceeded with the Canada-US free trade agreement and the Meech Lake constitutional accord when many in his own party and most senior bureaucrats would have been inclined to move more cautiously. Jean Chrétien kept Canada out of the Iraq War when the two foremost rivals for his office, Paul Martin and Stephen Harper, clearly signalled that they would have taken the country into the conflict. Chrétien also pushed ahead with the Clarity Act over the strong objections of members of his cabinet, his caucus, and his own staff. Countless other examples demonstrate that a prime minister can alter a government's trajectory, meaning that prime ministers are not interchangeable.

In the late twentieth and early twenty-first centuries, no Canadian historian contributed more to an understanding of Canadian prime ministers than John English, and he did so through the medium of biography. In his work, English illuminated a particularly Canadian style of political leadership, one that combines apparently contradictory qualities – at once transformational and uninspiring. Perhaps more than any other Canadian prime minister, Lester Pearson captures this paradox. Pearson's government accomplished more in five years than any other in Canadian history, yet both his contemporaries and historians often judged him to be a failure as leader. Even Pearson's own followers were dissatisfied. Tom Kent, his senior policy adviser, detected "feet of clay" and "weakness at the knees."[4] "Pearson was no leader," said Liberal MP Ralph Cowan. "He should never have left the groves of academe. He couldn't make a decision."[5] Another Liberal MP, Len Hopkins, said that Pearson was not "a decisive type of prime minister." "There is no question about his decency," Hopkins said, "but he was not the strong leader of the day."[6] The same view emerged from within Pearson's cabinet: in the view of forestry minister Maurice Sauvé, "Either to say 'no,' or to get rid of people, or to defend people – he was very weak."[7]

Historians have often repeated these critiques. Pearson "was not … a great success as prime minister," in the view of J.L. Granatstein. "His Cabinet leaked secrets like a sieve, his organizational talents were limited, and he was not forceful enough to direct firmly the work of his government."[8] Historian and Canadian studies scholar Jack Cardoso agreed: "Pearson was not much. He was a failure as prime minister, as a party leader, and as an administrator."[9] When Canadian historians were surveyed as part of an exercise to rank prime ministers in 2016, similar – though more measured – complaints emerged.[10] Respondent after respondent pointed to Pearson's lack of leadership skills. Yet there was a grudging respect for Pearson's many accomplishments – and a sense that there must be more to the story. "He was clearly more than the sum of his parts," Greg Donaghy said.[11]

Pearson's record as a party leader is stronger than the disparagement of his political skills would lead one to expect. He led the overhaul of the Liberal party after it had been reduced to forty-nine seats in the 1958 election, revitalizing its policies, recruiting new candidates, and leading the party back to power. These efforts allowed the Liberals to win many seats in traditionally Conservative areas, including Toronto. Ralph Cowan later criticized Pearson, but the backbench MP would not have won his riding of York–Humber had it not been for Pearson's shakeup of the party, which made the Liberals a formidable force in southern Ontario. According to Jack Pickersgill, Pearson's "most outstanding achievement was his leadership of the opposition," a role in which he was "every bit the equal of Mackenzie King."[12] Pearson continued to be an effective party leader as prime minister. One measure of his success is that, at the end of his tenure in 1968, he handed over the Prime Minister's Office to a successor in the same party, Pierre Trudeau, who was able to extend the Liberal hold on power for more than a decade. Only one other Canadian prime minster accomplished this feat, Mackenzie King, whom Canadian scholars ranked in 2016 as the top prime minister in Canadian history.[13]

Yet Pearson's strength is better measured in legislative than in electoral accomplishments. The Pearson Liberals completed the social safety net, implementing a national public health care program, the Canada Pension Plan, the Canada Student Loans program, the Guaranteed Income Supplement for seniors, and the Canada Assistance Plan, under which the federal government helped pay for provincial social programs, including nursing-home care and allowances for widows and needy mothers. The government lowered the retirement age from seventy to sixty-five. New programs fostered development in the poorest areas of the country. The last vestiges of racism were eliminated from Canada's immigration system. The government introduced bilingualism in the public service, strengthened the francophone presence in Ottawa, and adopted a flexible attitude toward Quebec and the other provinces. At last, Canada adopted a national flag and honours system. Pearson's government tripled the country's international aid budget and created the International Development Research

Centre. The armed forces were unified. Legislation created the Canadian Film Development Corporation and the Canadian Radio-Television Commission. In short, Pearson's government changed the face of Canada.[14]

Pearson did all this in the face of daunting circumstances. Under his leadership, the Liberals never held a majority in the House of Commons. Pearson withstood the attacks of John Diefenbaker, the most destructive Opposition leader in Canadian history, whose behaviour regularly shocked Pearson's sense of decorum.[15] And Pearson governed in the Sixties, a time of upheaval and unrest: anti-American sentiment was on the rise and Quebec nationalism was exploding, respect for established institutions was breaking down, and the voting public had come to expect government to solve the country's social problems.

How to explain the contradiction: a weak leader who accomplished so much? The answer is that Pearson's critics have misunderstood the meaning of leadership. Detractors have repeatedly pointed to Pearson's lack of administrative skill, as though leadership is merely high-level management. But leadership is not the same as management, though the two functions sometimes overlap. As John P. Kotter, a leading scholar of organizational behaviour, has argued, good management brings order to organizations to help them run effectively and efficiently. Managers plan, organize, staff, supervise, and direct. In contrast, leadership comes down to two things: first, establishing a vision and a strategy for achieving it, and second, aligning people and motivating them to work toward the vision by appealing to their needs, values, and emotions. In sum, management is about order; leadership often disrupts that order.[16] As social psychologist Abraham Zaleznik argued in a frequently quoted piece in the *Harvard Business Review*, "Leaders work from high-risk positions; indeed, they are often temperamentally disposed to seek out risk and danger, especially where the chance of opportunity and reward appears promising."[17]

Particularly important to Pearson's leadership was an understanding of the country and its evolution. As cabinet minister Bud Drury said, "He was more equipped with prescience than most of us."[18] Pearson understood that there were three revolutions under way in Canada and that government had to change to keep up. Prosperity fuelled the first revolution: a shift in the public outlook on the role of government. Canadians were coming to believe that the state was responsible for helping the less fortunate, including the poor, the sick, the elderly, the unemployed, and people with disabilities. As a liberal and a historian by training, Pearson had a sense of progress in society, which led him to support social programs.[19] "There is a moral obligation to assist," Pearson said. "It is part of the higher nature of man to help those who need help. It is only right for the strong to help the weak, for those who have to share with those who have not."[20] The second revolution was Quebec's Quiet Revolution, a change in views not only on the roles of church and state, but also on the province's relationship with the rest of the country. Long before most English Canadians, Pearson understood the rapidly evolving situation in Quebec and the need for the federal government to make accommodations or risk losing the country.[21] Pearson perceived that most French Canadians wanted a "true partnership" between anglophones and francophones, unlike most anglophones who thought of Canada as an English country with a sizable number of French speakers within a bilingual Quebec.[22] "Mr. Pearson knew well what our concern was," said Quebec premier Jean Lesage, the leading figure in the Quiet Revolution.[23] The third revolution was an even quieter revolution underway in English Canada, with most English Canadians no longer seeing themselves as British. With the arrival of large numbers of immigrants from Italy, Germany, and other parts of continental Europe, Canada became more multicultural, and the symbols of the country's British tie, including the flag, ceased to be sacrosanct.

Pearson's vision for Canada came from his determination to respond to these three transformations. Before he became party leader, Pearson's views on domestic issues were not well known. As a diplomat and minister of external affairs, he had spoken frequently on international issues but rarely on matters of purely domestic concern. Still, he could be identified as a social liberal.[24] In conversation with political aide Jim Coutts, Pearson confided that he would have joined the Co-operative Commonwealth Federation (the New Democratic Party's forerunner) rather than the Liberals had he not entered politics by joining the cabinet.[25] Pearson was determined that his government would complete the Canadian welfare state, providing public health care and generous pensions. He was equally committed to ensuring an equal place in Canada for those who spoke French. As prime minister, Pearson practised a flexible federalism that accommodated Quebec, and his government worked to see that francophones were properly represented in professional and administrative jobs in the public service. He might well have been the first prime minister to encourage ministers to speak French in cabinet meetings.[26] Pearson himself remembered, "My passionate interest when I was in government, apart from the ultimate question of peace and war, was in the national unity of our country. In some respects this was the most important issue of my career."[27] And Pearson was a "status nationalist," to use cabinet minister J.W. Pickersgill's phrase, determined that Canada abandon the last vestiges of colonialism.[28] Pearson wished for Canada to adopt the symbols of independence – a distinctive flag, a national anthem, and an honours system – and he wanted the federal government to negotiate with the provinces to create an amending formula for the constitution, so that Canada would no longer have to ask the British Parliament to amend the country's basic law.

Pearson aspired to do more than respond to the three transformations. He had hoped to improve both Canada's standing in the world and its relationship with the United States, which had suffered in the Diefenbaker years. A cheerful 1963 meeting between Pearson and US president John Kennedy signalled a new era in Canada-US relations, and the 1965 Auto Pact fostered trade in automobiles and automotive parts between the two countries. But there were limits to what Pearson could do. Canada tried to help the US extricate itself from the morass of the American war in Vietnam, but US officials were not interested in advice from Canadians, often perceiving it as self-righteous moralizing. On the broader world stage, it was difficult for the Pearson government to restore Canada's position to what it had been in the 1950s, when the rest of the world was recovering from the devastation of the Second World War and Canada enjoyed resources that most other countries lacked. Still, Pearson's government worked to increase Canada's military impact by unifying the armed forces and shifting resources from NATO and NORAD toward peacekeeping.

The Pearson government's accomplishments reached beyond the prime minister's vision. The government introduced major amendments to the Criminal Code, reforms that decriminalized abortion, the sale of contraceptives, and homosexual acts between consenting adults. New legislation made it possible for a woman to divorce a cruel or abusive husband, or one who had deserted her. These were not measures that the prime minister initiated. The only justice reform that was a high priority for Pearson was the abolition of the death penalty.

Pearson had the necessary strengths to implement his vision, or at least significant parts of it. He was willing to take risks, to move quickly, to make mistakes. He was hardworking, spending long hours either meeting with colleagues or thoroughly reviewing cabinet documents. He always arrived at meetings on time and well prepared.[29] He was patient and resilient. "Pearson had the ability to absorb an enormous amount of punishment in good spirits," in the words of Liberal MP John Reid.[30] And Pearson had remarkable recuperative powers. "Mike heals awfully fast," a former aide told journalist Peter C. Newman.[31] Pearson was charming, with an infectious sense of optimism, an endearing sense of humour, and an extensive store of self-deprecating stories. Cabinet minister Judy LaMarsh, who frequently clashed with Pearson and devoted much of her memoir to criticizing him, later called him "a darlin' man."[32]

Pearson had what we now call a high level of emotional intelligence.[33] He was able to control his own emotions while working to forge a consensus. He was a sensitive listener with a talent for putting others at ease and an intuitive awareness of their views and feelings. He kept an open mind and listened to cabinet ministers and caucus members. He welcomed different opinions. "He was extremely good," Coutts said, "at hearing what people had to say and understanding a point of view."[34]

Pearson was never jealous of his ministers, happily allowing them to take credit for accomplishments of the party and the government. So strong was his ability to make people feel needed and to make them believe that his achievements were theirs that his followers came to diminish his abilities as a leader, not recognizing his role in their success. Agriculture Minister Joe Greene contrasted the attitude of the MPs in Diefenbaker's caucus to those in Pearson's: Diefenbaker could look at his 208 MPs and say, "None of you would be here only for me." In contrast, Pearson's backbenchers looked at him and said, "Only for us, you wouldn't be there."[35] Mitchell Sharp echoed this sentiment: "When I sat around the cabinet table when Pearson was prime minister, I said to myself, 'The prime minister would not be here if we were not here.'"[36]

Pearson hated being disagreeable and would go to great lengths to avoid it, often to such an extent that others felt he had been dishonest with them. Marshall Crowe, deputy secretary to the cabinet, described Pearson as "a very slippery character."[37] LaMarsh's memoirs are bitter on this point:

> He usually appeared to have an open mind on any given question, but to be so greatly impressed with your advice or argument that he would probably follow it. It made everyone leave his office with a lovely feeling that he or she had had a most sympathetic hearing which would soon lead to the recommended action, although ... the whole interview was generally forgotten the moment the door had swung shut behind the caller.[38]

By 1964, senior aide Tom Kent was so frustrated with this trait that he wrote Pearson an extraordinary letter: "You should be franker in telling the person concerned what you think, instead of being nice to everyone ... What is needed is moral courage ... You are not being prime minister just to enjoy it."[39]

LaMarsh called Pearson "gutless," and others have derided his lack of courage, but this view was based on the mistaken belief that compromise is a sign of weakness.[40] In fact, Pearson repeatedly proved that he was capable of boldness. In January 1963, as Opposition leader, he reversed Liberal defence policy. The Liberals had been against Canada's acquisition of nuclear weapons, but Pearson argued that Canada had committed to take nuclear weapons when it accepted the Bomarc missile, which could only use nuclear warheads. A Liberal government, he said, would fulfill that obligation. This announcement angered countless Liberals and disappointed many of Pearson's old friends. It led three prominent Quebeckers – Jean Marchand, Gérard Pelletier, and Pierre Trudeau – to back away from their commitment to run for the party. It was a move that "took real nerve," LaMarsh admitted.[41] In 1964, Pearson chose to unveil his design for a new national flag at the annual meeting of the Royal Canadian Legion, purposely choosing the most hostile audience for this announcement. He did so without first consulting his cabinet or senior advisers, likely because he thought they would try to talk him out of it.[42] Pearson was roundly booed at the event, which was broadcast on CBC television. Then, when Pearson received an award from Temple University in Philadelphia in 1965, he used the opportunity to propose that the United States stop bombing North Vietnam, if only temporarily. Pearson knew the speech would anger US president Lyndon Johnson, but he went ahead with it, even though he was scheduled to meet with Johnson the day after the speech.[43] When the two met, Johnson berated the prime minister at length for criticizing US policy while on American soil. No doubt because of these and other instances, Lionel Chevrier believed he had never met a man of greater courage than Pearson.[44]

Pearson could be remarkably persistent. When a Conservative filibuster on the flag bogged down the House of Commons for six months, many cabinet ministers and close advisers counselled Pearson to drop the issue. Tom Kent considered it a "sideshow": it was not worth derailing the government's entire agenda for the sake of a symbol.[45] But Pearson persevered and eventually won the day. LaMarsh, a frequent critic of Pearson's lack of resolve, recognized his "single-minded determination to do away with the death penalty," noting that he "would bring up the death-penalty question again and again."[46] Pearson also succeeded in creating the Order of Canada, the country's highest honour, over the opposition of senior cabinet ministers Mitchell Sharp, Jack Pickersgill, and Walter Gordon, who believed it inappropriate for a democratic state to bestow distinctions on individuals. On the Canada Pension Plan, Pearson was, as Kent said, "the political leader with the courage to make a contentious proposal and the doggedness to ensure that it was fought through to an outcome close enough to his intention to satisfy a reasonable man."[47] Kent's conclusion is telling:

> He was entirely firm in the resolution that the essentials of the program for which he had come to office should be implemented ... To him it was always clear that the results were what mattered. To get them he was heavily dependent, because of his lack of organizing ability, on others. But they could not have been effective without the resolution that he gave to the program objectives. That is why his prime ministership achieved so much, why he made far more mark on Canada than have many ostensibly stronger men, with more aggressive personalities and more popular skills.[48]

Pearson recruited capable individuals to the Liberal party, including Marchand, Pelletier, and Trudeau, and did not feel threatened by them. The Trudeau case is particularly revealing. Trudeau had agreed to run for the Liberals in 1963 but backed out after Pearson changed the party's defence policy. Trudeau denounced Pearson in bitter terms, mocking him as "Pope Pearson," the man who changed party policy on nuclear weapons "one morning while eating his breakfast" without consulting caucus or his closest advisers. "The pope had spoken and all that remained to believers was to believe."[49] Yet when Trudeau ran, was elected, and joined the Liberal caucus in 1965, Pearson appeared to hold no grudge. He immediately appointed Trudeau as parliamentary secretary to the prime minister. Similarly, when talented people thought of leaving, Pearson convinced them to stay. In 1964, Jean Chrétien considered running provincially, but Pearson argued that if Chrétien believed in Canada, he should remain in Ottawa. Chrétien stayed.[50]

Pearson was sensitive and shrewd in his handling of Paul Martin, his rival in 1958 for the party leadership. When Martin pondered retiring from politics after losing the leadership, Pearson pressed him to stay. In both public and private, Pearson was generous in his praise for Martin's successes and, once in government, gave Martin the external affairs portfolio that he craved. The result was that Martin remained loyal to the man who had deprived him of the party leadership and of his chance to become prime minister.[51]

Pearson was able to attract and retain good people by letting them know they were needed. As Coutts said, "He made a great many people feel that they were part of the solution."[52] One of Pearson's techniques was a willingness to appear vulnerable. In Drury's words, "Mike, without ever asking for it ... got all kinds of help and support just through conveying an appearance – and it was only an appearance – of helplessness."[53] The result was to rally support to his side. According to Joe Greene, "You always felt, because he was an imperfect political dean, that he needs me."[54]

Pearson was rare among Canadian prime ministers in engaging in succession planning. The next three Liberal leaders – Pierre Trudeau, John Turner, and Jean Chrétien – all entered Parliament and cabinet under Pearson, who provided them with opportunities to advance their careers. Pearson, according to Turner, took an "avuncular attitude" toward him.[55]

Turner became a minister at the age of thirty-six, after only three years in Parliament, making him then the youngest member of cabinet. He learned much in his first cabinet post as a junior minister to transport minister J.W. Pickersgill, who knew more than anyone about how the system worked – and about how to work the system. Chrétien served as parliamentary secretary to Pearson and then to finance minister Mitchell Sharp, before being appointed to cabinet at the age of thirty-three. It was obvious to reporters at the time that Pearson was grooming Chrétien for a major role.[56] Pearson told Chrétien that he was apprenticing him with Sharp in the hope that the young MP would one day become the first French Canadian finance minister – a position Chrétien obtained in 1977.[57] Trudeau served as Pearson's parliamentary secretary before going on to be justice minister, an unusually senior portfolio for an MP with only seventeen months of parliamentary experience.

Pearson was especially talented as a leader of the Liberal parliamentary caucus. "I used to take caucus meetings very seriously and I was always available to members of the caucus for discussion," he later explained. "I never missed a caucus meeting if it was possible to be there … I used to encourage the frankest kind of questioning, however critical."[58] His followers were particularly generous in their praise on this point. Walter Gordon, a close friend who later fell out with his leader, described Pearson as "a master at handling the caucus."[59] According to Member of Parliament Ian Watson, Pearson brought three qualities to his leadership of the Liberal party: "He was forthright in caucus, he was fair to people, he was not autocratic."[60] Pearson was accessible to MPs, at times perhaps too accessible. "I just cannot conceive of any other prime minister whose door was open," remembered Larry Pennell. "Every backbencher who wanted to get in to see him on the smallest trifle, that door would open. And his patience was really immeasurable … He was never too busy to see people. And it must have taxed him almost beyond his powers of endurance."[61]

Yet Pearson's success with caucus was more than a matter of being available. The prime minister ensured that MPs had genuine input into government policy. "Caucus had a big focus on legislation and policy," remembered John Reid. "There was always debate, discussion, dissent."[62] When the younger members of caucus pushed for parliamentary committees to have more leeway, Pearson agreed, in the process expanding the role of backbench MPs.[63] Caucus was organized into advisory groups, one for each minister. When MPs complained that a minister would not meet with them, Pearson – who avoided reprimanding ministers directly – encouraged them to raise the issue in caucus. Then he would look at the minister and say, "Joe, you'd better see this crowd now. They mean business."[64] Inevitably, this would solve the problem.

The same traits characterized Pearson's approach to cabinet. Not only was he easily accessible, but he took the views of others seriously. As Coutts later said, "He was extremely good, perhaps because of his training, at hearing what people had to say and understanding a point of view that they were bringing to the cabinet or to his office or wherever it was."[65] He created conflict among his ministers by recruiting people of different – often incompatible – views and encouraging them to express these views in the cabinet room, where he purposely maintained an informal atmosphere.[66] All the while, he worked to prevent the conflict from overheating. "Pearson allowed free discussion at cabinet," Paul Martin recalled. "If things got sticky, he used to tell a baseball anecdote to calm things down."[67]

Pearson was not a conflict avoider, as has often been said. He simply did not resolve conflicts head-on and refused to be rushed into decisions. His method of conflict resolution was to refuse to take sides and to show sympathy to everyone, making people think he agreed with them, even when he did not.[68] "I can see both sides of a question when, as is usually the case, there are two sides," he joked, "unless there are four or five."[69] As journalist Grattan O'Leary later wrote, Pearson had the "ability to place himself in the other person's position: he had all the tricks of a negotiator. Finding out how one side felt, then playing it back to the other side, and vice versa."[70] Pearson would patiently and pragmatically negotiate a solution, always preserving his own freedom as much as possible. This meant that his approach was seldom straightforward, as diplomat Charles Ritchie observed:

> He approached his objectives indirectly, not by method of head-on confrontations. He was incredibly persistent as, for instance, later on in the flag question. That was absolutely typical of the way he approached things. He would back away from something and then ...

> come around to it again. It was fascinating to watch. It was a form of gamesmanship of the most accomplished kind, and his footwork ... was expert and very seldom was there a fumble.[71]

One example of Pearson's method was his reaction to a cabinet deadlock over Dominion Steel and Coal's announcement that it was closing the mill in Sydney, Nova Scotia, a decision that would throw eight hundred people out of work. Trade minister Robert Winters strongly opposed any federal aid, while cabinet colleagues Jean-Luc Pépin and Allan J. MacEachen were in favour. Pearson announced that Sharp, MacEachen, Pépin, and Winters would meet with Premier Ike Smith when he came to Ottawa to discuss the issue. "And then he [Pearson] dropped the bomb," remembered Pépin: "Mr. Winters will lead the Canadian group." MacEachen and Pépin were dismayed, but when the meeting took place, Winters backed away from his dogmatic position. Pépin then realized how clever Pearson had been. As head of the Canadian delegation, Winters had been forced to represent the national interest. He no longer had the luxury of promoting his personal view.[72] That broke the impasse.

Another example came during a critical point in the negotiations over the Canada Pension Plan. Pearson sent forestry minister Maurice Sauvé and policy adviser Tom Kent to Quebec City to negotiate directly with the provincial government. Not only did he fail to send the responsible minister, Judy LaMarsh, he also did not even tell her about the negotiations. After the deal was finalized, he dispatched Kent to break the news to LaMarsh, who exploded, throwing a framed picture of Pearson on her desk, where the glass shattered, sending shards flying. As her memoirs make clear, LaMarsh never forgave Pearson. Yet the objective had been achieved.

Despite a reputation to the contrary, Pearson had a well-developed talent for making decisions. There are rarely votes in the Canadian cabinet room. Instead, the prime minister listens to the discussion and then announces a decision, but in doing so must ensure that all ministers are willing to support it in public, even if they oppose it in private. Pearson had a knack for finding a formula that would satisfy the entire cabinet and leave no ministers feeling that they had lost.[73] In part, this was because his decision was not always expressed with perfectly clarity.[74] "I never saw anyone who could sum up and get the substance of the consensus of a meeting at the cabinet table," said Larry Pennell. "He could really sum it up, and have the consensus of that meeting – or at least make us believe it was a consensus of the meeting, because sometimes I wondered whether it was or not."[75]

Although Pearson had a skill for forging agreement, it was not the case, as J.L. Granatstein has written, that "compromise was always the goal."[76] Pearson's approach depended on the issue. On matters that were important to him and where he had expertise, compromise was never an end unto itself. He was careful to find a settlement that could move the country toward his vision.[77] In Pearson's words, a leader should not look for "the political line of least resistance along which drift those without the courage of their convictions, or simply without convictions." He believed in finding common ground – "the middle way," he called it. But finding it was not enough: "It is necessary to go somewhere." The middle way had to emphasize "the integrity and worth of the individual" as well as the objectives of "equality of opportunity" and "raising the living standards of all."[78] Pearson, according to Kent, understood "that most problems don't get literally solved, but if you can find some ways, some compromise, some agreement that gets you on the way towards a solution, then that's all you can do today."[79] Pearson was ahead of his time in understanding what business schools and public administration programs now call *wicked problems,* difficult situations where the best hope is not a solution, but some level of improvement.[80]

Time and again, Pearson compromised to achieve his objective. He had come up with his own proposal for the Canadian flag: three conjoined red maple leaves on a white background with blue bars on each side. But he left Liberal MPs free to vote for whichever option they preferred, with the result that the Commons flag committee unanimously voted for a different design, the one that became Canada's flag. Pearson was not even slightly troubled. The point was to create a symbol behind which Canadians could unite. The specific design was much less important. When the Pearson Liberals came to office with a draft for a contributory pension plan, they quickly discovered that Quebec was developing its own plan and was much further along than the federal government. Pearson jettisoned his government's proposals and created a pension plan on the Quebec model. For Pearson, the contribution levels, benefits, and the funding formula for the pension plan mattered little, so long as Canada had a contributory pension plan. Likewise, Pearson faced strong cabinet opposition to his proposal for an Order of Canada with three ranks. He backed down and accepted an order with just one grade and a limited number of recipients (no more than 150 at any time). Five years later, the government of Pierre Trudeau decided that the order needed to recognize more Canadians and different types of service. In 1972, the order was revised to create three levels – Companion, Officer, and Member of the Order of Canada – as Pearson had originally intended.

On issues beyond Pearson's vision and outside his area of expertise – what Kent called Pearson's "blank areas" – the prime minister was less sure-footed.[81] These included most economic issues, labour relations, and agriculture. In these fields, Pearson tended to seek compromise for the sake of compromise. When finance minister Mitchell Sharp and his predecessor Walter Gordon clashed over revisions to the *Bank Act,* Pearson sought peace at any cost. The issue was whether the Mercantile Bank, Canada's only foreign-owned chartered bank, should reduce its foreign ownership to 25 percent or 10 percent, and whether it could continue to expand as it increased the number of shares held by Canadians. In the midst of the dispute, both Sharp and Gordon threatened to resign. On Pearson's request, national revenue minister Ben Benson acted as mediator, brokering a complicated settlement that required each side to compromise. At no point did Pearson intervene to discuss the merits of the issue. His role was devoted entirely to keeping both Gordon and Sharp in cabinet.[82]

This approach to economic problems got Pearson into trouble on the issue of foreign ownership of Canadian companies. In 1960, Pearson told Walter Gordon he agreed completely with his friend's views on a wide range of policy issues, including the need to limit foreign investment, even at the expense of lowering Canada's rate of economic growth.[83] At the Kingston conference of liberal thinkers in 1960, Pearson described foreign investment as "a major problem" and pledged "that there is something we, as a party, can do about it and should – and will."[84] While Opposition leader, Pearson responded to letters on the issue by saying that he would implement measures not only to discourage foreign takeovers but also to encourage foreigners to sell their Canadian assets back to Canadians.[85] In 1963, Pearson supported Walter Gordon's first budget, which included measures to discourage the foreign takeover of Canadian firms. But when the financial community attacked the budget and when cabinet ministers refused to speak out in support of the contentious measures, Pearson retreated. The budget was amended to cleanse it of its nationalist elements. Pearson thought of removing Gordon from the finance portfolio but shied away from demoting a minister who had an enormous following in the Liberal caucus.

When Gordon resigned in 1965 for having failed as campaign chair to win a majority in that year's election, Pearson was no doubt relieved. Later, in late 1966, Pearson found himself under pressure from his Ontario MPs to bring Gordon back to cabinet. Pearson agreed to Gordon's demand that cabinet strike a committee to draft a policy statement on foreign investment, but Pearson appointed ministers to the committee, including Mitchell Sharp and John Turner, who rejected Gordon's views on the issue. As a result, the committee could not agree on a policy direction for the government. Gordon resigned from cabinet in frustration, feeling that Pearson had betrayed him – and not for the first time. Sharp summarized the problem: "My impression of Mr. Pearson on economic questions was that his principal concern was to achieve a consensus. He didn't start out with his own ideas. He spent some time in trying to reconcile the various points of views of ministers."[86]

The Pearson government had a reputation for being disorganized – and it often was. But, as Chrétien later noted, the appearance of chaos did not mean that the government lacked direction: "There would be great storms during the Cabinet meetings, with ministers pounding the table and raging at each other. Eventually, the prime minister would say, 'It's time to go to lunch, so I'll take care of the matter.' He had his own views and, for the most part, he just did what he wanted to do."[87] In his memoirs, defence minister Paul Hellyer recounts an episode where the prime minister polled ministers on a wage increase for St. Lawrence Seaway workers, and having found that they were almost unanimously against the increase, decided in favour of it anyway. Hellyer concluded sardonically that decisions in the Pearson cabinet were arrived at by consensus, with consensus defined as "one or more ministers, of whom the prime minister is one."[88] All of this disproves the frequent claim that Pearson was indecisive and ruled by consensus and compromise. Instead, the Pearson cabinet was a decision-making body when the ministers could agree. When they could not agree, it was a focus group, providing the prime minister with different points of view that he could take into account when *he* made the decision. He led his cabinet by charm and force of reason but was not beyond imposing his will when necessary.

Pearson was willing to delegate, giving ministers space to operate. He played a central role on certain issues: federal-provincial relations, the flag, bilingualism, capital punishment, the Order of Canada, and some key diplomatic files. But in other areas, he allowed ministers to take the lead. He later explained his approach:

> My philosophy was to let a Cabinet minister, as far as possible, run his own show and that it was not my job to be interfering in details. I felt that I should, in most cases, let Cabinet ministers take the initiative in policy discussions in their areas and defend their initiatives in Cabinet. I would then have to make the decision if there was a division of opinion.[89]

Pearson had "an intelligent, sophisticated" approach to leadership, according to Bud Drury. "If the machine will run itself, let it. If it doesn't, however, then you've got to move in. And he was prepared to move in, and did."[90] When there was no chance of a consensus, Pearson simply made the decision. He later recalled two examples: the flag and the timing of the implementation of medicare. "The caucus and cabinet were divided on both issues. I heard arguments on both sides and then decided."[91] Usually, though, ministers had considerable freedom – so long as they did not blunder.

The flip side to this – one could say the dark side – was that Pearson did not stand up for his ministers when they were in trouble. "Pearson just let his ministers lie where the axes had felled them," in LaMarsh's words.[92] Once ministers had served their political usefulness, they were allowed to leave or were pushed out. Chrétien compared Pearson to a hockey coach: "Have a power play and the guy's not producing, we bench him." Pearson has repeatedly been portrayed as weak, but Chrétien believed that he "was *very* tough if someone's political utility was expended."[93] Liberal fundraiser John Godfrey agreed: "I don't think there was anything wishy-washy about Mike Pearson. He could be very tough and could be quite ruthless on occasions."[94]

Justice Minister Guy Favreau was hounded from office – and, his friends insisted, to an early death – after allegations of bribery against the senior political aide to the minister of citizenship and immigration. The aide had been fired but was not charged because Favreau believed a conviction unlikely. The judicial inquiry into the case faulted Favreau not for misconduct but for poor judgment: he should have consulted his department's legal advisors before deciding not to lay charges. Not only did Pearson fail to defend Favreau, but for weeks he also refused to correct the record after mistakenly saying that the minister had only told him of the scandal the day before it broke, not two months earlier, as had been the case. Day after day, the Opposition and the media attacked the minister for not informing the prime minister, while Favreau refused to account for himself, not wanting to contradict Pearson publicly. Finally, after two weeks, Pearson set the record straight. For Pickersgill, the failure to correct the mistake immediately, abandoning Favreau to his critics, "was the worst thing Pearson did."[95]

The pattern repeated itself several times. Justice minister Lucien Cardin, Favreau's successor, told the media that a low-level Soviet spy, George Victor Spencer, would remain under RCMP surveillance but would not be charged because he did not have long to live. The decision was controversial, with some critics attacking the surveillance as a violation of Spencer's right to privacy, while others condemned the minister for not pursuing a case against a known spy. At first, Pearson appeared to defend the minister, telling the Commons that an inquiry was not needed. But a few days later, in the midst of a heated Commons debate where three Liberal MPs had defended Cardin and insisted that no inquiry was necessary, Pearson changed his mind and announced there would be an inquiry into the case. Jean Marchand walked over to Pearson and said, "If you ever do to me what you've just done to Cardin, all hell will break loose."[96] Cardin was about to resign but was talked out of it by colleagues who feared that others would follow and the government would fall.

Equally telling was Pearson's treatment of Maurice Lamontagne and René Tremblay. The two ministers had purchased furniture on credit and still owed money, a large amount in Lamontagne's case, to the furniture company when it went bankrupt. In Tremblay's case, some of the furniture was never delivered. "There was no scandal, no impropriety, or even carelessness" on Tremblay's part, according to Pearson.[97] Privately, he told the two men that they had been "victims of unjust attacks."[98] Pearson believed that they were "honourable and honest men of great ability," but that "they had difficulty in defending themselves." As a result, they had been "so undermined as politicians that their usefulness had been practically destroyed. They had to go because they were now ineffective."[99] According to Chrétien, Pearson "loved Maurice Lamontagne" but felt that he "had no more political usefulness."[100] Pearson has come under considerable criticism, much of it well deserved, for this unwillingness to risk his own position to defend ministers, even when they were falsely accused. As Kent noted, "The Pearson charm ... concealed a strongly developed instinct for self-preservation."[101]

Pearson was a deeply private man who did not reveal himself to others. A fellow diplomat described him as "a deep one whose secret self very few, if any, can know."[102] It is impossible to know when Pearson acted out a conscious strategy and when he reacted instinctively to situations. He might well not have realized that his leadership technique was to use his considerable interpersonal skills to align and motivate his followers in pursuit of a common vision.

It is also difficult to know why Pearson seemed not to care about the administration of his office or the cabinet. When Pearson offered Coutts a job in the Prime Minister's Office, Coutts asked: "Well, what would I do? What would my job be?" Pearson's response betrayed his failure to think about the structure of his office: "I haven't any idea, but I've got eight empty offices out there, and I have to fill them up. Would you like to sit in one of them?"[103] Before 1966, there was no chief of staff to whom the others would report, and Pearson had an "old habit of assigning a task to whomever was at hand," to quote Tom Kent. As a result, for much of Pearson's time as prime minister, his office was "chaos and confusion, with everyone falling over everyone else in frantic efforts to cope with one of the crises of the moment."[104] Senior public servant Arnold Heeney's comment on Pearson's time in the Department of External Affairs is equally apt for his tenure as prime minister: "Pearson had little time, indeed little taste, for administrative problems. His real flair was for developing and negotiating avenues of solution, for action at the policy level."[105]

Pearson did not simply lack an aptitude for management. Government-by-crisis seemed to suit him. He was, in the words of Liberal MP John

B. Stewart, "prepared to run quite a sloppy cabinet operation because he knew that at the end of the day he was quite capable of making what he would regard as the correct decision."[106] Pearson's fellow diplomat, Hume Wrong, agreed: "Mike is like Houdini – put him in the middle of a crisis and he will get himself out of the mess, and in the process will help others to get out of it too."[107] As his friend, journalist Grant Dexter, often remarked, Pearson was "happiest when he's clinging to a precipice and just about to fall off."[108] One of Pearson's favourite quips was "We'll jump off that bridge when we come to it," and he frequently quoted a line from G.K. Chesterton: "Don't be afraid of getting into hot water; it keeps you clean."[109]

Not only was Pearson able to remain calm in the middle of a crisis, but his particular talents also meant that he often came out of the crisis better than anyone else. He saw crises as opportunities.[110] After a failed federal-provincial meeting, Jim Coutts commented that the event had gone badly. "No," responded the prime minister, "it is worse than that – it is a disaster – now maybe we can get something done."[111] Member of Parliament Donald Macdonald came to wonder if Pearson was purposely managing events to create crises that he could then exploit. "I, of course, had a commitment to what he was doing, but his style used to make me nervous."[112] Jean-Luc Pépin remembered the impact of government-by-crisis on the cabinet: "It shakes everybody, everybody is wrecked by it, but the objective is attained."[113]

Pearson was uninspiring and never could fire up a crowd. He rejected the call for dramatic or exciting leadership, saying that it had a large element of "escapism" about it.[114] The chaos of the Pearson years, when the government seemed to lurch from crisis to crisis, left many people, including members of the Pearson cabinet, deeply disenchanted. Too often scholars have taken these complaints at face value. Yet a thorough review of the Pearson government's accomplishments – and the prime minister's role in those achievements – leads to a different conclusion. Pearson was a leader in touch with his times. He knew where he wanted to take the country. He possessed the necessary skills to recruit a group of highly talented individuals and to convince them to work toward common objectives, the flexibility to overcome seemingly insurmountable obstacles, and the interpersonal skills to keep a team together in the face of otherwise dispiriting challenges. If one accepts that the job of a leader is not to prevent minor crises, but to move people toward a shared goal – even if achieving that goal entails a great deal of disruption – then it follows that the best way to judge a political leader is not by examining the process by which policies were made but by examining the policies themselves. By that measure, Lester Pearson was an extraordinarily successful leader.

NOTES

Acknowledgments: I am grateful to Aaron Goldstein-Storseth, Kurt Montgomery, and David Cooper for their assistance with the research for this essay. This piece would have been impossible but for John English, Greg Donaghy, and Norman Hillmer, with whom I spent many hours talking about Lester Pearson. Professor Hillmer also provided extensive and incisive commentary on an earlier version of the manuscript.

1 John English, "Political Leadership in the First World War," in *Canada and the First World War: Essays in Honour of Robert Craig Brown*, ed. David MacKenzie (Toronto: University of Toronto Press, 2005), 77.

2 James MacGregor Burns, *Leadership* (New York: Harper and Row, 1978).

3 Michael Holroyd, "Parasites and Peddlers," *Times* [London], 31 March 1999, 20. For more on the role of biography in historical and leadership studies, see James Walter, "Biographical Analysis," in *The Oxford Handbook of Political Leadership*, ed. R.A.W. Rhodes and Paul 't Hart (Oxford: Oxford University Press, 2014), 314–27; and Lucy Riall, "The Shallow End of History? The Substance and Future of Political Biography," *Journal of Interdisciplinary History* 40, 3 (Winter 2010): 375–97. Patrick K. O'Brien's views are typical of those who see little value in biography; see his "Political Biography: A Polemical Review of the Genre," *Biography* 21, 1 (Winter 1998): 50–57.

4 Tom Kent, *A Public Purpose: An Experience of Liberal Opposition and Canadian Government* (Montreal/Kingston: McGill-Queen's University Press, 1988), 81.

5 Ralph Cowan, interview with Stursberg, 14 July 1976, 43, file 16, vol. 28, MG 31 D78, Peter Stursberg fonds, Library and Archives Canada (hereafter LAC).

6 Len Hopkins, interview with Tom Earle, 4 and 11 October 1989, 8 and 30 November 1989, 25 January 1990, 7 February 1990, and 14 March 1990, 27, file 3, vol. 2571, R1026, Library of Parliament fonds, LAC.

7 Maurice Sauvé, interview with Stursberg, 15 December 1976, 57, file 18, vol. 31, Stursberg fonds, LAC.

8 J.L. Granatstein, *Canada, 1957–1967: The Years of Uncertainty and Innovation* (Toronto: McClelland and Stewart, 1986), 199.

9 Jack J. Cardoso, review of *The Worldly Years: The Life of Lester Pearson*, vol. 2, *1949–1972*, by John English, *American Review of Canadian Studies* 23, 4 (Winter 1993): 617.

10 The results of the survey were published as Stephen Azzi and Norman Hillmer, "King among PMs: Historians and Scholars Weigh In on Canada's Best and Worst Prime Ministers," *Maclean's,* 17 October 2016, 19–23 (online as "Ranking Canada's Best and Worst Prime Ministers," 7 October 2016, www.macleans.ca/politics/ottawa/ranking-canadas-best-and-worst-prime-ministers); and Stephen Azzi and Norman Hillmer, "Ranking Prime Ministers: Canada in a Commonwealth Context," *Journal of Imperial and Commonwealth History* 49, 1 (February 2021): 22–43.

11 Greg Donaghy, response to 2016 survey distributed by Stephen Azzi and Norman Hillmer.

12 J.W. Pickersgill, *The Road Back, by a Liberal in Opposition* (Toronto: University of Toronto Press, 1986), 32.

13 Azzi and Hillmer, "King among PMs," 19–23; Azzi and Hillmer, "Ranking Prime Ministers," 22–43.

14 For more on the government's accomplishments, see Stephen Azzi, "Lester Pearson and the Substance of the Sixties," in *Mike's World: Lester B. Pearson and Canadian External Affairs,* ed. Asa McKercher and Galen Roger Perras (Vancouver: UBC Press, 2017), 107–29.

15 "I didn't think a man could act the way he did," Pearson once declared. John Godfrey, interview with Tom Earle, 11 June 1985, 57, file 9, vol. 2564, Library of Parliament fonds.

16 John P. Kotter, *A Force for Change: How Leadership Differs from Management* (New York: Free Press, 1990). For a brief review of the literature on the relationship between leadership and management, see Bernard M. Bass, with Ruth Bass, *The Bass Handbook of Leadership: Theory, Research, and Managerial Applications,* 4th ed. (New York: Free Press, 2008), 653–59. On the frequent confusion of leadership with management, see Joseph C. Rost, *Leadership for the Twenty-First Century* (New York: Praeger, 1991), chap. 6.

17 Abraham Zaleznik, "Managers and Leaders: Are They Different?" *Harvard Business Review* 55, 3 (May–June 1977): 72.

18 Bud Drury, interview with Stursberg, 19 October 1976, 33, file 20, vol. 28, Stursberg fonds, LAC.

19 Kent, *Public Purpose,* 255.

20 Lester Pearson, "The Case for Cooperation," in *The Crisis of Development* (New York: Praeger, 1970), 32.

21 Jim Coutts, "Windows of Opportunity: Social Reform under Lester B. Pearson," *Policy Options,* November 2003, 14. Pearson was one of the few prominent English Canadians to advance this issue. When he was planning to give his speech on bilingualism in December 1962, prominent members of the Leader's Advisory Committee, including Tom Kent and J.W. Pickersgill, were skeptical. Peter Stursberg, *Lester Pearson and the Dream of Unity* (Toronto: Doubleday, 1978), 9.

22 Pearson laid out his vision for improved relations between English and French Canadians in *House of Commons Debates: Official Report,* 25th Parl., 1st Sess., 17 December 1962, 2722–26.

23 Jean Lesage, interview with Stursberg, 3 May 1977, 16, file 5, vol. 30, Stursberg fonds, LAC.

24 A.W. Johnson, "Consistency," in *Pearson: The Unlikely Gladiator,* ed. Norman Hillmer (Montreal/Kingston: McGill-Queen's University Press, 1999), 172.
25 Coutts, "Windows of Opportunity," 17. Coutts also notes that in 1965, Pearson authorized high-level discussions over the possible merger of the Liberal party and the NDP.
26 Paul Martin, *A Very Public Life,* vol. 2, *So Many Words* (Toronto: Deneau, 1985), 374.
27 Lester B. Pearson, *Mike: The Memoirs of the Rt. Hon. Lester B. Pearson,* vol. 3, *1957–1968,* ed. John A. Munro and Alex I. Inglis (Toronto: University of Toronto Press, 1975, 2015), 236.
28 J.W. Pickersgill, interview with Christina McCall-Newman, 13 November 1981, quoted in Christina McCall-Newman, *Grits: An Intimate Portrait of the Liberal Party* (Toronto: Macmillan, 1982), 45.
29 On Pearson's preparation, see Martin, *Very Public Life,* 2:374.
30 John Reid, author interview, 5 May 2016.
31 Quoted in Peter C. Newman, *The Distemper of Our Times,* Carleton Library edition (Toronto: McClelland and Stewart, 1978), 61.
32 Judy LaMarsh, review of *Mike: The Memoirs of the Rt. Hon. Lester B. Pearson,* vol. 3, *1957–1968,* by Lester B. Pearson, *Dialogue* [Liberal Party of Canada], Autumn 1975, 20. According to secretary to the cabinet Gerald Stoner, Pearson "could charm the birds right out of the trees." Stoner, author interview, 28 November 1994.
33 The pivotal work on this topic is Daniel Goleman, *Emotional Intelligence: Why It Can Matter More Than IQ,* 10th anniversary ed. (New York: Bantam, 2005). Several studies suggest that individuals with high emotional intelligence tend to be more effective leaders. See Hyejin Kim and Taesung Kim, "Emotional Intelligence and Transformational Leadership: A Review of Empirical Studies," *Human Resource Development Review* 16, 4 (December 2017): 377–93.
34 James Coutts, interview with Stursberg, 22 April 1977, 34, file 15, vol. 28, Stursberg fonds, LAC.
35 Joe Greene, interview with Stursberg, 28 July 1976, 40, file 7, vol. 29, Stursberg fonds.
36 Mitchell Sharp, quoted in Allan Levine, *Scrum Wars: The Prime Ministers and the Media* (Toronto: Dundurn, 1993), 248.
37 Marshall Crowe, author interview, 22 March 1995.
38 Judy LaMarsh, *Memoirs of a Bird in a Gilded Cage* (Toronto: McClelland and Stewart, 1969), 26. Tom Kent made a similar observation: "Quite frankly, he did have a great capacity to leave the last men he talked to feeling that that was the view with which he agreed, and quite often it was the view with which he agreed for the next hour or whatever. I am afraid there is just no escape from that. That was the way he worked. And it had some considerable political advantages. It also had some great disadvantages at times." Kent, interview with Stursberg, 30 March 1977, 86–87, file 19, vol. 29, Stursberg fonds, LAC.
39 Kent to Pearson, 21 June 1964, box 3, Tom Kent fonds, Queen's University Archives, cited in John English, *The Worldly Years, The Life of Lester Pearson,* vol. 2, *1949–1972* (Toronto: Vintage, 1992), 295.
40 Judy LaMarsh, quoted in Levine, *Scrum Wars,* 248. LaMarsh's comment to Levine contradicts what she wrote in her memoirs: "It isn't that he lacks courage, he just prefers to talk rather than to fight." LaMarsh, *Memoirs,* 6.

41 LaMarsh, *Memoirs,* 28.
42 Kent, *Public Purpose,* 323.
43 Brendan Kelly, "Lester B. Pearson's Temple University Speech Revisited: The Origins and Evolution of the Proposal for a Bombing Pause," *American Review of Canadian Studies* 47, 4 (2017): 377.
44 Lionel Chevrier, "The Practical Diplomacy of Lester Pearson," *International Journal* 29, 1 (Winter 1973/74): 130.
45 Coutts, "Windows of Opportunity," 11. See also Mitchell Sharp's comment that Pearson's enthusiasm for the flag "was not shared very widely by his colleagues." Sharp, quoted in Stursberg, *Dream of Unity,* 160.
46 LaMarsh, *Memoirs,* 230.
47 Kent, *Public Purpose,* 255.
48 Kent, *Public Purpose,* 119.
49 Pierre Elliott Trudeau, "Pearson ou l'abdication de l'esprit," *Cité Libre,* April 1963, 7.
50 Jean Chrétien, foreword to *Mike: The Memoirs of the Rt. Hon. Lester B. Pearson,* vol. 1, *1897–1948* (Toronto: University of Toronto Press, 2015), vi.
51 On the Pearson-Martin relationship, see Greg Donaghy, *Grit: The Life and Politics of Paul Martin Sr.* (Vancouver: UBC Press, 2015), especially 171–72.
52 James Coutts, interview with Stursberg, 22 April 1977, 34, file 15, vol. 28, Stursberg fonds, LAC.
53 Bud Drury, interview with Stursberg, 19 October 1976, 33, file 20, vol. 28, Stursberg fonds, LAC.
54 Joe Greene, interview with Stursberg, 28 July 1976, 40, file 7, vol. 29, Stursberg fonds, LAC.
55 John Turner, quoted in McCall-Newman, *Grits,* 245.
56 Anthony Westell, *The Inside Story: A Life in Journalism* (Toronto: Dundurn, 2002), 176. As Chrétien remembered, Pearson used the post of parliamentary secretary to prepare promising MPs for cabinet rather than as a reward to be rotated among the backbenchers. Jean Chrétien, *Straight from the Heart* (Toronto: Key Porter, 1985), 30.
57 Chrétien, foreword to the 2015 edition, *Mike,* 3:vii; Chrétien, *Straight from the Heart,* 49.
58 Lester B. Pearson, interview with Thomas A. Hockin, in *Apex of Power: The Prime Minister and Political Leadership in Canada,* 2nd ed., ed. Thomas A. Hockin (Scarborough, ON: Prentice-Hall, 1977), 257–58.
59 Walter Gordon, interview with Lentner, 13 June 1974, 4, file 7, vol. 2, R11232, Howard Lentner fonds, LAC.
60 Ian Watson, interview with Tom Earle, 12 January 1986, 9, file 4, vol. 2565, Library of Parliament fonds.
61 Lawrence Pennell, interview with Stursberg, 2 May 1977, 32–33, file 9, vol. 31, Stursberg fonds, LAC. See also Martin, *Very Public Life,* 2:374.
62 John Reid, author interview, 5 May 2016.
63 See Paul Litt, *Elusive Destiny: The Political Vocation of John Napier Turner* (Vancouver: UBC Press, 2011), 51. Pearson's speech in support of the reforms can be found in *House of Commons Debates: Official Report,* 26th Parl., 3rd Sess., 19 May 1965, 1474–83.
64 James Walker, interview with Stursberg, 16 September 1976, 17, file 7, vol. 32, Stursberg fonds, LAC.

65 James Coutts, interview with Stursberg, 22 April 1977, 34, file 15, vol. 28, Stursberg fonds, LAC.
66 According to Pearson, "My style of conducting cabinet meetings was relaxed and informal, more so, I believe, than was the case with my predecessors." Pearson interview with Hockin, in Hockin, *Apex of Power,* 261.
67 Martin, *Very Public Life,* 2:375.
68 According to Mitchell Sharp, Pearson "was very good in cabinet. However, you were never quite sure what his view was. And that probably was a good thing. You could never be sure which side he was going to come down on. And that contributed, I think, to freedom of discussion." Sharp, interview with Stursberg, 26 July 1976, 29, file 1, vol. 32, Stursberg fonds, LAC.
69 Pearson, *Mike,* 3, 109.
70 Grattan O'Leary, *Recollections of People, Press, and Politics* (Toronto: Macmillan, 1977), 137.
71 Charles Ritchie, interview with Stursberg, 18 May 1978, 14, file 15, vol. 31, Stursberg fonds, LAC.
72 Jean-Luc Pépin, interview with Stursberg, 29 December 1976, 48–49, file 10, vol. 31, Stursberg fonds, LAC.
73 Marshall Crowe, interview with Tom Earle, 25 and 27 April, 3, 10, and 16 May 1995, 40, file 14, vol. 2574, Library of Parliament fonds, LAC.
74 "It wasn't always easy to know exactly what had been decided, because discussion was rambling and not organized," recalled Gordon Robertson, secretary to the cabinet. Robertson, interview with Tom Earle, 12, 19, 26 January, 9 February 1996, 38, file 18, vol. 2574, Library of Parliament fonds, LAC.
75 Larry Pennell, interview with Stursberg, 2 May 1977, 33, file 9, vol. 31, Stursberg fonds, LAC.
76 Granatstein, *Canada, 1957–1967,* 198. Compare Granatstein's comment with Mitchell Sharp's: "He was a very decisive man on certain issues like the flag, things on which his heart was set, or the National Arts Centre. But on many other things he appeared to be indecisive." Sharp, interview with Stursberg, 26 July 1976, 30, file 19, vol. 31, Stursberg fonds, LAC.
77 "Certainly for Mike the thing was to get an agreement," Tom Kent later said. "But I don't think it was *just* to get an agreement. It was normally to get an agreement which served at least to move in the direction of solving the problem." Kent, interview with Stursberg, 30 March 1977, 108, file 19, vol. 29, Stursberg fonds, LAC.
78 Lester B. Pearson, "The Implications of a Free Society," speech to the Canadian Institute of Public Affairs at Lake Couchiching, 13 August 1949, in Lester B. Pearson, *Words and Occasions: An Anthology of Speeches and Articles* (Toronto: University of Toronto Press, 1970), 91.
79 Tom Kent, interview with Stursberg, 30 March 1977, 108, file 19, vol. 29, Stursberg fonds, LAC.
80 In the policy world, the term *wicked problem* dates to 1973. Horst W.J. Rittel and Melvin M. Webber, "Dilemmas in a General Theory of Planning," *Policy Sciences* 4 (1973): 155–69.
81 Tom Kent, interview with Stursberg, 30 March 1977, 109, file 19, vol. 29, Stursberg fonds, LAC.

82 Stephen Azzi, *Walter Gordon and the Rise of Canadian Nationalism* (Montreal/Kingston: McGill-Queen's University Press, 1999), 117–18, 152–55.
83 Walter L. Gordon, *A Political Memoir* (Toronto: McClelland and Stewart, 1977), 81; Denis Smith, *Gentle Patriot: A Political Biography of Walter Gordon* (Edmonton: Hurtig, 1973), 64–70.
84 Pearson address at the banquet of the Study Conference on National Problems, Kingston, 6 September 1960, 24, June–Sept. 1960 file, vol. 19, MG 26 N9, Lester Pearson fonds, LAC.
85 Memorandum to members of the Liberal caucus, 15 October 1962, vol. 38, N6, Pearson fonds, LAC.
86 Mitchell Sharp, interview with Stursberg, 26 July 1976, 28, file 19, vol. 31, Stursberg fonds, LAC.
87 Chrétien, foreword to the 2015 edition, *Mike,* 3:vii. See also Chrétien, *Straight from the Heart,* 53; and Pierre Elliott Trudeau, *Memoirs* (Toronto: McClelland and Stewart, 1993), 108.
88 Paul Hellyer, *Damn the Torpedoes: My Fight to Unify Canada's Armed Forces* (Toronto: McClelland and Stewart, 1990), 169.
89 Pearson, interview with Hockin, *Apex of Power,* 260–61.
90 Bud Drury, interview with Stursberg, 19 October 1976, 32, file 20, vol. 28, Stursberg fonds, LAC.
91 Pearson, interview with Hockin, *Apex of Power,* 262.
92 LaMarsh, *Memoirs,* 92.
93 Jean Chrétien, interview with Stursberg, 6 January 1977, 40, file 10, vol. 28, Stursberg fonds, LAC.
94 John Godfrey, interview with Tom Earle, 11 June 1985, 57, file 9, vol. 2564, Library of Parliament fonds, LAC.
95 J.W. Pickersgill, author interview, 5 October 1994.
96 Jean Marchand, quoted in Newman, *Distemper of Our Times,* 397.
97 Pearson, *Mike,* 3:161.
98 Pearson, *Mike,* 3:162.
99 Pearson, *Mike,* 3:214.
100 Jean Chrétien, interview with Stursberg, 6 January 1977, 40, file 10, vol. 28, Stursberg fonds, LAC.
101 Kent, *Public Purpose,* 340.
102 Arnold Heeney diary, 24 September 1955, quoted in Heeney, *The Things That Are Caesar's: Memoirs of a Canadian Public Servant,* ed. Brian D. Heeney (Toronto: University of Toronto Press, 1972), 137n5.
103 James Coutts, interview with Stursberg, 22 April 1977, 6, file 15, vol. 28, Stursberg fonds, LAC.
104 Kent, *Public Purpose,* 338, 339.
105 Heeney, *Things That Are Caesar's,* 98.
106 John B. Stewart, interview with Tom Earle, 11 June 1987, 17, file 15, vol. 2566, Library of Parliament fonds, LAC.
107 Hume Wrong, quoted in Granatstein, *Canada, 1957–1967,* 199.
108 Grant Dexter, quoted in Bruce Hutchison, *Mr. Prime Minister, 1867–1964* (New York: Harcourt Brace, 1964), 358.

109 Pearson, quoted in Newman, *Distemper of Our Times,* 43; Pearson, *Mike,* 3:187. See also Richard J. Gwyn, *The Shape of Scandal: A Study of a Government in Crisis* (Toronto: Clarke Irwin, 1965), 12.

110 Donald S. MacDonald, interview with Tom Earle, 10, 11, 18, 20, and 21 April 1989, 14, file 13, vol. 2569, Library of Parliament fonds, LAC.

111 Pearson, quoted in James A. Coutts, "An Insider's Review of the Pearson Government," 1 May 2013, Pearson Centre, https://perma.cc/E7JZ-ZTG4.

112 Donald S. MacDonald, interview with Tom Earle, 10, 11, 18, 20, and 21 April 1989, 14, file 13, vol. 2569, Library of Parliament fonds, LAC.

113 Jean-Luc Pépin, interview with Stursberg, 29 December 1976, 41, file 10, vol. 31, Stursberg fonds, LAC.

114 Lester B. Pearson, *Politics and Participation,* Dominion-Chalmers 4th National Capital lecture (Ottawa: Dominion-Chalmers United Church, 1968), 4.

CHAPTER 6

SCANDAL AND THE DECENTRING OF CANADIAN BIOGRAPHY

The Case of Gerda Munsinger

P.E. Bryden

Biography, for historians, exists at the crossroads: it is the form of historical scholarship most palatable to the public, yet derided by academics as elitist, frequently sexist and colonial, and unquestionably old-school. It offers the possibility of popularity, the avenue through which real insights into the past can reach a broader public, but also the pitfalls of parochialism, ingenuousness, and egotism. But as a genre, it retains its allure, offering the historian a structure through which to interpret the past and the reader an individual through which to understand it.[1]

In recent years, biography has undergone something of a renaissance. Transformed in the hands of a new generation of historians committed to examining history from below, biography has evolved from its "great man" roots into a form that offers a window into ordinary lives, or provides a skeleton for understanding broader notions of transnationalism, identity, or colonization.[2] The subjects of biographies have changed dramatically in the last few decades too as historians have broadened their understanding of appropriate lives to examine.

The form of biography has changed just as dramatically in the same period. Where formerly the life itself would provide structure to the historical study – the subject was born, and influenced, and held power of whatever sort (political or economic or social, for example), and lost power, and died – new strategies for understanding the significance of a life began to emerge at the end of the twentieth century. Indeed, it was John English, with his magisterial studies of, first, Lester Pearson and, then, Pierre Trudeau, who shaped the modern approach to biography as much as anyone working in the genre in Canada or abroad. Certainly, his characters were great men, traditional topics of biography in that they held political power and left voluminous records; but unlike in other biographies of prime ministers, English's studies were careful windows into much broader subjects. Like the new biographers, English used his characters to shine light on the ordinary by following his subjects' gaze, and on identity by showcasing their anxieties, psychologies, and pathologies, and on the transnational by illuminating their cultural touchstones and their ever-changing worlds. English not only made his characters dance, but also used them in new and compelling ways to write real histories of the postwar world.

By infusing the writing of biography with new energy, English has inspired historians to contemplate new ways in which the genre can be used as a tool to understand the past. In particular, he has showcased the magnificent possibility of perspective. By standing in another's shoes, English not only brought them to life, but also used that vantage point to analyze another world – sometimes a political or international world, but also, often enough, a world of art or literature or philosophy.

In the story I will tell in the following pages, I want to use the tools that English introduced and examine some of the characters he wrote about, as a way of illustrating something about the nature of politics and society in 1960s Canada. The wide-angle story that appears here is one that is familiar to all Canadians of a particular generation but never fails to fascinate those that have followed: it is the tale – the quasi-biography – of the woman at the centre of one of Canada's only sex scandals. Gerda Munsinger was, for a time, the most talked about woman in Canada. She was a femme fatale and a double agent, a sign of the times whether one viewed Canada from the perspective of the 1950s or looked forward to the 1970s. Indeed, her story, and the scandal she inspired, sheds a great deal of new light on a world that John English introduced to us so eloquently in his biographies of both Mike Pearson and Pierre Trudeau.

Much of what we know about Gerda Munsinger comes to us through others or through her own faulty recollection. In this, she is comparable to most other private figures, who leave little in the way of a paper trail. Her biography is thus fragmentary and often contradictory. What we know about her comes almost exclusively from reports and conversations and testimony in 1966, the year in which the scandal that bore her name erupted. Her biography, as it was told then, tells us a great deal about the nature of that scandal, even as it still shrouds in mystery the woman herself. Gerda Munsinger does not change the picture that English has drawn of this time period, but she does insist that our gaze move from the centre to the periphery and that we take a place beside her on the outside looking in.

Examined from the standpoint of 1966, we see that there are easily three different narratives around the biography of Gerda Munsinger, each of which will be examined here. Whether we get any closer to understanding the woman herself is doubtful, but the results certainly shed some light on the stories people wanted to hear and hint at some of the reasons why; there are also, more clearly from the perspective of the twenty-first century, stories that people did not want to hear, and considering why that might be the case is also illuminating. So what follows are multiple biographies of one very shadowy figure and some new perspectives, as a result, on Canada's 1960s.

Munsinger's story was told in three very different locations in the 1960s, and told to three very different audiences. Most broadly, it unfolded in the pages of the North American press, where it was told in great detail in Canada, which should come as no surprise, but also in American newspapers such as the *New York Times,* which is surprising. It was told too, much more luridly, by the German tabloid *Neue Illustrierte,* where it obviously was designed to appeal to a vastly different reading public. Finally, the details of Gerda Munsinger's life were read into the court record of the inquiry into the scandal itself. Not really meant for widespread public consumption, this version of her biography nevertheless flew off the shelves like the latest thriller when it was published in 1967.[3]

Before there was much known about the woman Gerda Munsinger beyond her own circle, there was a scandal; her life story then, when it was told, was already being shaped to fit within the narrative arc of that scandal. Erupting in the already heightened environment of Lester Pearson's second minority government, at what was close to the pinnacle of Cold War anxieties and in a world often preoccupied by the convulsions of racial, sexual, and linguistic rights movements, the titillating details of scandal fell on fertile ground. For a public that had been living through the Cold War for two decades, replete with spies and double agents, conspiracies and coverups, and that had recently gawped at the Profumo sex scandal at the heart of the British Parliament, the time was ripe for a homegrown scandal.[4] That it touched on all the anxieties of a modern world made it all the more attractive.

At first, it was little more than a tidbit of gossip, perhaps inadvertently dropped into an exchange in the House of Commons following an acrimonious argument about various Liberal scandals. Richard Gwyn, without the benefit of hindsight, had called this trio of Liberal scandals "the winter of discontent," not realizing that what would follow in the spring would become much more memorable.[5] Riled by continuous jabs about government chaos by the Opposition, Liberals accused the Conservatives, when in government under John Diefenbaker, of knowing about and covering up an affair between associate minister of national defence Pierre Sévigny and an East German woman named Gerda Munsinger, who quite possibly had ties to Soviet espionage. Diefenbaker, claimed justice minister Lucien Cardin, was "the very last person in the house who can afford to give advice on the handling of security cases in Canada ... [given his] participation in the Monseignor [sic] case when he was prime minister of this country."[6] The press, at least, took notice of the statement, even as debate moved quickly on to other Liberal shortcomings.

Ottawa is and always has been abuzz with gossip and rumours and suggestions of wildly inappropriate behaviour. Rarely do these stories emerge from behind the scenes of the capital. For an actual political scandal to develop, a number of factors need to exist – not only does a potentially inappropriate or unacceptable event have to have happened, but it also has to have been made public, and the public has to care.[7] To break out of the backrooms and backstairs of Ottawa, there has to be some sense in the media that there might be wider interest in the events and that that wider interest is apposite. Broken marriages and ill-advised dalliances, unusual sexual practices, and unexpected partners litter the halls of most institutions, with government no exception, but an unspoken code of conduct for reporters meant few of these were ever widely reported. According to one scholar, changes to the professionalization of journalism in the twentieth century, combined with privileged access to the new political elite, explain much of the reason behind this hesitation to report sexual improprieties as they came to light.[8] This remained true long after the 1960s and continues even today. Certainly, in the Canada of 1966, however, much was known, or at least suspected, and little was reported. Finally, the only reason that the public ends up caring about the event, the "transgression," is because it involves people with reputations that would have suggested different behaviour, or because it taps into some existential fears of the moment and resonates with a broader cultural anxiety. In the case of Gerda Munsinger, it was both. Her story, then, the one that was told in newspapers and tabloids and commissions of inquiry in 1966 after the initial revelations in the House of Commons, was a story told to fit the anxieties of the age. And those concerns were different depending on whether the story was being told in Europe or in North America.

The biographies of Gerda Munsinger – not the true one, but the only ones that were told in that heated environment of 1966 and, therefore, the only ones we have – illustrate a great deal about Canada on the cusp of its second century; Munsinger herself remains far more elusive. "Olga" Munsinger, as she was first identified in the press, was surprisingly peripheral to the arc of the scandal.[9] At first, Cardin maintained in the House of Commons that he was under the impression that she had died in East Germany, perhaps of leukemia, sometime in 1963 or 1964. The convenience of death was soon removed, however, when *Toronto Star* reporter Bob Reguly found her alive and well and living in Munich. From that point on, she became a real character in the drama but one shaped by the narratives of those around. Newspapers described a "shapely" blond woman who was, by 1966, thirty-seven years old. The details of her biography were scant: after the Second World War, she had married an American soldier named Mike Munsinger, but they had been denied entry when the couple tried to return to the US and were thus divorced sometime in the 1950s. "With the help of a Canadian Government loan," she came to Canada in 1955 as a landed immigrant. She ultimately moved to Montreal and lived in "a modern apartment building with a smart lobby." On several occasions in 1958, 1959, and 1960, she met with Pierre Sévigny, then associate minister of national defence, "visited his Ottawa hotel suite and [went] with him to the races in Boston in a Government plane."[10] Much was made of Munsinger's current living arrangements. Her apartment was "chintzy," according to the *Star*, and located in an affluent part of Munich. She also, apparently, continued to wear a birthstone ring that Sévigny had given her years earlier.[11]

There was surprisingly little of substance in the initial descriptions of Munsinger beyond a few words describing her appearance, her clothes and, her apartment, and a few quotes regarding the extent to which she knew Conservative cabinet ministers in the late 1950s and early 1960s. She "attended an election banquet in the Windsor Hotel in Montreal," she told Reguly, and she still "knows and can call many people" in the Social Registry.[12] But despite being described as a "sex and security scandal," there were scant details about either sex or security. Simply showing photographs of Munsinger, noting her attractiveness, and establishing that she did indeed know Sévigny was sufficient to link the cabinet minister and possibly others in the Diefenbaker government to the German woman in a "sex" scandal. Acquaintances in Montreal, scoped out during the first heady days following the bombshell in the House of Commons, had various tales to tell: she was "a high-flying party girl with a heart of gold"; she was a "woman with connections" who could secure top-notch medical care when it was needed in 1960; she was "a laughing lady with a puckish sense of humour" who attended political dinners in Ottawa and "seemed amused at being so near the wives of some ministers."[13]

More information came out over the next few weeks. As the story moved from the House of Commons to the press to the courtrooms of the inquiry, Pearson was forced to call into question what the Diefenbaker government knew and when. But Munsinger herself was never at the centre of the story. Instead, she was a "playgirl" and a "swinger with a heart of gold"[14] whose mere existence seemed to hint of improprieties. By the time that Sévigny took his turn on the stand, she was increasingly being referred to in the press as a "prostitute," a characterization that was never entirely proven and yet came to become the standard description of the woman, even long after her death.[15] He took issue with that depiction. Stating point blank that "Mrs. Munsinger was never my mistress," Sévigny explained that "she was certainly not the despicable person she has been represented to be in the press in recent weeks." No, he said, she was instead "charming," she "dressed well," was "well-liked by all," and was "accepted and admired in Montreal's finest clubs and hotels."[16] When confronted with the information that on the evening of 26–27 November 1960 he had been the fourth man to visit Munsinger, and that the previous three had "paid a fee," Sévigny responded that she could only have resorted to such behaviour during her final desperate few weeks in Canada.[17]

As events unfolded in the spring of 1966, sex was never very far from the surface. The scandal was repeatedly called a "sex and security" scandal, the woman at the heart of it was identified using language that emphasized her appearance and her sociability, and the men at the centre agreed that they knew Gerda Munsinger "socially." The nods, the winks, the suggestions all pointed to an affair, but it remained elusive and ill-defined even if it was obvious to all but the most naïve. Indeed, there was an active effort to keep particularly salacious details quiet. Some cabinet ministers in the Diefenbaker government, for example, had been aware that the Chief had an RCMP recording of a "meeting" between Sévigny and Munsinger, presumably a sex tape, that he would play back to Sévigny when he felt the need to humiliate him.[18] None of this was known, or apparently demanded, at the time. More interesting than the fact that the details of any sex remained blurry was that there seemed relatively little public appetite for anything more.

The security features of the Munsinger story are similarly obscured, but here the public seemed much more interested. Most of the details about Munsinger's potential threat to national security came as a result of the hearings into the case and were leaked drip by drip to the press. In the report by Justice Wishart Spence on the Munsinger affair, she was described as having a "checkered career." In summarizing RCMP reports on Munsinger, Spence reported that she had been refused a visa for immigration to Canada in 1952 because she was "a self-admitted espionage agent [who] had a record of convictions as a common prostitute, a petty thief, and a smuggler." The crimes, such as they were, seemed to relate to incidents in the 1940s when she took clothing from a home in which she was employed as a maid, and when she "rifled through the pockets of a United States Army private who had befriended her." She was, the commission found, someone who could "very easily betray those who trusted her." The commission based its version of Gerda's pre-Canadian life on RCMP files, which themselves indicated that her "espionage activities" had been of a "minor character."[19] The RCMP accounts were, in turn, based on a report of the American West German Border police, who had stopped Gerda at one point in 1949 as she moved back and forth across the border in an effort to survive.

Once the initial excitement over finding Munsinger alive and well and living in Munich had worn off, the story came to be told firmly within the context of the Cold War. Whether or not Munsinger was a security risk was incidental to the central issue, as it was clear that little effort had been made to uncover her early history in East Germany or to verify her contacts with Soviet intelligence. Instead, it was clearly sufficient to establish that she *might* have been a security risk and that the prime minister knew that was the case. The real focus of the Munsinger inquiry was on Diefenbaker's Progressive Conservative government, not on the shadowy woman who gave her name to the scandal.

As Canadians both gazed at Munsinger through the tumultuous run of the Spence inquiry in the spring of 1966 and turned away in awkward embarrassment, the biography of the woman herself remains painfully incomplete. But by shifting to Munsinger's viewpoint and to her perspectives on Canada, and on government and the West in general, we can begin to understand the scandal and the times more completely. Her observations of Canada are just as obscured as the Canadian view of her, but each provides us with a bit of insight into the times themselves.

Munsinger sold her version of her story to the German tabloid *Neue Illustrierte* for the princely sum of $45,000, shoehorning it into a "formulaic melodrama" format that kept Munsinger at its centre.[20] From this perspective, the scandal is not really about espionage or even really about sex, although Munsinger and the writers at *Neue Illustrierte* were wise enough to cater to those themes. Instead, it is a romantic narrative about hopes and dreams and the ways in which neither are ever really fulfilled. If there is a scandal at all in Munsinger's version of events, it is of the mundane variety, more disappointment than outrage, more private than public.

Gerda Heseler was born sometime around 1929 in the German city of Königsberg, which became the Soviet city of Kaliningrad after the Second World War. In the years between the end of the war, which Gerda spent evading arrest, and 1948, when she fled to West Germany with her mother, it is unclear entirely what she did. By her own account, told much later, "I was 16 when the war was over … long blond pigtails … [the Soviets] ruined my life because of those three years. I had quite a lot of operations. My whole life has been ruined with it." There is the implication that she suffered physical abuse, possibly sexual, but in her telling she remains vague. In 1966, the public was quite prepared to believe Soviet atrocities and just as likely to be scandalized by the abuse of pigtailed children at the hands of a communist state. For Gerda, this scenario explains her desire to come to Canada – "to get away from all this … there was so much I couldn't forget here. I wanted to get away from the country."[21]

Gerda's story is not unlike many in postwar Canada and fits with a narrative of new starts in a new country, an immigrant story that was particularly popular in the 1950s.[22] Munsinger crafted a version of her own need for a new start in the details of her life in the 1950s that she offered the German gossip magazine. "I worked at the time for one hundred and thirty Marks and free meals and board … I got up at six o'clock in the morning and fell exhausted to bed at midnight," she recalled. But in Munsinger's version, there was romance behind the bleakness of her postwar Germany. "In my unheated room in the attic," she continued, "I dreamed of beautiful clothes, of jewelry, of elegant men, of romantic nights in far away countries."[23] She also cast herself as a bit-player in another intrigue, the high-profile case of Otto Praun, allegedly killed by a woman with "a social aristocracy that could be honored and envied."[24] The parallels with Munsinger's own case as it unfolded in Canada were obvious and meant to be made by the German reading public.

Munsinger's role in the Praun case is incidental, and quite probably fabricated, but it does shed some light on how she remembered her aspirations before coming to Canada. She met a man at a dance, reputedly Otto Praun's son, who put her in touch with Canadian immigration officials, who indicated that there was still space in the Canadian quota system for housemaids and lumberjacks. She opted to apply as the former, although even then her preference would have been to marry the man, whoever he was, who she had met at that dance.[25] Clearly, the version of the story that Gerda told, and the way the reporter opted to tell it, was spun for the enjoyment of a postwar European audience. The hardscrabble existence that confronted the survivors of the Second World War was familiar, as was the mention of a local scandal. Moreover, many readers would have considered flight to Canada, familiarly presented as the caricature of an unpopulated northern nation. Of course, in this German retelling of the story, Canada would need *lumberjacks*!

Munsinger's story of her Canadian life emphasized sex in a variety of different iterations – romantic, transactional, and illicit. Her year of working for a family outside Montreal, necessary in order to repay the government loan that brought her to Canada in the first place, was described briefly and positively. They were "nice people" who "tried everything for me," she said. "The woman even wanted to learn to speak German because of me."[26] But despite having maintained that her sole goal in coming to Canada was "to make money, whatever I could make, and then return," rather than to take advantage of the "places where there were three thousand men and not a single woman," she soon headed to Montreal to seek her fortune.[27]

Her first lover was a waiter named Johnny from Montreal's infamous Ruby Foo's, *the* place to "see and be seen" in the late 1950s, when it was, according to its own hype, "class personified, fun and lively."[28] And Johnny was "more than a man for me," claimed Munsinger. He "was Canada. Rough and hard and, in the evenings, when the cold wind blew from the mountains, as tender as the strings of the guitars of the lumberjacks of this country."[29] From the outset, Munsinger casts nations as characters, equating Canada with adventure, opportunity, and love. But Johnny, like Canada perhaps, was fickle and soon moved on to other women.

The tabloid went on to devote considerable attention to Munsinger's account of her affair with Progressive Conservative trade minister George Hees, an encounter that did not play a particularly large role in the Canadian rendition of events. Indeed, Justice Spence noted that although "many wild rumours" and "livid stories" had appeared in the "foreign press" regarding Hees, he would pay them little notice.[30] The attention that Munsinger herself gave to her encounters with Hees, however, suggests that they were important to her characterization of her life in Canada.

Hees was one of "two love-hungry ministers [who] followed me with their eyes," she told *Neue Illustrierte*. The two are presented as opposites: her affair with Hees was brief and apparently not particularly fulfilling. After mediocre sex, Gerda shooed the cabinet minister back to the House: "Half past two already. Go govern your people now. Perhaps you can do that." Hees was just an opening act, though, for the other "love-hungry minister," Pierre Sévigny:

> I met him in the Le Hunt cocktail lounge of the Sheraton Hotel in Montreal, the best cocktail bar in the city. Between 5 and 7 o'clock in the afternoon all the important people of the city can be seen there. Millionaires who own mines in the central parts of the country, lawyers who want to discuss a lost procedure while sipping a whiskey. Mannequins, reporters, secretaries, players, jockeys, and even the manager of the supermarket across the road. [Sévigny] was a gentleman from head to heel. A man whom one could dream of but never conquer. We spoke only a few words on that first afternoon. But [my friend Jackie] saw from my shining eyes what the few words had meant to me.[31]

Their relationship developed slowly – "he must court me if he really liked me" – and, according to Gerda, did so tenderly, lovingly, romantically.

As told in the pages of *Neue Illustrierte,* this was unquestionably a story about sex, recounted with considerable innuendo but also at considerable length. Not only did she describe meals and walks and travels with Sévigny, but she also detailed her relationship with others in Germany before her emigration and more harrowing subsequent encounters with hard-drinking men who beat her and others involved in racketeering who ended up either dead or in jail.[32] Much of the story was surely embellished, but it hinted at what Munsinger's world looked like – an ultimately futile adventure in making a living in the new world, where men were judged on the way they treated women and the way they made their money. In fact, Munsinger's conclusions about North America turn her story into something of a morality tale:

> There are three kinds of millionaires in America. There are those who have inherited their millions ... In most cases these people have just one idea in their heads and that was to hand out money. They usually hang out in the company of companions of misfortune who all consider it a matter of prestige to spend their dollars in the most original ways.

> There are then the men who have made their millions through hard work, which has given them no opportunity for anything else. It has often taken twenty to twenty-five years. They refused all fun from life until they stood at the summit of their careers.
>
> Then all of a sudden they become hungry for life. They wanted to catch up with everything. They wanted to have everything, especially women, entertainment and love. When they met women they wanted, they did not let her loose until they had obtained their goal, and they again started to chase a new woman.
>
> The meanest kind are the racketeers, gangsters and pushers. They have made their millions through dark affairs, blackmail and covert robberies.[33]

The writing marks *Neue Illustrierte* as melodramatic fluff, but it also hints at some of the ways in which Munsinger wanted to control her story. In this delineation, Sévigny emerges as one of those men especially hungry for life and living in a world where that hunger could be satiated by women other than his wife without attracting opprobrium. Canada in the 1960s was clearly still one in which a gentleman's code of honour enabled extramarital liaisons. He clearly comes across more positively than any other man in this version of Munsinger's story, probably because he treated her better than they did and continued to do so under the scrutiny of the inquiry. Where others refused to acknowledge the degree of their contact in the 1950s and early 1960s, notably Hees (to his discredit in the German account), Sévigny at least appeared to take some responsibility. He admitted the affair to his wife, who, according to Munsinger, was apparently "so happy that everything between us is clear again." Munsinger concluded that "these Sevignys are really great human beings. Especially when considering how this man Hees acted."[34] But if Pierre Sévigny is not cast as the villain in Munsinger's account, he nevertheless comes across as both covetous and certain of his right to be so. Everyone else who Munsinger meets in North America is portrayed similarly. The European audience for which this version was written would certainly have found this a familiar stereotype of postwar western excess.

In the only telling of the Munsinger story where sex plays a prominent role, there is little in the way of scandal. *Neue Illustrierte* reports her musing about the possibility that her case was bigger than the Profumo affair in Britain and that "a government may now fall because of me," but such talk was designed to sell magazines. The government most obviously entangled in the Munsinger affair had fallen in the 1963 general election, and there was little chance of Pearson's government becoming implicated, even if the public increasingly regarded its decision to launch a judicial inquiry as unbecoming and inappropriate.[35] The scandal, in Munsinger's version, was the failure of North America to fulfill the dreams she had as a young woman in East Germany in the years immediately following the Second World War.

In Canada, the press responded somewhat differently. Munsinger's Canadian sojourn was not really about her at all – it was all about the tawdriness of Canadian politics, where accusations and counteraccusations of impropriety dominated House of Commons debate to such an extent that almost half of Canadians indicated in a Gallup poll that they thought neither Pearson nor Diefenbaker were worthy of leading the nation. In fact, for the Canadian press, Munsinger was not the central character but rather the prize at the end of the tunnel. Initial reports, when the Munsinger affair broke in the House in the spring of 1966, were that the woman in question was dead. That left the politicians to argue about other things and the public to grow increasingly weary of the decline of civility in public life. But then she showed up, alive and well in Germany. She was a mystery, an enigma, a femme fatale – that stock character of 1960s movies. Sex was alluded to, but more prominent in the stories that hit the press were suggestions of her other identity as a spy. Were Canadians uninterested in sex? The domestic press reporting suggests that even in the raucous 1960s, sex was not necessarily the ticket to selling newspapers. The mystery of Gerda Munsinger was good copy, and the suggestions of espionage clearly fell on receptive ears, but details about whatever transpired between Sevigny and Munsinger, with an emphasis either on the romance or the sex, received relatively little play in the Canadian press.

If we move Gerda Munsinger to the centre of the story that was told in 1960s Canada, there is not much of a scandal. There was, though, a quiet condemnation of the postwar West, where the much-hyped opportunity was for men, and men only, and often appeared in the form of women. Someone such as Munsinger could hardly expect to have her dreams fulfilled in that West, despite what the press might suggest. Her story, in fact, has a happy ending only in East Germany, where she "found a man who is serious about me ... and only shakes his head when I tell him about my adventures."[36] Munsinger herself centres sex at the heart of this story, not the scandal, which others created and which revolved almost entirely around unfounded suggestions of espionage. Her telling of the story begins to intimate a double standard and suggests that sex was, indeed, at the heart of what was problematic about government interactions, or power more generally, in the 1960s. That was not the story that anyone heard when the Munsinger case dominated the media, though. In Canada, it was a tale of Cold War hostilities, neither about illicit nor modern sex.[37] Had anyone listened to Gerda Munsinger herself, they might have heard a different story of what was wrong with Canada in 1966.

Biography, a form that John English has used masterfully, offers a structure to the historical narrative; it gives us a life on which to hang the events of the past. But there are many ways to tell the story of a life, as this examination of the Munsinger affair suggests, just as there are many ways to read a scandal. Biography thus provides more than simply structure to the historical narrative. It also gives us the perspectives from which to view the events of the past. Gerda Munsinger's life story was told in multiple ways; even her autobiography unfolded differently, depending on the audience, the moment, and the demands of a good story. Biography becomes not just an organizational tool, as English so clearly demonstrates, but also an interpretive tool, and one whose capabilities are only just beginning to be tapped.

NOTES

1 See Stephen Brook, "Subjects of Interest: Biography, Politics and Gender History," *Journal of the Canadian Historical Association* 21, 2 (2020): 21–28; and Rod Barman, "Biography as History," *Journal of the Canadian Historical Association* 21, 2 (2010): 61–75.

2 See Laurel Thatcher Ulrich, *A Midwife's Tale: The Life of Martha Ballard Based on Her Diary, 1785–1812* (New York: Knopf, 1990), one of the first of the new use of biography as a tool to understand the ordinary. More recently, see Adele Perry, *Colonial Relations: The Douglas-Connolly Family and the Nineteenth Century Imperial World* (Cambridge: Cambridge University Press, 2015); Cameron Duder, *Awfully Devoted Women: Lesbian Lives in Canada, 1900–1965* (Vancouver: UBC Press, 2010); and Maya Jasanoff, *The Dawn Watch: Joseph Conrad in a Global World* (London: William Collins, 2017).

3 See Bryan D. Palmer, *Canada's 1960s: The Ironies of Identity in a Rebellious Era* (Toronto: University of Toronto Press, 2009), 76.

4 On security scandals, see J.L. Granatstein and David Stafford, *Spy Wars: Espionage and Canada from Gouzenko to Glasnost* (Toronto: McClelland and Stewart, 1990); on Profumo, see Richard Davenport-Hines, *An English Affair: Sex, Class and Power in the Age of Profumo* (London: HarperCollins, 2013).

5 Richard Gwyn, *The Shape of Scandal: A Study of Government in Crisis* (Toronto: Clarke, Irwin, 1965), 3.

6 Lucien Cardin, quoted in House of Commons, *Debates*, 1st session, 27th Parliament, vol. 2, 4 March 1966, 2211.

7 See John B. Thompson, *Political Scandal: Power and Visibility in the Media Age* (Cambridge: Policy Press, 2000), 5.

8 John H. Summers, "Whatever Happened to Sex Scandals?: Politics and Peccadilloes, Jefferson to Kennedy," *Journal of American History* 87, 3 (Dec. 2000): 826; see also Joshua Gamson, "Normal Sins: Sex Scandal Narratives as Institutional Morality Tales," in *Public Affairs: Politics in the Age of Sex Scandals,* ed. Paul Apostolidis and Juliet Williams (Durham, NC: Duke University Press, 2004), 40–41.

9 Geoffrey Stevens, "Cardin Charges PCs Hid Sex, Spy Scandal," *Globe and Mail,* 5 March 1966, 1.

10 "'Is It about Sevigny?' Said the Shapely Frau in the Comfy Flat," *Globe and Mail,* 12 March 1966, 10.

11 Bob Reguly, "Gerda's Story," *Ottawa Citizen,* 12 March 1966, 10.

12 Ibid.

13 Robert McKenzie and John Brehl, "Blonde Gerda a Swinger with a Heart of Gold," *Toronto Daily Star,* 12 March 1966, 13.

14 "Playgirl Worked in NATO Claims German Newspaper," n.d., file: Spence Inquiry – press clippings – 1966, vol. 110, MG 32 B11, E.D. Fulton fonds, Library and Archives Canada (hereafter LAC); and McKenzie and Brehl, "Blonde Gerda a Swinger with a Heart of Gold."

15 Michael Posner, "Reporter Found Hal Banks, Gerda Munsinger," *Globe and Mail,* 5 March 2011, S12.

16 Anthony Westell, "Gerda Not His mistress, Sevigny Says at Inquest," *Globe and Mail,* 10 May 1966, 1.

17 "Sevigny Fourth Male Visitor Says Counsel," *Kamloops Daily Sentinel,* 10 May 1966, 1.

18 Anthony Westell, *The Inside Story: A Life in Journalism* (Toronto: Dundurn Press, 2002), 149.

19 Justice Wishart Flett Spence, *Report of the Commission of Inquiry into Matters Relating to One Gerda Munsinger* (Ottawa: Queen's Printer, 1966), 3–4.

20 Palmer, *Canada's 1960s,* 102.

21 Gerda Munsinger, quoted in Jay Walz, "Mrs. Munsinger Denies She Was a Spy and Says Russians Ruined Her Life," *New York Times,* 16 March 1966, 14.

22 See, for example, Franca Iacovetta, *Gatekeepers: Reshaping Immigrant Lives in Cold War Canada* (Toronto: Between the Lines, 2006), 21–47.

23 Gerda Munsinger, quoted in *Neue Illustrierte* 14, 3 April 1966 (translated at RCMP Headquarters), vol. 3, RG 33, LAC.

24 Flora Lewis, "Trial Bares Seamy Side of Bavarian High Life," *Washington Post*, 5 June 1962, 5.
25 *Neue Illustrierte* 14, 3 April 1966.
26 Gerda Munsinger, quoted in Ibid.
27 Ibid.
28 Hotel Ruby Foo's, "Learn about Our Iconic History," https://www.hotelrubyfoos.com/about.html.
29 Gerda Munsinger, quoted in *Neue Illustrierte* 14, 3 April 1966.
30 Spence, *Report of the Commission of Inquiry into Matters Relating to One Gerda Munsinger*, 35.
31 Gerda Munsinger, quoted in *Neue Illustrierte* 14, 3 April 1966.
32 *Neue Illustrierte* 19, 8 May 1966 (translated at RCMP Headquarters), vol. 3, RG 33, LAC.
33 *Neue Illustrierte* 17, 24 April 1966 (translated at RCMP Headquarters), vol. 3, RG 33, LAC.
34 Gerda Munsinger, quoted in *Neue Illustrierte* 14, 3 April 1966.
35 "The Public Has Had Enough," *The Telegram*, 12 March 1966, 1.
36 Gerda Munsinger, quoted in *Neue Illustrierte* 19, 8 May 1966.
37 The best account of the Munsinger scandal appears in Palmer, *Canada's 1960s*, chap. 3, in which he clearly positions the scandal within the context of Cold War anxieties.

CHAPTER 7

HERB GRAY AND THE FOUNDING OF THE FOREIGN INVESTMENT REVIEW AGENCY

Jennifer Levin Bonder

When Herb Gray retired, he was the longest continuously serving member of Parliament in contemporary Canadian history, having worked with eight prime ministers from two parties. Gray won thirteen back-to-back elections in his home riding of Windsor West between 1962 and 2002 and held eleven cabinet posts, including the portfolios of national revenue; industry, trade and commerce; and Treasury Board. He was unceremoniously shuffled out of cabinet three times and still went on to roles as government House leader, interim leader of the Opposition, solicitor general, and deputy prime minister.[1] From 2002 to 2010, Gray was the Canadian chair of the International Joint Commission. This, the oldest Canadian-American intergovernmental organization, was established by the Boundary Waters Treaty of 1909 mainly to deal with transborder air and water pollution issues in the Great Lakes region. His work on the environment, as those closest to him would say, was his proudest achievement.

Gray's passionate interest in environmental issues – he played a key role in the negotiation of the Kyoto Protocol on climate change – reflected a man ahead of his time. He was also the first person, recalled Prime Minister Paul Martin, to bring the issue of the treatment and compensation of children at residential schools to cabinet. Martin, a fellow Windsorite, said that Gray talked about issues with integrity, whether or not they were politically expedient.[2] Gray was a feminist too, before Justin Trudeau popularized the notion in 2015. Cabinet colleagues were sometimes annoyed that his wife, Sharon Sholzberg-Gray, a health policy advocate and, later, president of the Canadian Healthcare Association, appeared before parliamentary committees to criticize her husband's government for funding cuts. This miffed many, but not Gray. His constituency office listed his mother's phone number should anyone in Essex West have matters to discuss. While it was common for parliamentarians' wives to deal with local affairs while the husbands tended to "real business" in Ottawa, this was not something Sharon, a trained lawyer, was interested in.[3]

Yet, in other ways, Gray reflected his era. His attitudes about the economy and foreign investment were undeniably products of his time. They reflected that tumultuous period of economic nationalism that peaked in the late 1960s and early 1970s. With an abundance of natural resources but a low population, Canada historically has had high capital needs and relied on foreign investment and trade to grow. But the long economic boom that followed the Second World War finally gave Canadians confidence to question the need for high levels of foreign money, particularly American money, which by 1950 accounted for 75.5 percent of direct investment in Canada.[4]

Canadian economic nationalism found its form in two flagship policies of Liberal prime minister Pierre Trudeau's Third Option, in 1972. The Foreign Investment Review Agency (FIRA) began reviewing the foreign takeover of Canadian firms in 1974 and lasted with varying degrees of efficacy until it was renamed Investment Canada in 1985 under Progressive Conservative prime minister Brian Mulroney, and its mandate was drastically reduced. Six years after FIRA was founded, the National Energy Program (NEP) was designed to achieve energy self-sufficiency, a redistribution of wealth, and greater Canadian ownership by funding oil expeditions in remote areas. Instead, it alienated Western Canada.[5]

But Gray's nationalist reputation hardly captured the whole story. This chapter puts Gray at the centre of its study of Trudeau's economic nationalist policies. Making use of Gray's recently opened personal papers, clippings, and speeches, this biographic accounting highlights the pragmatism that tempered his nationalism, and in doing so underlines the ambiguities of the government's policy and, indeed, of Canadian economic nationalism during this era. Canada's paper of record introduced Gray to the nation as the “chunky, Jewish lawyer from Windsor, the border city that is a prime laboratory for the foreign-ownership way of life, what it means to Canada and what it costs.”[6] What follows is a look at how this one man tried to mitigate these costs and became representative of the fears of an entire nation.

Gray was born in Windsor, Ontario, on 25 May 1931 to Eastern European immigrant parents. He grew up in the riding he would later represent. His father, Aaron Gurarie, arrived in Windsor and adopted the anglicized name when an immigration officer thought that it sounded like Gray; his mother was a nurse in Detroit before marrying. She and her husband opened a department store together on Windsor’s Ottawa Street.[7] He worked in the store, studied Yiddish, and became an accomplished pianist. And after seeing Liberal prime minister Louis St. Laurent at a rally, he wrote in his high school yearbook that he wanted to become prime minister.[8] He soon sought the advice of his hometown Liberal cabinet minister, Paul Martin Sr., the member of Parliament for Essex East, on how to make it happen.

Taking Martin’s advice, Gray attended McGill University, in Montreal (after a year at the University of Western Ontario), where he earned a bachelor’s degree in commerce and simultaneously improved his French. He then studied law at Osgoode Hall, in Toronto, and returned to article with Martin’s Windsor law firm. Martin adopted Gray as his protegé and increasingly relied on him to safeguard his interests in Essex West, one of three ridings in the Windsor area. Gray backed Martin at the 1958 Liberal leadership convention, and Martin backed Gray for the Liberal nomination in Essex West in 1962.

Gray’s political longevity was largely due to his commitment to constituency matters, and he probably adopted at least some of his practices in this regard from Martin who, even as external affairs minister, paid attention to local minutiae. On one occasion, Gray launched an inquiry under the federal Combines Investigation Act into the National Hockey League when the Detroit Red Wings imposed a television blackout in Windsor to boost ticket sales.[9] As one of Gray’s electoral opponents recalled, “Everyone had a similar story: my uncle had a problem with such and such and Herb Gray fixed it; my friend had a problem with such and such and Herb got it straightened out.”[10] His personal papers are replete with constituency letters where Gray and his staff cited obscure regulations and tracked down past commitments on behalf of his voters.

It is worth emphasizing that Windsor is a border city; in fact, Detroit-Windsor is North America's largest cross-border conurbation.[11] The young Herb Gray saw the United States every day and watched the steady flow of people and goods crossing the Detroit River. But he could not always see, or trust, the Americans to respect all the rules that came with their trade and investments.

Foreign ownership in Ontario was higher than the national average in the manufacturing and mining sectors and close to or above average in most other sectors.[12] Stephen Azzi, biographer of economic nationalist Walter Gordon and author of Chapter 5 of this volume, has shown that Windsor and the Southwestern Ontario corridor was the strongest hub of economic nationalism in the 1960s and 1970s. As the wealthiest part of the country, it was precisely the region that could most afford to discriminate against future investment.[13]

But in the late 1950s, it was an economic recession hitting his hometown that inspired Gray's political run against the incumbent Progressive Conservatives.[14] Gray's suspicions lasted his entire life. In 2004, he contributed to the public service report on Canada-US relations, which argued that there was "an enormous store of goodwill" between the countries but concluded that "this goodwill does not necessarily translate to policies that are more favourable to Canada than to other nations."[15]

Despite his extensive and varied career, little has been written about Gray. What has, namely a chapter in a 2007 book on *The Jews of Windsor, 1790–1990,* focuses on his role as Canada's first Jewish cabinet minister. Yet political scientists have noted that Gray did not seem to fit the mould of more flamboyant Jewish political stereotypes.[16] Nor, as John English has concluded in his Trudeau biographies, did Gray's speeches deal with issues specific to Jewish interests.[17] By all accounts, he was a secular Jew concerned with social justice, and it was a surprise to both him and his wife that one of their children became an orthodox Jew.[18] At a special parliamentary tribute at his retirement, Gray summed up the impact of his Jewish heritage, saying he had "always been inspired by the words of the Hebrew prophets when they called out for us to do judgement and justice."[19]

What Gray became known for was actually the opposite of that prophetic Jewish charisma. His name was inversed to Gray Herb to reflect his monotone dullness. *Maclean's* political writer Paul Wells dubbed him the "Gray Fog" for his ability to deflect Opposition questioning with dry verbiage and to camouflage explosive issues in monotone mists.[20] He has also been labelled "the godfather of politics," "the Liberal Party's version of the Rock of Gibraltar," and "the most effective non-answerer of Question Period."[21] He used his dullness as a weapon, but this proved to be a double-edged sword. His personality is important because it was, arguably, the reason he was sacked from his promising political career. Twice. Yet Gray was far from intolerably dull. He loved rock 'n' roll and political satire, exhibited by his political cartoon collection and appearance on CBC's Royal Canadian Air Farce.[22] At a 1990 press gallery dinner, he joked about running for the Liberal leadership with the slogan "Paint the town Gray!" in a performance that Brian Mulroney ranked a perfect ten. When he died, in 2014, a deluge of obituaries and articles reflected on "Herbalmania," a play on Trudeaumania, itself a play on Beatlemania.[23]

Elected in June 1962, Gray first came to notice as a capable member of Parliament for his efforts as an observer and member of Canada's delegations at meetings of the International Monetary Fund, World Bank, NATO parliamentarians' conference, Canada-US interparliamentary conference, and the Inter-American conference of ministers of labour. He was named chair of the important House of Commons finance committee in February 1966 and proved himself during the Kennedy Round tariff negotiations. It was reported in the papers as a stepping stone to parliamentary secretary, which he was named, to finance minister Edgar Benson, in August 1968. Although disappointed that he was not selected for Trudeau's cabinet, his hometown paper confidently reported that "the future still looks bright for Mr. Gray."[24]

The *Windsor Star* was right, and Pierre Trudeau named Gray as a minister without portfolio in October 1969. In Trudeau's thirty-person cabinet, Gray would continue to work in association with Benson on policies and legislation concerning financial institutions. He would also assume the day-to-day responsibilities for tariff policy and loan programs. Without an assigned portfolio, Gray would also become responsible for "breaking in new material," a "favourite Trudeau formula," reported the press.[25] The young minister soon stirred up controversy with his foreign investment policy review that led, in 1972, to the release of a major study known commonly as the Gray Report and officially titled *Foreign Direct Investment in Canada*.[26] Gray's name became synonymous with the issue. As the prime minister explained:

> Let's say you don't want to have a trade deficit with us, therefore you want to sell us more than you buy from us. Yet we have to pay interest and dividends – I think it is more than a billion and a half of net outflow (we might check this figure but it's in that area) every year. How are we going to pay for it if it's not by selling you goods? And if it's not by selling you goods are you going to buy up more and more of our country? This is the Herb Gray problem.[27]

So, it was Herb Gray's problem and his job to fix. Trudeau was not an economic nationalist and was less interested in economic matters.[28] Mark MacGuigan, Martin's successor as Member of Parliament for Essex East, recalled that Gray had irritated Trudeau during this time by looking to him too often for direction.[29]

The Trudeau government was in the midst of a foreign policy review, which resulted in six colourful booklets, none of which talked about the United States. The party line was that the review did not discuss Canada's pre-eminent bilateral relationship because other studies were in progress, namely Gray's.[30] The Americans had just conducted their own foreign policy review with no mention of Canada, so the countries were even.[31]

What is evident is that Gray's report and the anticipation of Gray's report became more than a culmination of a routine policy debate; it represented years of heightened public consciousness on the issue of foreign control. Interest had been bubbling over after numerous Canadian Radio-television and Telecommunications Commission rulings, the external affairs review, a report on the Canadian securities industry, the legislation before Parliament regarding a Canada Development Corporation (CDC), and growing provincial attention on the issue.[32]

Gray's report outlined in earnest the rationale and framework for the future FIRA. It reflected both his nationalist concerns about the problem of foreign direct investment, as well as his sensibilities as a son of a border city. It concluded that a screening body to review incoming investments would ensure that foreign investors brought significant benefits to Canada. Rather than declaring certain sectors off-limits to foreigners or creating mandatory participation rules – like 51 percent Canadian ownership – a screening body was thought to be the least protectionist option; the least likely to provoke retaliation by the Americans; and the most flexible vehicle to respond to changing conditions and national priorities: thus, a moderate and conservative approach. Cabinet, advised by the minister of industry, trade and commerce, would make final decisions. Only those who "paint the choices in very straight black and white colours" believe "we must either retain the status quo or cut off foreign investment entirely," explained Gray's memorandum to cabinet.[33] A screening process would be a little gray.

None of what the report said is nearly as interesting as the circumstances under which it was written, leaked, leaked again, and received across the country. The *Toronto Star* published a special report on the contents of the leaked Gray Report and concluded that the saga was "a mini-version of the Pentagon Papers,"[34] a leak then rocking the United States. A mini-version of America is exactly what the Gray Report was trying to avoid.

The committee responsible for the Gray Report consisted of nine members, with four student assistants.[35] Joel Bell chaired, fresh from postgraduate studies at Harvard and eventually one of the principal architects of Petro-Canada, a signature project of the economic nationalist era. The *Globe* even ran a story headlined "Joel Bell – the real author" and labelled him a "pragmatic nationalist."[36] As Gray's closest staffer, Bell approached the topic, like Gray himself, imbued with a pragmatic concern of what to do, if anything, about foreign investment. The relationship was close and trusted; Bell earlier knew Gray through Sharon, who was a year behind him in law school.[37]

They drew on research findings from two previous government studies and a royal commission, as well as from work of the House of Commons external affairs committees and many economists in Canada and abroad.[38] One glaring problem with data available was the overall lack of information on multinational corporations; no federal government department maintained even a simple listing of US-subsidiary firms in Canada. It was estimated that around 80 percent of all US foreign direct investment was accounted for by some two hundred firms, such as General Motors, Chrysler, Ford, Singer, and Esso. Direct foreign investment was concentrated in the resource-based industries and the manufacturing sectors. What numbers were available were staggering: in the petroleum and coal industries, ownership was 99 percent foreign; 95 percent in book publishing (but much of that was British); 93 percent in rubber; 67 percent in mining; 64 percent in electrical products; 82 percent in chemicals; 87 percent of transportation equipment; and even 86 percent of professional hockey teams were controlled by Americans.[39]

The stakes were equally high for investors and those wanting the government to do little, and for nationalists and those wanting the government to do a lot. And since it was still unclear where Trudeau stood on the matter, the working group tried to stay away from prying eyes. Of all of Gray's portfolios, the Gray Report was the only time his wife Sharon remembers meetings taking place at their home. A lot of thought had gone into the timing of its release – after 5:00 p.m. to mitigate any impact on the financial markets and to allow External Affairs to notify Canadian consulates in the United States before its release.[40]

Finalizing the report took much longer than expected, giving rise to rumours that Trudeau's government was weakening in its resolve to make the document public. Walter Gordon wrote to Gray in early 1971 that he had heard through the "grapevine from Ottawa" that Gray was still struggling with proposals to put before cabinet. Gordon reiterated his nationalist views as honorary chair of the Committee for an Independent Canada, a citizens' group promoting Canadian economic and cultural independence.[41] On behalf of its claimed 250,000 members, Gordon pressed for measures to increase the proportion of Canadian ownership of the national economy; a federal agency to supervise foreign-controlled operations in Canada and any new takeovers, with particular attention to the energy sector; and the establishment of a nationally funded CDC to develop and maintain Canadian-controlled companies in the private sector.[42]

The media was equally agitated by the delay, prompting the frustrated editors of the leftish *Canadian Forum* to publish a leaked version of the Gray Report in the December 1971 issue of its magazine.[43] "There was either a theft in the dark of night because of slipshod and slovenly security or we have here the tattletale 'Gray' of a deliberate leak," claimed one member of Parliament.[44] Hundreds of government employees, from cabinet ministers to mailroom clerks, had access to the draft report. Some editorials speculated the leak was engineered by the Prime Minister's Office itself, allowing the press and professors to debate a leaked version before the government decided what to do.[45] Or maybe the leak was meant for an international audience – warning the Americans of "what visions of sugar plums are dancing in Canadian heads."[46] Abraham Rotstein, the magazine's editor, refused to disclose the source but said it did not come from a civil servant or cabinet minister. Rotstein himself was an unpaid editor. "Was he bribed?," wondered reporters.[47] Unlikely. But there are two things for certain: first, the leak put Gray on the political map; and second, within the next six months, the government would have to decide on the future direction of Canada's trade relations with the United States.

At a press conference held by the *Forum*'s editors, they provided their own explanation for publishing the report. The "Old Guard in the Cabinet," they raged, was "sleepwalking into the future."[48] A spokesperson for the prime minister said that the Gray Report was merely one draft and in no way an official statement of government policy.[49] Gray publicly proclaimed he did not know how the *Forum* got the story. Again, using an American phrase, Gray was harangued by the media for keeping quiet and "pleading the fifth."[50]

A week after the initial leak, the *Montreal Gazette* published on 16 November a second top-secret cabinet document revealing that the government agreed with the report's finding and would soon establish a screening mechanism to deal with foreign ownership.[51] Unlike typical government leaks, the difference this time was that it was not merely verbal.[52] And unlike the Gray Report, only the members of Trudeau's twenty-nine-person cabinet, plus a handful of aides and advisors, had direct access to cabinet documents which were typically guarded with the utmost secrecy.[53] The breach prompted Progressive Conservative Opposition leader Robert Stanfield to call for a narrowly defeated adjournment vote.[54] Gray provided a trademark "gray-out" answer, in the *Globe*'s terms, when he refused to acknowledge the existence of a screening agency in his report or as government policy, because such an agency could not be established until cabinet had made a decision and no final decision had been taken.[55]

In fact, key decisions had been taken. The second leak confirmed that the Trudeau government had adopted a plan of action as early as 19 July and then changed course, either temporarily or for good. Something shocking must have happened.

On 15 August, President Richard Nixon abruptly ended ties between the American dollar and gold, which had been the foundation of the international economic system since the end of the Second World War. At the same time, he unilaterally imposed a 10 percent surcharge on imports to try to fix America's balance of payments. The Department of Industry, Trade and Commerce believed that the United States accounted for 70 percent of Canada's export market, and one quarter of that would be affected by Nixon's tax, amounting to roughly $2.5 billion.[56] Worried that Nixon might see Canadian measures to restrict foreign investment as retaliation, Trudeau's government decided not to release Gray's report and its recommendations for fear of making matters worse.

Yet, reaction across Canada remained strongly favourable toward the leaked foreign investment regulations. A Gallup poll in November 1971 revealed that 69 percent of Canadians approved of Gray's proposal for an investment screening process, 15 percent rejected the idea outright, and 16 percent were undecided.[57] Taking no chances, Trudeau ordered Gray to visit each provincial premier to sell the agency, starting first in the Atlantic provinces.[58] The Liberal premier of Nova Scotia, Gerry Regan, responded that he could not afford the luxury of being economically nationalist.[59] Saskatchewan's premier proposed that US subsidiaries be bought up by the government, but the cost made this suggestion unfeasible. Expanding the mandate of the CDC to get more Canadian money invested in the country's resources was favoured over screening by the premier of Manitoba.[60] Another alternative idea was allowing Canadian companies to deduct interest payments from their income, as their US counterparts could do, when borrowing to buy up other Canadian firms. Although the new tax legislation in the *Competition Act* allowed for this, the report concluded these preventive measures would have little impact. Mel Watkins, a University of Toronto economist and author of a previous report on the topic, derided the screening mechanism as a "Mickey Mouse solution."[61]

Several cultural factors explain the report's popular reception in Quebec, notably the prioritization of Québécois nationalism over economic nationalism.[62] It was celebrated in *Le Devoir* as the most exciting document of the Trudeau administration.[63] The Quebec ministers in particular – Jean Marchand, regional economic expansion; Jean-Luc Pépin, industry, trade and commerce; and Jean Chrétien, Indian affairs and northern development – wanted the government to proceed slowly as they saw a continuing heavy reliance on foreign capital and technology for growth.[64] The moderate stance of the Gray Report aligned with a province that was less threatened both by American cultural domination and with foreign ownership below national levels in all sectors.

In the federal election that followed, in October 1972, heavy Liberal losses in Ontario – the hub of economic nationalism – highlighted the need for a wider scope and a stronger foreign investment bill than the one outlined in the Gray Report. A minority Liberal government was elected with the New Democratic Party (NDP) holding the balance of power. Indeed influenced by public opinion and powerful lobby groups such as the Committee for an Independent Canada, the NDP opposed the moderate screening measures and insisted on stronger actions as the price of its support.[65] Robert Stanfield, leader of the Opposition and an ex-premier of Nova Scotia, tried to adjourn Parliament because of the leaks, disapproved of the government's secrecy, and analogized the policy to an "octopus structure" that would be foisted on provincial governments.[66] The Progressive Conservatives, he declared, would fight any mechanism that cut off investment capital to provinces that still needed it.[67]

The Gray Report was largely free of ideological prejudices or slogans and presented moderate and practical policy recommendations when it was introduced in May 1972. It required that the foreign acquisition of businesses in Canada meet the criteria of "significant benefit." Largely due to the pressure exerted by the left-wing nationalist minority within the NDP, the Waffle, reviews were expanded to apply to the establishment of new businesses under the *Foreign Investment Review Act* the following year.[68]

But Gray's own views have remained ambiguous in the minds of commentators – at the time and since. It was natural to conflate the man with his report; that was a reasonable judgment. Indeed, as early as 1970, Gray was already seen in Ottawa as being synonymous with the question of controlling foreign investment. Numerous members of Parliament forwarded to Gray the December 1970 cover story of the American magazine,

Forbes. It appeared to them to be the first alarm bell by American business leaders about the discussions happening north of the border.[69] The magazine editors came to this conclusion:

> Two great trends are in conflict: the tendency for the world to become one economically; and the strengthening everywhere of nationalism. The two are at war in Canada. Which will win? A good deal may depend on how the US Government, US businessmen and the US press handle the situation. To refuse to compromise with Canadian economic nationalism will be to encourage it. To go along with it will entail some loss of profit and privilege by US business, yet that course will almost certainly prove to be the most sensible of the alternatives.[70]

In the same article, the American deputy assistant secretary of commerce, Harold Scott – and the US official most closely concerned with Canadian investment and trade on a day-to-day basis – warned Canadians not to take a strong line on emotional nationalism. The Americans noted the real underlying irony of any policy: at the same time as Canada was weighing limiting foreign investment at home, it was still campaigning for foreign investment abroad.[71]

As public pressure on economic nationalism mounted, Gray made three matter-of-fact speeches on the subject in three cities comfortable to him: in Toronto, at Osgoode Hall in April 1970, in Windsor, in March 1971, and in Montreal, at McGill in August 1971.

At his law school alma mater, Gray distinguished between legal sovereignty and politico-economic sovereignty, which he believed to be less familiar to most. Historically, in developing Canada's trade policy, he argued, "the Canadian people have consciously and implicitly accepted a form of limitation of their theoretically absolute autonomy in order to achieve certain other well-defined national objectives," which was true of Canadian political development as a whole. This link between political and economic power, including the problem of extraterritoriality, was what he pinpointed as the biggest threat. In the public policy realm, the further the ability to make economic decisions falls out of Canadian hands, he said, the greater the limitations of Canadian governments to do anything about it. This was seen when the US administration, grappling with its own balance of payments problems, enacted regulations meant to slow down the flow of American dollars abroad, and subsidiaries of American firms automatically regarded the rules as applying to them. Crises in the Canadian financial markets ensued, and important exemptions had to be negotiated in 1963, 1965, and 1968, examples of what historians R.D. Cuff and J.L. Granatstein called Canada's "exemptionalist" culture. But the criticism remains of having to negotiate with a foreign government in the first place about business behaviour within Canada.[72] In this first big statement on the topic, Gray highlighted the fundamental questions Canadians needed to answer about the importance of the citizenship of those who own and control Canadian business activity; the appropriate level of foreign investment; and the steps to be taken to encourage Canadian participation and Canadian entrepreneurship.[73]

Nearly a year later, Gray revisited the topic in Windsor. Noting that his report had been delayed, he explained that it was because the foreign investment problem had to be addressed as a whole. "Policy on foreign investment cannot be developed in isolation," he argued. The appropriate level of foreign investment was not a yes or no question, but depended on how much, in what sectors, under what terms, and to meet what national objectives. In this speech in his industrial (American investment) and unionized (American dominated) hometown (Canada's most important border crossing for imports and exports), he declared himself to be more skeptical than most about the risks of the multinational enterprise. "Unless appropriately regulated by governments," multinationals were "in a position to be able to circumvent national laws and policies and bring about entrenched world oligopoly rather than provide more fully the benefits of a more efficient form of economic organization."[74]

In the McGill speech later that summer, but still before the leaks, Gray melded his ideas about politico-economic sovereignty and the risks of multinationals from his prior speeches. He reiterated that Canada's abundance of natural resources and expanding market for the products of manufacturers made the country highly desirable for multinationals. But the "benefits now being promised by the theoreticians of the multinational enterprise are not unlike those which were promised in the past by the theoreticians of international trade." Not all countries were benefiting equally from trade and multinationals came with substantial costs, which included the extraterritorial application of foreign law, the erosion of cultural distinctiveness, directed procurement, and restrictions on export sales. Furthermore, domestic innovation would be gradually stultified, like "a kind of tread-mill situation" where a past reliance on foreign entrepreneurship and technology would lead to a perpetual need for them. But Gray recognized there were also benefits from foreign direct investment, which is how he was able to conclude that Canada's strategy required recognition "that both sovereignty and economic growth are vital and necessary national objectives" whereby the achievement of one was not inconsistent with the achievement of the other.[75]

Collectively, these speeches show Gray's tempered and measured assessment of the certain gains and also calculations of the risks around foreign money operating in Canada. After months of speculation, when Gray officially announced government policy in the House of Commons in May 1972, he explained, "If takeovers created only problems it would be a simple matter to deal with them – they could all be blocked. But takeovers can be of benefit to Canada," and ensuring they brought significant benefits to the country would be the general policy.[76] This seems a natural conclusion for someone from Windsor.

Throughout this period of negotiation and leaks, Gray had become minister of national revenue in 1970 and minister of consumer and corporate affairs in 1972. But two years later, at the age of 43, his fortunes abruptly changed. The Liberals regained a majority in the July 1974 election, but Trudeau decided that he had too many cabinet ministers from Windsor and relieved Gray of his duties in a cabinet shuffle critically dubbed the Tuesday Night Massacre.[77] Gray was stunned, as were other parliamentarians and the national media. It was widely assumed that Trudeau's advisers had convinced him that Gray simply lacked the pizzazz for a high-profile post.

Out of office, Gray reinvented himself as a spokesman on consumer issues, foreign investment, and economic regulation more generally. He did so in a constructive way, he explained, to encourage the government to stick to its Liberal policies and not drift to the political right. Many acknowledged that he also liked to see his comments reported favourably in the press. When asked how he felt about his new role, he explained he was acting "the way US senators act, identifying issues and problems, speaking out on them, making them national concerns."[78] He also felt that he was expressing the views of small-*l* liberals in the caucus and in the country concerned with social justice.

His warnings that the party was losing touch with the electorate seemed to be confirmed in 1979 when the government was defeated by Joe Clark's Progressive Conservatives. Now in opposition, Trudeau turned to Gray again, giving him the high-profile role of finance critic. This put Gray on the front lines attacking the minority government's budget, which triggered the 1980 election and the Liberal Party's return to power. Gray became the minister of industry, trade and commerce, and the media attention was less favourable, as the *Globe and Mail* editors complained that he had "tunnel vision" and only saw things through an economic nationalist lens.[79] This was not a fair criticism according to English, but it did reflect the increasingly conservative attitude of Canada's financial centre.[80]

Gray maintained his pragmatic approach to foreign investment. This was especially evident in his response to the crisis in Canada's auto industry during the early 1980s, when the largest employer in his hometown tottered on the brink of collapse as a result of poor quality and growing offshore competition. Gray convinced Trudeau to join the American government in saving the debt-ridden Chrysler Corporation, negotiating federal loan guarantees to keep the company afloat and preserving approximately ten thousand local jobs in the most successful public bailout in Canadian history. The federal loan guarantees he negotiated brought further aid from the US government and were widely credited with saving the company.[81] It meant Chrysler's untried new vehicle, the minivan, would be made exclusively at its Windsor plant.[82]

Then, in 1982, Gray became Treasury Board president and maintained the post once John Turner became prime minister. As noted in the official history of the Department of External Affairs by John Hilliker, Mary Halloran, and Greg Donaghy, the 1982 shuffle that moved Gray from the Department of Industry, Trade and Commerce to Treasury Board signified a shift toward economic ministers that favoured more conservative, free-market principles.[83] But this statement did not necessarily reflect the views of the new prime minister.

Turner and Gray had a longstanding personal relationship: Turner took credit for Herb's marriage, having introduced him to Sharon. In 1968, when Turner ran for the Liberal leadership, he was tremendously worried about American influence. His famous declaration in 1988 that free trade would eliminate Canada with a stroke of a pen was not a flippant belief.[84] For example, Turner was on the special cabinet committee that received the first government-sponsored study on foreign ownership; of the five members, he was the only one that supported the report with only minor reservations.[85] Throughout his entire political career, Turner recognized the urgent problems foreign investment posed for Canadian independence. Perhaps, as his biographer argued, Turner's political fortunes really were a matter of poor timing. By 1984 the country was less frightened of trading with the Americans, and the Liberals were crushed by Brian Mulroney's Progressive Conservatives. Gray was the only Liberal in Southwestern Ontario to survive.[86]

When the Liberals regained power in 1993, Prime Minister Jean Chrétien named Gray both government House leader and solicitor general and, in 1997, deputy prime minister. His political career ended abruptly in 2002 when Chrétien shuffled him out of cabinet to, seemingly, give his ministry a more youthful appearance.[87]

So, was Herb Gray really an economic nationalist, or has his name become linked to beliefs that were just one eponymous government report in a long career of civil service? First, it is important to remember that holding elected office for forty years is only possible if you can compromise. The Liberal Party was never fully committed to the nationalist cause and was therefore unwilling to make firm decisions on foreign investment. Indeed, the key adjective echoing throughout the formation of FIRA was "flexible."[88] The following years demonstrated Gray's ability to adapt to the times. Nevertheless, in some areas Gray did not compromise. He was always a left-leaning Liberal on social issues and strongly backed the country's social safety net. But when Mulroney gutted FIRA and other nationalist efforts of the Trudeau era after 1984, Gray seemed to have accepted this.[89] He fought fiercely against free trade in 1988 but embraced globalization in the 1990s.

Gray was successful in getting acts passed because he could bring different views together. This is the second important piece. The key political actors of Canada's economic nationalist moment, including Trudeau, Walter Gordon, and cabinet minister Alastair Gillespie, had different perspectives on foreign investment. Trudeau was willing to experiment with policy measures, but he boldly stated that no trading nation should practice economic nationalism.[90] Gordon put the issue of foreign investment on the political agenda with his royal commission in 1957, and his attitudes are clear from the title of his second book, *A Choice for Canada: Independence or Colonial Status*.[91] Gillespie would become the minister of industry, trade and commerce – the department responsible for creating and overseeing FIRA. In his memoirs, as in many of the accounts by the economic nationalists, Gray is barely mentioned. In Gillespie's memoirs, he shows up just once.[92] Turner and Martin Sr. were both close colleagues and mentors of Gray. While Turner's views on the economy weighed heavily nationalistic, Martin's leaned more purely political; Gray was probably somewhere in the middle. His position usually represented one side of an issue, so he had to accept – and did accept – that he would compromise his own views.

If you asked Gray if he was an economic nationalist, he would probably answer instead about his concern for the development of Canada's economic sovereignty. The Gray Fog would dull the sharpness the phrase implies. He disliked labels and complained often that questions about American control of the economy had become "bound up with emotion rather than objective analysis."[93] The greatest benefit of FIRA was moving away from ad hoc decisions to a comprehensive review where "people knew where they stand."[94] The only label he seemed to know for sure was that "Canada came into being because some North Americans did not want to become United Statesers [sic]."[95]

Gray believed Canada and the United States were different countries and wanted to stay different. His views, regardless of how strongly they were held, did cause some difficulty with the Americans. Former ambassador to the US Allan Gotlieb said Gray was "actually persona non grata – nobody wanted to see him" in Washington.[96] Paul H. Robinson Jr., American ambassador in Ottawa from 1981 to 1985, echoed this view and recalled sidestepping Gray, who he felt was "stonewalling him" in terms of trade.[97]

Gray was a progressive Liberal from a working class, industrial city. At the start of his career in 1962, Gray won the riding from the Conservatives; since his retirement to at least the 2021 federal election, the riding has been

NDP. He combined the intellectual with the political; he read every cabinet document and wrote in the margins what was wrong with it.

In 2012, the Windsor-Essex Parkway was named The Right Honourable Herb Gray Parkway[98] – a little bit ironic considering this transportation system brings Windsor and Detroit closer together. The title, Rt. Hon., should be noted, as it is normally reserved for prime ministers and chief justices of the Supreme Court. Before his death, Gray also served as Carleton University's tenth chancellor and became the first recipient of the Laurier Leadership Award for his many years of public service.[99]

If he provides a lesson to members of Parliament on longevity, it is to pay attention to the ridings. He was never too preoccupied with matters of state to care about the latest toll increase over the local Ambassador Bridge to Detroit. Gray was a troubleshooter and mediator when handling cabinet disputes, coordinating policies, and watching over the government's legislative agenda. John Diefenbaker, no stranger himself to political failings, remarked after the first leak that it looked like "Gray's eulogy."[100] But this was only his first ouster from government, and Gray would continue to survive for another four decades in government.

If he provides a lesson in economic nationalism, it is the need for an industrial strategy. And no matter how forcefully he believed these ideas, Gray gave Canada something resembling one. His report's screening policy seemed to be the most realistic and the most flexible. This was the time when the postwar boom was ending, when the Nixon shocks were compounded by the oil crisis, when the Russian purchase of American and Canadian wheat created a food crisis, and when Britain's entry into the European Economic Community threatened the preferential trade arrangement proffered by the Commonwealth. Rather than simply a question of bureaucracy and a history of FIRA, biography is the lens that adjusts the image from demagogue to pragmatist. Gray was a man of the economic nationalist times. But he was also a man of many others.

NOTES

1 "The Right Hon. Herbert Eser (Herb) Gray, P.C., Q.C., C.C., M.P.," Parlinfo, Library of Parliament of Canada, https://lop.parl.ca/sites/ParlInfo/default/en_CA/People/Profile?personId=14023.

2 "Paul Martin on Herb Gray; The Former PM Remembers a Liberal Titan," *Maclean's*, 25 April 2014, streaming audio, 11:07, http://www.macleans.ca/politics/ottawa/paul-martin-herb-gray-audio/ (accessed 19 September 2019); Gloria Galloway, "Obituary: Former Cabinet Minister Herb Gray was Noble in Public Life," *Globe and Mail*, 22 April 2014.

3 Sharon Sholzberg-Gray, interview with author, 4 May 2018.

4 Michael Bliss, "Founding FIRA: The Historical Background," in *Foreign Investment Review Law in Canada*, ed. James M. Spence and William P. Rosenfeld (Toronto: Butterworths, 1984), 2.

5 G. Bruce Doern and Glen Toner, *The Politics of Energy: The Development and Implementation of the NEP* (Toronto: Methuen, 1985).

6 Clair Balfour, "A Special Feel for the Issue: The Non-Writer," *Globe and Mail*, 13 November 1971.

7 Jonathan V. Plaut, *The Jews of Windsor, 1790–1990: A Historical Chronicle* (Toronto: Dundurn, 2007), 86.

8 "Longtime Former MP Herb Gray Dies at 82," *Windsor Star*, 21 April 2014, http://windsorstar.com/news/herb-gray-dies-at-82.

9 Greg Donaghy, *Grit: The Life and Politics of Paul Martin Sr.* (Vancouver: UBC Press, 2015), 198–99, 215–16.

10 "Longtime Former MP Herb Gray Dies at 82."

11 "The Canada-U.S. Border: By the Numbers," CBC News, 7 December 2011, https://www.cbc.ca/news/canada/the-canada-u-s-border-by-the-numbers-1.999207; Detroit Regional Chamber, "Global Logistics," Detroit Regional Chamber, http://www.detroitchamber.com/destinationdetroit/global-logistics-2/ (accessed 12 June 2019).

12 Stephen Azzi, "Foreign Investment and the Paradox of Economic Nationalism," in *Canadas of the Mind: The Making and Unmaking of Canadian Nationalisms in the Twentieth Century*, ed. Norman Hillmer and Adam Chapnick (Montreal/Kingston: McGill-Queen's University Press, 2007), 76.

13 Stephen Azzi, "Intuitive Nationalist: Walter Gordon as Thinker," *Journal of Canadian Studies* 34, 4 (Winter 2000): 121–35.

14 Plaut, *The Jews of Windsor*, 163.

15 Jeff Heynen and John Higginbotham, *Advancing Canadian Interests in the United States: A Practical Guide for Canadian Public Officials*, CSPS Action-Research Roundtable on Managing Canada-US Relations (Ottawa: Canada School of Public Service, 2004), https://publications.gc.ca/site/eng/9.687099/publication.html.

16 Jennifer Tzivia MacLeod, "Herb Gray: A Trailblazing Parliamentarian," *The Canadian Jewish News*, 17 July 2017, http://www.cjnews.com/culture/canada-150/herb-gray-trailblazing-parliamentarian.

17 John English, *Just Watch Me: The Life of Pierre Elliott Trudeau*, vol. 2, *1968–2000* (Toronto: Knopf, 2009), 191–92, 268–69.

18 Sharon Sholzberg-Gray, interview with author, 4 May 2018.

19 Herb Gray, Canada, *House of Commons Debates*, 37th Parl., 1st Sess., Num. 155, 13 March 2002, 1535, https://www.ourcommons.ca/DocumentViewer/en/37-1/house/sitting-155/hansard#SOB-165355.

20 Paul Wells, "Gray Fog Works Magic in House – and All Is Quiet," *National Post*, 23 October 1999.

21 Paul Wells, "The Gray Fog Rolls Out: Paul Wells Remembers Herb Gray, the Veteran MP Who Passed Away," *Maclean's*, 21 April 2014, http://www.macleans.ca/politics/ottawa/the-gray-fog-rolls-out/; "Herb Gray: Like the 'Rock of Gibraltar,'" CBC Digital Archives, 2:21, https://web.archive.org/web/20180308143658/http://www.cbc.ca/archives/entry/herb-gray-like-the-rock-of-gibraltar.

22 Sharon Sholzberg-Gray, interview with author, 4 May 2018.

23 Robert Lee, "Herbalmania Sweeps Press Dinner; Herb Gray Smash Hit at Off-the-Record Event," *Ottawa Citizen*, 30 April 1990.

24 Quote from Robert Hull, "Bigger Tasks for Windsor MP," *Windsor Star*, 11 September 1968. See also Maurice Jefferies, "Gray and Whelan Head Major Committees," *Windsor Star*, 18 February 1966; Robert Hull, "Our Herb Busy Guy Come Fall," *The Windsor Star*, 26 July 1966; Robert Hull, "'Plums' for Half of Grit MPs," *Windsor Star*, 11 July 1968.

25 Quote from John Best, "Stanbury Does Right Thing at Right Time," *Windsor Star*, 5 November 1969. See also Robert Hull, "Windsor's Gray in the cabinet," *Windsor Star*, 16 October 1969; Ken Caunce, "Hard Work Opens Cabinet Door for Herb," *Windsor Star*, 16 October 1969.

26 Canada, *Foreign Direct Investment in Canada* [The Gray Report] (Ottawa: Information Canada, 1972).

27 Prime Minister P.E. Trudeau, file Speech on Foreign Investment by Prime Minister – 13 Feb 1971, box 36, Herb Gray fonds, Library and Archives Canada (hereafter LAC).

28 English, *Just Watch Me*, 2:542; Pierre Elliott Trudeau, *Memoirs* (Toronto: McClelland and Stewart, 1993), 205.

29 Interview with Mark MacGuigan, quoted in Robert Bothwell and J.L. Granatstein, *Trudeau's World: Insiders Reflect on Foreign Policy, Trade, and Defence, 1968–84* (Toronto: UBC Press, 2017), 78.

30 Mitchell Sharp, "Canadian Foreign Policy and the Third World" (speech, University of Toronto, Toronto, Canada, 18 September 1970), file Foreign Investment Speeches 1970, box 37, Herb Gray fonds, LAC.

31 Terrance Wills, "Report Discusses Canada: U.S. Expects Consultation on Investment Controls," *Globe and Mail*, 27 March 1971.

32 Memorandum to Cabinet, "Domestic Control of the National Economic Environment: The Problems of Foreign Ownership and Control," 9 October 1970, file Study Group on Foreign Investment 1970, box 37, Herb Gray fonds, LAC; Joel Bell, Memorandum to Herb Gray, "The Report of the Moore Committee and the Tentative Reaction of the Department of Finance," 7 August 1970, file Foreign Ownership Study Group 1970–1972 Part II of II, box 47, Herb Gray fonds, LAC.

33 Memorandum to Cabinet, "Domestic Control of the National Economic Environment."

34 The *Toronto Star* devoted its Saturday front page and Insights section on 13 November 1971 to the leaked Gray Report. For a discussion of the comparison with the Pentagon Papers, see, for example, "Canada Gets Its Own 'Pentagon Papers,' Associated Press, 13 November 1971; Robert Hull, "Leak less serious than embarrassing," *The Windsor Star*, 13 November 1971; Douglas Fisher, "And the issue will go on and on," *The Windsor Star*, 18 November 1971; "Federal employees told lock papers away," *The Leader-Post*, 26 November 1971.

35 List of Members of the Working Group on Foreign Ownership and Control, n.d., file Study Group on Foreign Investment 1970, box 37, Herb Gray fonds, LAC.
36 Stanley McDowell, "Joel Bell – the Real Author," *Globe and Mail,* 13 November 1971, B6. See also Peter Desbarats, "An Unemotional Man Drafted the Report on Canada's Future," *Toronto Star,* 2 May 1972, 8; James Rusk, "Joel Bell: 'Policy Activist but Not Political Activist,'" *Globe and Mail,* 26 November 1982, 9.
37 Joel Bell, interview with author, 25 February 2021.
38 The question of foreign ownership was squarely put on the political map by Canada, *Final Report: Royal Commission on Canada's Economic Prospects* (Ottawa: Queen's Printer, 1957). Urgency and attention on the issue grew with each further report, listed chronologically here: Privy Council Office, *Foreign Ownership and the Structure of Canadian Industry: Report of the Task Force on the Structure of Canadian Industry* [The Watkins Report] (Ottawa: Information Canada, 1968); House of Commons Standing Committee on External Affairs, *The Eleventh Report of the Standing Committee on External Affairs and National Defence Respecting Canada-US Relations* [The Wahn Report] (Ottawa: Queen's Printer, 1970).
39 Minister of Industry, Trade and Commerce, *Annual Report of the Minister of Industry, Trade and Commerce under the Corporations and Labour Unions Returns Act (Part I. Corporations), Report for 1968* (Ottawa: Department of Labour, 1971), Statement 6. Average Asset Size of Foreign-owned and All Corporations, by Industries, Non-financial Industries Only, 33, https://publications.gc.ca/site/eng/9.809455/publication.html.
40 Joel Bell, Memorandum to Herb Gray, "Communications of Foreign Ownership Policy," 27 December 1971, file The Minister Part I: Introduction and Background to the Study of Foreign Direct Investment in Canada, box 27, Herb Gray fonds, LAC; Harvey Lazar to Herb Gray, "Timing of the Report for Publication," 29 December 1971, file The Minister Part I: Introduction and Background to the Study of Foreign Direct Investment in Canada, box 27, Herb Gray fonds, LAC; Mike Gillan to Herb Gray, "Announcement Day Plans," 25 April 1972, file Foreign Ownership 1972, box 261, Herb Gray fonds, LAC; Office of the President of the Privy Council, Memorandum to Herb Gray, "Re: Procedural Aspects of the Foreign Investment Announcement," 9 May 1972, file Foreign Ownership 1972, box 261, Herb Gray fonds, LAC.
41 Walter Gordon to Herb Gray, 16 February 1971, file 12 1971 Foreign Ownership (Miscellaneous), box 3, Herb Gray fonds, LAC.
42 "A Committee of 200 'to Save Canada,'" *The Toronto Telegram,* 17 September 1970; "Text of Independent Canada Committee Statement," *Toronto Star,* 17 September 1970; John Doig, "Time Running Out for Free Canada Nationalists Told," *Toronto Star,* 11 December 1971; Michael Lavoie, "MPs Split on Joining Committee for Independent Canada," *Toronto Star,* 12 May 1971; Anthony Westell, "Nationalism/Gordon's Irregulars Lack a Leader," *Toronto Star,* 8 July 1971.
43 "Gray Report: Publish It Fully," *Toronto Star,* 16 July 1971.
44 G.W. Baldwin, Canada, *House of Commons Debates,* 28th Parl., 3rd Sess., Vol. 9, 15 November 1971, 9550, https://parl.canadiana.ca/view/oop.debates_HOC2803_09/700.
45 Dalton Camp, "Did the PM's Office Leak the Report?" *Toronto Star,* 29 November 1971.

46 "Many Had Chance to Leak Report Official Believes," *Toronto Star,* 13 November 1971. See also "Unthinkable, Very Nearly," *Globe and Mail,* 15 November 1971.
47 Paul Kidd, "Now Gray's in Black and White ... No More Scoops for This Editor," *Ottawa Citizen,* 24 November 1971.
48 In bright red letters on a glossy black cover, the magazine proclaimed: "A Citizen's Guide to the Herb Gray Report: Domestic Control of the National Economic Environment," *Canadian Forum* 51, December 1971.
49 George Bain, "Light through the Clouds," *Globe and Mail,* 17 November 1971.
50 Robert Hull, "Sharp-Gray Hour in Commons," *Windsor Star,* 16 November 1971.
51 Arthur Blakely, "Foreign Control Report True: 'Leak Obvious': Sharp," *Montreal Gazette,* 17 November 1971; Stanley McDowell, "Sharp Confirms Cabinet Favors 'Screening' Board," *Globe and Mail,* 17 November 1971; Eric Malling, "Screening Agency Decided by Cabinet Last July: Sharp," *Toronto Star,* 17 November 1971.
52 Arthur Blakely, "Cabinet Leak of Foreign-Owned Report Violates Long Word-of-Mouth Tradition," *Montreal Gazette,* 19 November 1971.
53 Michael Lavoie, "2nd Leak on Foreign Ownership Rocks Ottawa: Probe Covers the Entire Cabinet," *Toronto Star,* 17 November 1971.
54 "Stanfield Nearly Adjourns House," *Montreal Gazette,* 17 November 1971; Canada, *House of Commons Debates,* 28th Parl., 3rd Sess., Vol. 9, 15 November 1971, 9553–59, https://parl.canadiana.ca/view/oop.debates_HOC2803_09/703; Canada, *House of Commons Debates,* 28th Parl., 3rd Sess., Vol. 9, 16 November 1971, 9593–601, https://parl.canadiana.ca/view/oop.debates_HOC2803_09/743; Myra Aronson, Memorandum to Herb Gray, 17 November 1971, file 2 Question Period – Foreign Ownership – Leak 2/3, box 20, Herb Gray fonds, LAC; Stanley McDowell, "Denies House Was Misled: Sharp Confirms Cabinet Favors 'Screening' Board," *Globe and Mail,* 17 November 1971.
55 Stanley McDowell, "Gray-Out on Foreign Ownership Report," *Globe and Mail,* 16 November 1971. See also Patrick Fellows, "Gray Says No Final Decision Made on Foreign Ownership," *Toronto Star,* 17 November 1971; "National Strategy: All Shades of Gray," *Toronto Star,* 16 November 1971.
56 John Hilliker, Mary Halloran, and Greg Donaghy, *Canada's Department of External Affairs,* vol. 3, *Innovation and Adaptation, 1968–1984* (Toronto: The Institute of Public Administration of Canada and University of Toronto Press, 2017), 124–25.
57 "Gray Report: Shock, Dismay, Approval," *Toronto Star,* 13 November 1971.
58 Pierre Trudeau, letter to all provincial premiers, "Domestic Control of the National Economic Environment," 25 April 1972, file Foreign Ownership 1972, box 261, Herb Gray fonds, LAC.
59 Background Information Foreign Takeovers Review Process, 2 May 1972, file [Foreign Takeovers Review Process 1972], box 261, Herb Gray fonds, LAC.
60 "The Gray Report: Keep Canada for Canadians," *Ottawa Citizen,* 17 November 1971.
61 "'Mickey Mouse' Solution: Economist Watkins," *Toronto Star,* 3 May 1971; Melville Watkins, "The Great Debate – 'The Gray Report Is Good but Trudeau Failed Us,'" *Toronto Star,* 22 November 1971.
62 Dominique Clift, "Quebec Happy with Gray Report," *Montreal Star,* 4 May 1972; Derek Hill, "Premier Eyes Quebec Control for Ownership," *Montreal Gazette,* 4 May 1972.

63 "Gray Report Could Transform Canadian Society, Le Devoir Says," *Toronto Star,* 17 November 1971; "Le Devoir Says Report Neglects Quebec Problem," *Toronto Star,* 17 November 1971; Claude Lemelin, "Pas de contrôle de l'économie sans action directe de l'État," *Le Devoir,* 13 November 1971; Claude Ryan, "Le Rapport Gray et le Québec," *Le Devoir,* 16 November 1971.
64 "'More Time Is Needed to Form Ownership Policy': Trudeau," *Toronto Star,* 28 July 1971; David Crane, "Canada's Foreign Ownership Policy Paper May Be Headache of Trudeau's First Term," *Globe and Mail,* 17 September 1970.
65 NDP Federal Council, "National Economic Policy," 4 February 1972, file Foreign Ownership Study Group 1970–1972 Part I of II, box 47, Herb Gray fonds, LAC; Stanley McDowell, "NDP Leader Brands Draft Bill a Betrayal," *Globe and Mail,* 3 May 1972.
66 Ben Tierney, "I'll Fight Screening Plan – Stanfield," *Ottawa Citizen,* 18 November 1971; "Stanfield Rejects 'Octopus' to Screen Foreign Investing," *Toronto Star,* 18 November 1971.
67 Robert Stanfield (speech to the Annual Meeting of the Nova Scotia Progressive Conservative Association, Lord Nelson Hotel, Halifax, Canada, 5 February 1972), file Foreign Ownership Study Group 1970–1972 Part I of II, box 47, Herb Gray fonds, LAC.
68 House of Commons, Bill C-201 Foreign Takeovers Review Act, 28th Parl., 3rd Sess., 1972; House of Commons, Bill C-132 Foreign Investment Review Act, 29th Parl., 1st Sess., 1973.
69 D. Gordon Blair to Herb Gray, n.d., file 12 1971 Foreign Ownership (Miscellaneous), box 3, Herb Gray fonds, LAC.
70 "Yankee Go Home?" *Forbes,* 1 December 1970, 28.
71 "Ottawa Not Surprised by U.S. Position," *Globe and Mail,* 29 March 1971.
72 R.D. Cuff and J.L. Granatstein, *American Dollars–Canadian Prosperity: Canadian-American Economic Relations, 1945–1950* (Toronto: Samuel Stevens, 1978).
73 Herb Gray, "Ensuring Sovereignty and Growth – Toward a Policy on Foreign Ownership for Canada" (speech to the John White Society, Osgoode Hall Law School, Toronto, Canada, 8 April 1970), file Foreign Ownership (material for information) 1970–1972, box 46, Herb Gray fonds, LAC.
74 Herb Gray (speech to the Independent Canada Seminar of the University of Windsor, Windsor, Canada, 6 March 1971), file Foreign Ownership (material for information) 1970–1972, box 46, Herb Gray fonds, LAC.
75 Herb Gray, "Legal, Economic and Managerial Aspects" (speech to the International Conference on Nationalism and the Multi-national Enterprise, McGill University, Montreal, Canada, 23 August 1971), file Foreign Ownership Study Group 1970–1972 Part I of II, box 47, Herb Gray fonds, LAC.
76 Herb Gray, Statement to the House of Commons, "Foreign Takeovers Review Policy," May 1972, file 8 [Press releases, speeches, misc. material re foreign takeovers, 1969–1972.], box 8, R 14567, Herb Gray fonds, LAC.
77 Donaghy, *Grit,* 335; Peter Thomson, "Pressure Mounts for Trudeau to Shuffle His Cabinet," *Ottawa Journal,* 30 March 1974; Lubor Zink, "Trudeau's Cabinet Shuffle," *Toronto Sun,* 9 August 1974; Bothwell and Granatstein, *Trudeau's World,* 323–24.
78 Plaut, *The Jews of Windsor,* 225.
79 "Little to Choose From," *Globe and Mail,* 4 March 1980, 6.

80 English, *Just Watch Me,* 2:466.
81 Dimitry Anastakis, *Autonomous State: The Struggle for a Canadian Car Industry from OPEC to Free Trade* (Toronto: University of Toronto Press, 2013), 132, 162–83.
82 "Herb Gray, Former MP and Deputy Prime Minister, Dead at 82," CBC News, updated 22 April 2014, http://www.cbc.ca/news/politics/herb-gray-former-mp-and-deputy-prime-minister-dead-at-82-1.2617214.
83 Hilliker, Halloran, and Donaghy, *Canada's Department of External Affairs,* 3:392.
84 "Mulroney Battles Turner on Free Trade in 1988," CBC Digital Archives, 4:36, https://www.cbc.ca/player/play/2653709009.
85 Alastair Dow, "MPs Get Report on Foreign Investment," *Toronto Star,* 15 February 1968; "Canada-First Response Urged to Counter U.S. Domination: Ownership Study Political Bomb," *The Chronicle Herald,* 16 February 1968.
86 Paul Litt, *Elusive Destiny: The Political Vocation of John Napier Turner* (Vancouver: UBC Press, 2011).
87 Joel Baglole, "Canadian Prime Minister Chretien Makes Major Changes to Cabinet," *Wall Street Journal,* 15 January 2002.
88 Bliss, "Founding FIRA: The Historical Background," 11.
89 Michael Hart, "Free Trade and Brian Mulroney's Economic Legacy," in *Transforming the Nation: Canada and Brian Mulroney,* ed. Raymond B. Blake (Montreal/Kingston: McGill-Queen's University Press, 2007), 66.
90 "Trudeau Runs … and Opposes Gordon Policy," *Toronto Star,* 16 February 1968.
91 Walter L. Gordon, *A Choice for Canada: Independence or Colonial Status* (Toronto: McClelland and Stewart, 1966).
92 Alastair W. Gillespie, with Irene Sage, *Made in Canada: A Businessman's Adventures in Politics* (Montreal: Robin Brass Studio, 2009), 146.
93 Gray, quoted in Michael Lavoie, "Independence a Fragile State: Gray's Refrain," *Toronto Star,* 13 November 1971.
94 "Ottawa Not Surprised by U.S. Position," *Globe and Mail,* 29 March 1971.
95 Notes for a Lecture on Existing Restrictions on Foreign Ownership by David B. Greenspan delivered by Herb Gray to the Practicing Law Institute, Toronto, 14 January 1972, file Foreign Ownership Study Group 1970–1972 Part I of II, box 47, Herb Gray fonds, LAC.
96 Interview with Allan Gotlieb, quoted in Bothwell and Granatstein, *Trudeau's World,* 223.
97 Paul H. Robinson Jr., quoted in Bothwell and Granatstein, *Trudeau's World,* 228–29.
98 Transport Canada, "Governments of Canada and Ontario Mark Completion of the Rt. Hon. Herb Gray Parkway," News Release, Government of Canada, https://www.canada.ca/en/transport-canada/news/2015/12/governments-of-canada-and-ontario-mark-completion-of-the-rt-hon-herb-gray-parkway.html.
99 "Long-Time Liberal MP Named Chancellor of Carleton U," CBC News, 28 November 2008, http://www.cbc.ca/news/canada/ottawa/long-time-liberal-mp-named-chancellor-of-carleton-u-1.752411.
100 J.G. Diefenbaker, Canada, *House of Commons Debates,* 28th Parl., 3rd Sess., Vol. 9, 15 November 1971, 9555, https://parl.canadiana.ca/view/oop.debates_HOC2803_09/705.

CHAPTER 8

THE FINE BALANCE INTENDED

Allan J. MacEachen and Canadian Diplomacy in the Middle East, 1974–84

Greg Donaghy

Victory in the federal election of July 1974 freed Pierre Trudeau to turn his attention south, toward the impoverished and restless masses of the developing world. Long interested in decolonization and its messy aftermath, the Liberal prime minister wanted to shift the focus of Canadian foreign policy. "In the years immediately ahead," he instructed his new external affairs minister, Allan MacEachen, "we must choose consciously to express our concern about the widespread inequalities found in the world ... a strong moral fibre must appear increasingly to be a fundamental ingredient of our foreign policy."[1] One of the regions where MacEachen would soon apply this philosophy was the ever unstable and chaotic Middle East. The government's decision to join the UN Emergency Force that ended the Arab-Israeli War of October 1973, the staggering new riches of Arab oil producers, and the rising Palestinian clamour for global recognition made an updated policy urgent. The challenge seemed tailor-made for MacEachen, who came to office with a solid reputation as a progressive policy heavyweight. Yet unvarnished success eluded the veteran minister. The region's complexity, a challenging policy-making landscape at home, and the shrinking limits of ministerial autonomy conspired to frustrate his diplomatic ambitions.

Allan MacEachen was already a well-known quantity – with a resumé that included strong progressive credentials, evidence of intellectual heft, and long political experience – when Trudeau named him secretary of state for external affairs on 8 August 1974. The son of a Cape Breton coal miner, MacEachen was born in 1921 and grew up in the impoverished company town of Inverness, Nova Scotia. Fleeing the mines, he enrolled in St. Francis Xavier University in 1941, where he soon came under the "liberating influence" of Fr. Moses Coady's Antigonish movement.[2] For the devout MacEachen, Coady's radical Catholic activism, which combined an attack on the existing social and economic order with a cooperative program of self-help, was welcome evidence that "social and economic change was possible, legitimate, and justified."[3] It made a lasting impression on the young MacEachen and would define his progressive approach to politics and public policy.

In 1953, after doctoral work in economics at the Massachusetts Institute of Technology, MacEachen was elected to the House of Commons for the riding of Inverness-Richmond. By the early 1960s, he had become a close ally and admirer of Liberal Opposition leader Lester Pearson, whom he often advised on economic questions and parliamentary procedure. Following the 1963 election, he joined Pearson's cabinet as minster of labour, before becoming minister of health and welfare in the second Pearson government. As a minister, MacEachen solidified his reputation as a member of the Liberal Party's progressive wing and was responsible for legislation that established Canada's first minimum wage and brought into being the Canada Assistance Plan and medicare. Hopeful that he could win progressive and Maritime votes, he ran for the Liberal leadership in 1968, placed seventh in a field of eight, and threw his support behind the eventual victor.

Trudeau rewarded MacEachen with Manpower and Immigration, a difficult portfolio in the late 1960s, and one that left him outside the prime minister's inner circle. The two men drew closer after 1970, when Trudeau recruited MacEachen as House leader, where he remained to shape Liberal strategy in the minority government, from 1972 to 1974. He proved a wily and shrewd parliamentary tactician. Progressive Conservative MP John Crosbie described him as "slippery as a cod tongue in a barrel of cod's liver."[4] The Liberal backroom strategist Senator Keith Davey called MacEachen "the best House Leader I have ever seen."[5] Following the 1974 victory, it was understood by the prime minister that MacEachen would be freed from the daily grind of the House and given a ministry with a little more glamour: External Affairs was his reward.

MacEachen was an experienced politician, with clearly defined views on the proper role of ministers and officials. He respected the expertise that he found in External Affairs, but he was leery of its diplomats. "Getting along with the bureaucracy," he wrote, "does not mean becoming its puppet."[6] While most officials enjoyed working with MacEachen, who was shy but good humoured, he was perceived as remote and distant. "The old mysterious bachelor, elusive as ever," one later wrote.[7] His habit of returning memoranda without comment and his frequent visits to his Cape Breton home generated whispered accusations of laziness. His cautious and deliberate approach to decision-making, which sometimes left officials without instructions, reinforced both impressions.

Yet the department's shrewdest observers knew better. "Avec MacEachen," recalled diplomat Michel Dupuy, "j'avais appris que ne pas décider est une forme de décision."[8] Allan Gotlieb, who watched MacEachen manoeuvre from afar, first as deputy minister in rival departments (Communications and then Manpower and Immigration) and then as ambassador to Washington, concurred. "The hesitancy, evasiveness, and unwillingness to lead are not really those things at all," he exclaimed.[9] MacEachen's background in economics at MIT and his political experience gave him standing at External Affairs. It also helped that he was bright, well read, and good at absorbing his briefs. He liked his job and projected a solidly competent air that ensured good relations with other foreign ministers, including Americans Henry Kissinger in the 1970s and George Shultz in the 1980s.

Updating Middle Eastern policy to take into account recent developments in the region as well as Canada's quickening relations with the Arab world was one of the first issues to confront the minister. As an active regional peacekeeper, Canada had long sought a balanced attitude toward the Arab-Israeli conflict. But by the summer of 1974, the diplomats in External Affairs were fearful that Canadian policy was increasingly anti-Arab just when the region's economic resources were of growing significance, and they looked to MacEachen for change. He was not constrained, as his predecessor was, by a pro-Israel lobby in his riding and a shaky parliamentary minority. Moreover, he was reputed to welcome the aspirations of developing countries and likely to support policies that hewed more closely to Arab views.[10]

Change seemed especially urgent in the case of Canada's attitude toward the problem of the Palestinian people, whom Ottawa historically viewed as solely a humanitarian and refugee issue, avoiding any acknowledgment of collective Palestinian political rights. Those rights, however, appeared at the top of the global agenda in October 1974, when the UN General Assembly (UNGA) invited Yasser Arafat, leader of the Palestine Liberation Organization (PLO), to join its deliberations on Palestine. Though MacEachen abstained from supporting the invitation, which conflicted with Canada's established position of refusing to "prejudge" who should represent the Palestinian people, his officials welcomed the debate as an opportunity to update Canadian policy.[11]

Canadian diplomats were certainly aware of the intense pressure MacEachen would probably face over any policy change, and they moved gingerly. Acting undersecretary John Halstead recommended that Canada deliver a modest statement at the UNGA with just "an implicit reference to the existence of a Palestinian personality." Canada would not recognize PLO claims or acknowledge any Palestinian right but would employ such words as "legitimate," "interests," "concerns," and "aspirations" to imply that some kind of Palestinian entity existed. This small shift in language and policy would acknowledge the logic behind Palestinian demands for a voice in regional affairs, bring Canadian policy into line with its European allies, and encourage moderate Palestinians to pursue their cause peacefully.[12]

As MacEachen weighed the recommendation, his earlier decision to abstain from voting on the resolution inviting Arafat to attend the UNGA came under vehement attack. While some critics thought that he ought to have gone further in recognizing PLO claims, most condemned the vote as a sop to terrorism. In the House of Commons, the Liberal MP for York Centre, Robert Kaplan, demanded to know whether "Canada accepts the legitimacy of this gang of self-confessed murderers and terrorists?"[13] Former Progressive Conservative leader John Diefenbaker denounced the vote as a "slap in the face for Israel" that "placed the Jewish people in a shameful position."[14] A few days later, John Roberts, another Toronto Liberal MP, joined the assault.

MacEachen cast about for a compromise. He met with the Israeli and Arab ambassadors on 21 October and with the Canadian Jewish

Congress four days later, and he arranged for consultations with his predecessor as Secretary of State for External Affairs Mitchell Sharp and with Roberts. The result was a weaker text designed to reassure Israel and the Canadian Jewish community that Canada understood Israeli security needs, while acknowledging "the concept of a distinct Palestinian entity and personality."[15] In MacEachen's absence, the draft was shown to both the prime minister and Sharp.[16] Trudeau approved it without amendment, but Sharp suggested extensive changes. With the prime minister's backing secured, and convinced that he had already met his critics halfway, MacEachen refused, reluctant to upset "the fine balance intended."[17]

Yet the statement failed to have the impact that MacEachen wanted. Though it acknowledged the "legitimate concerns of the Palestinians," it was hedged with language designed to safeguard the Israeli position.[18] While the Arab world reacted with predictable annoyance, even Western observers were surprised by the pro-Israeli tone, a disappointing reaction that determined how MacEachen would vote on the two resolutions under discussion at the UNGA. The minister opposed a motion according the PLO observer status at the UN in keeping with existing policies on both the PLO and the status of NGOs at the UN. The second resolution, defining Palestinian rights in anti-Israeli terms, was more problematic. Its content clearly merited a negative vote, but coming so soon after the minister's statement, diplomats worried that a negative vote might be interpreted as marking too sharp a shift toward Israel. MacEachen had little choice but to abstain.[19]

In the wake of MacEachen's controversial UN debut, Barney Danson, the minister of state for urban affairs, brought the matter to cabinet. Many Canadians, he warned, were anxious about policy toward the PLO. His remarks generated a chorus of complaints. Several ministers were concerned with the growing tendency of the nonaligned movement to use its majority to run roughshod over the UN. Others were upset by MacEachen's failure to persuade Canadians to support the government's current policy on the PLO, Israel, and the Middle East. Accordingly, cabinet instructed the minister to work harder at explaining policy and asked him to return with papers on policy in the Middle East and on the situation at the UN. Finally, with PLO observers now part of the UN network, cabinet asked the minister of manpower and immigration for a memorandum on admitting members of known terrorist organizations into Canada.[20]

MacEachen's first instinct was to duck. He and Halstead asked staff for a simple document reviewing Canada's traditional Middle East policy, explaining the sour UN atmosphere, and seeking approval for the current policy of "balance and equidistance."[21] But the diplomats pushed back. Michel Dupuy, assistant undersecretary for economic affairs, insisted that the paper must address the growing economic weight of the Arab world. Geoffrey Pearson, whose experience in UN affairs had left him with strong views on Arab-Israeli relations, endorsed this judgment. Since domestic pressures made it so hard for Canada to pursue an objective policy, he added, perhaps it was time to explore other options.[22] Heads of Canadian missions across the Middle East also chimed in. However balanced in conception, they argued, Canadian policy was too often perceived as anti-Arab, and they urged headquarters to adopt a more flexible policy toward the PLO and do more to bring about regional peace.[23]

These views were echoed in a surprising quarter. In March 1975, after Israeli prime minister Yitzhak Rabin scuttled Kissinger's recent efforts to broker a Middle East settlement, the US secretary of state invited MacEachen to lunch. Following their meal at the State Department, where the conversation fixed on the "goddamn mess" in the Middle East, Kissinger drew his colleague aside, asking "if Canada could approach Israel to urge it to adopt a more flexible attitude."[24] Trudeau, with whom MacEachen discussed the region on his return home, agreed and encouraged the minister to bring a paper to cabinet for discussion.[25] In April, the undersecretary told Pearson to pull together a final draft.[26]

Pearson's draft promised a sharp departure in Canada's approach to the Middle East. While continuing to insist on the importance of balanced policy, a prerequisite for an effective peacekeeping role, the memorandum implied that the balance had tilted too much toward Israel. To correct this, the government should embrace initiatives such as Kissinger's suggestion that Canada moderate Israeli policy, even if that meant courting the anger of the Canadian Jewish community. After all, as the paper pointed out at length, the surging economic and political strength of the Arab world had obvious offsetting benefits. While maintaining its "balanced and objective approach" to regional conflict, Canada must free itself to take "initiatives as occasions arise to contribute towards substantive negotiations." More generally, Ottawa should expand bilateral relations with all countries in the region, emphasizing commercial and economic opportunities.[27]

MacEachen's tardiness in preparing his Middle East memorandum meant that the paper from the Department of Manpower and Immigration on the PLO's admissibility arrived first at the powerful cabinet Committee on Priorities and Planning. And this paper, which had been the subject of bitter interdepartmental wrangling since early spring, framed the problem of Canada's relations with the Middle East in very different terms. The two central issues at stake were already apparent at the first interdepartmental meeting in February, when John Hadwen, director general of consular services, and Yvon Beaulne, director general of African and Middle Eastern affairs, met with Jean Edmonds, an assistant deputy minister from manpower and immigration. On the first question, the two departments agreed that individual PLO members could enter Canada under a minister's permit for specific events and that the PLO, by virtue of its new status as a UN observer, could send delegates to the 5th UN Congress on Crime, scheduled for September, in Toronto.

Crucially, the departments differed on the second issue: whether or not the PLO was a terrorist organization whose members should be automatically denied entry into Canada. From the perspective of the Department of Manpower and Immigration, it was obvious that membership in the PLO constituted sufficient grounds to refuse admittance. Hadwen and Beaulne demurred. Basing themselves on recent intelligence assessments, they argued that the PLO was not a terrorist organization per se, though some of its sub-units clearly engaged in terrorist activities. A complete ban on the organization, the two diplomats warned, "could provoke a negative reaction by Arab states and could jeopardize Canada's increasingly important political, commercial, economic and financial interests in the Arab Middle East."[28] The meeting adjourned with this question unresolved, but within days the deputy minister of manpower and immigration, Allan Gotlieb, had decided to press on unilaterally with his cabinet memorandum.

As Gotlieb's paper moved forward, the PLO's status became a public and controversial issue. In April, the Law Society of Upper Canada announced that it would boycott the UN Crime Congress if the PLO was allowed to attend. A month later, Ontario premier Bill Davis warned Trudeau that his province, which had co-sponsored the initial offer to host the UN conference, would pull out if the PLO participated. The letter was leaked to the *Globe and Mail* on 30 May, just days before ministers were to discuss the issue, raising the spectre of a full-blown domestic political crisis.[29] Against this background, MacEachen made no headway convincing his colleagues to refrain from banning the PLO outright or from excluding only those subgroups that were engaged in terrorist activities. On 3 June, the cabinet Committee on Priorities and Planning decided that the PLO was indeed a prohibited organization, although individual members without terrorist ties would be admitted to Canada under a minister's permit to attend UN conferences or if invited by a "reputable Canadian organization."[30]

Cabinet's discussion of the PLO cast a shadow over MacEachen's efforts the following week to secure approval for a more active and pro-Arab policy. Despite some support from Trudeau, who welcomed the effort to reassess Canadian policy and thought that a tougher line on Israeli intransigence might be warranted, MacEachen encountered stiff opposition. Israel, argued Sharp, considered Canada a good friend and was satisfied with its current policy in the region. He warned the external affairs minister, who cabinet gossips suggested was out of touch with the Canadian Jewish community, that it was important to ensure that Jewish leaders understood the government's motives and policies. His colleagues agreed and turned back the memorandum, asking MacEachen for clearer policy options with all the international and domestic implications worked out.[31]

A more serious setback soon threatened. Cabinet's decision to permit limited entry of the PLO was not what MacEachen wanted, but it at least allowed the UN Crime Congress to proceed. Ministers were even hopeful of convincing the Jewish community and its supporters in the Liberal caucus to go along with the decision. That optimism evaporated as soundings were taken in mid-June. After meeting Jewish leaders and the caucus, MacEachen judged their support lukewarm and suggested postponing any public announcement.

With MacEachen on a trade mission to Japan, Sharp held a second round of talks with Jewish leaders, including the national director of the

Canada-Israel Committee, the executive director of the Canadian Jewish Congress, and members of Canadians Against PLO Terrorism (CAPLOT).[32] Struck by their fierce opposition to admitting the PLO into Canada under any terms, Sharp recommended withdrawing the offer to host the UN Crime conference. Trudeau struck a defiant note: "He personally felt that the proposal to admit PLO members by Minister's Permit under controlled conditions was the correct course ... He believed the Canadian position should be very firm. There could be no compromise with the principles of universality of states' membership in the UN."[33] The question would have to be reviewed when the minister returned.[34]

MacEachen, outlining steps taken to counter potential critics, held his own when cabinet reconsidered the issue on 3 July.[35] Pending a final decision, which was postponed for another week, he continued to meet with national representatives of the Jewish community, while urban affairs minister Danson arranged for meetings with regional and local Jewish leaders. A bloody terrorist attack by a PLO-linked group on 4 July, however, suddenly rendered these efforts redundant. This was confirmed later that week when MacEachen met with outraged Jewish leaders and local cabinet ministers in Hamilton and Toronto.[36] Trudeau, too, was repulsed by the PLO attack and told ministers on 10 July that he had changed his mind and "was not prepared to tolerate further violence." The prime minister added "that he would prefer the support of the Canadian people than admiration from certain international quarters." Cabinet promptly withdrew the invitation to host the UN Crime Congress.[37]

This was a bitter defeat for MacEachen, who told friends that he was "very unhappy." The prime minister, he complained, had acted without "due consultation."[38] But worse was coming. Within a week, MacEachen was back in cabinet with a plan to ask the UN to postpone its Crime Congress for a year on the grounds that Middle East tensions and the politicization of international conferences had made it impossible to host a successful conference. After amending the proposal to remove any implication that Canada might host the conference if the requested delay was rejected, ministers approved MacEachen's script for a face-saving retreat.[39] UN secretary-general Kurt Waldheim was not so accommodating. When MacEachen met him two days later in New York, it was clear that the UN would not postpone the conference.[40] Canadian editorialists saw through the minister's gambit and added to his discomfort by denouncing the government for failing to act decisively either in support of its UN commitment or in opposition to the PLO.[41]

Despite this public setback, a new Middle East policy remained a priority for MacEachen, who decided in late July to visit Egypt, Iran, Saudi Arabia, and Iraq, where an embassy was to be opened later in the year. The visit was largely intended to expose the minister directly to the region, focusing attention on its growing economic links with Canada. MacEachen also hoped that the trip would permit him to signal a renewed era in relations with the Middle East, a step for which he wanted a mandate from cabinet.[42] A revised memorandum on Canada and the Middle East began to take shape in September.

The task of drafting the memorandum was handed to Michael Shenstone, Canada's ambassador to Saudi Arabia. Home on annual leave, Shenstone worked for a few extra weeks to produce a draft with a modest set of policy proposals. Stressing the growing importance of economic relations with the Middle East, the memorandum tried to separate the Arab-Israeli conflict from Canada's bilateral relations with individual states in the region "without doing so in a way which would make [ministers] feel that they were being asked to choose materialistically between Israelis and Arabs, between God and Mammon." The memorandum recommended that Canada maintain its current "balanced and objective" approach to the Middle East, acknowledging that "circumstances ... dictate caution about a more active role for Canada at present." Instead, Canada should focus on developing a dialogue with the region's leading oil producers, giving trade promotion a "high priority."[43]

Aware that these recommendations were likely to disappoint a minister who wanted to play an active role in the Arab-Israeli dispute, Shenstone warned MacEachen that any effort to address this role would draw unwanted attention from his cabinet colleagues and risk derailing the rest of the paper. Of course, he added, this was a political decision that only a minister could make. If MacEachen decided that a "bolder approach" was politically feasible, Shenstone recommended moving toward recognizing the PLO as the legitimate representative of the Palestinian people, acknowledging their "rights" in Palestine, and perhaps even allowing a PLO office in Canada.[44]

MacEachen accepted the main thrust of the memorandum but remained determined to address the Palestinian issue. In discussions with departmental officials, he helped work out a series of recommendations that would have Ottawa acknowledge nonspecific Palestinian "rights" as well as the PLO's role as their "most authoritative spokesman" provided the organization accepted Israel's right to exist within safe and secure borders.[45] MacEachen wisely delayed cabinet consideration of the policy in the fall of 1975, worried that it might be swept up in the emotions surrounding the bitter UN debate on a motion, which Canada opposed, equating Zionism with racism.[46]

As a result, the memorandum was overtaken by the minister's trip to the Middle East in January 1976. Without cabinet's endorsement, MacEachen avoided Palestinian issues during the tour, which highlighted the mutual benefits of closer bilateral commercial relations. Despite this narrow agenda, the visit was thought to be a solid success, reassuring evidence of the wisdom of engaging the Arab world more closely.[47] Encouraged by this small victory, and with the prime minister once again back in his corner, MacEachen pushed his revised Middle East memorandum through cabinet in February. Having felt little pressure during his trip to recognize the PLO, he resisted demands from his colleagues that he make a public statement of the government's new position.[48] Fatefully, he tucked it away until needed.

Trudeau moved MacEachen out of External Affairs in the fall of 1976 to reprise his role as House leader, followed by a short stint on the Opposition benches and an unhappy spell as finance minister. During his absence, his Middle East policy remained unfulfilled as Canada's approach to the region tilted toward Israel under MacEachen's three successors: Don Jamieson, Progressive Conservative Flora MacDonald, and Mark MacGuigan. Keeping his promise to give MacEachen another shot at diplomacy, Trudeau returned him to External Affairs in August 1982 just as the Middle East climbed to the top of the international agenda. The region had simmered all summer following Israel's invasion of southern Lebanon in June, drawing Trudeau's ire and arousing Liberal backbenchers and the public, who pressed the government to redress what many considered its pro-Israeli tilt. The prime minister wanted an updated policy paper on Canada's relations with the Middle East too, a view he made clear to his new minister and his officials.

MacEachen had shed none of his progressive instincts during his six-year absence from External Affairs. On taking office, he discovered that few of his "forward and innovative" policy initiatives from 1976 had actually been implemented, and he promptly authorized Canadian diplomats to engage secretly with overseas PLO personnel. Though closer than ever to Trudeau and wielding extra clout as his deputy prime minister, he approached the prospect of a Middle East policy review more carefully than ever, perhaps wary of another bruising cabinet battle. To avoid cabinet scrutiny, he and Michael Shenstone, now assistant deputy minister for African and Middle East affairs, agreed to prepare a paper for the prime minister alone, the distribution of which would be tightly controlled. They would start with a paper on Palestinian self-determination as a prelude to a fuller memorandum on Arab-Israeli relations.[49]

Under Shenstone's guidance, the Middle East division set about its drafting work, which was carefully safeguarded and not shared with the other ministers, parliamentary secretaries, or even other units in External Affairs.[50] Canadian policy on self-determination, the division's paper contended, was no longer consistent, lagged behind West European policies, and ought to be changed. Since 1945, Canada had accepted the right of people to self-determination in a broad range of circumstances. More recently, it had acknowledged the Palestinians as a people with "legitimate rights and just requirements." Though this was tantamount to accepting their right to self-determination, Ottawa had avoided this final step, which was often associated with the idea of a Palestinian state. To resolve this contradiction, the paper recommended that Canada accept the Palestinian right to self-determination within the West Bank and Gaza Strip "in a manner consistent with the principles of [UN Security Council] Resolution 242," which guaranteed Israel's security and right to exist. This qualified acceptance, which would bring Canada into line with its European allies, would merely confirm the recent "drift" in the government's Middle East policy and would be unlikely to run into much domestic or international opposition.[51]

Endorsed by deputy minister De Montigny Marchand and blessed by MacEachen, the memorandum was sent to Trudeau in early 1983. MacEachen's uneventful appearance before the Standing Senate Committee on Foreign Affairs in February 1983 allayed fears that there might be insurmountable opposition to amending Canadian policy. The minister was outspoken in his criticism of Israel's occupation of Lebanon and of Jewish settlements in the West Bank. He also revealed the government's policy of maintaining contacts with the PLO, hinting that these might be raised to the ambassadorial level. Despite his frankness, MacEachen emerged unscathed.[52] Trudeau's reaction to the memorandum on self-determination was equally encouraging. The prime minister read it "with great interest" and indicated that he was looking forward to the cabinet memorandum on Canada and the Arab-Israeli dispute.[53]

This memorandum, reviewed by MacEachen in March, was circulating within a confined group in External Affairs by May.[54] It began with the observation that Canada retained its important historic stake in the Arab-Israeli dispute, which might at any time spark a direct Soviet-American conflict and lead to nuclear war. Though Canada had little regional influence, it could still contribute to the peace process by adopting forward positions on several issues. At the general level, argued the draft, while Canada maintained its strong support for Israel's existence, it ought to indicate greater sympathy for Arab, especially Palestinian, nationalism. Canada should do this by endorsing Palestinian self-determination in the West Bank and the Gaza Strip, linked with an affirmation of Israel's right to peace and security. More specifically, the memorandum recommended adjusting Canadian policy toward the three main parties in the dispute. First, Ottawa must remain a friend of Israel, though it should no longer hesitate to criticize its settlement policy and the Lebanese occupation, and should refuse any new bilateral initiatives. Second, the government should maintain and extend its contacts with the region's Arab states. Third, it should acknowledge the PLO as a representative of the Palestinian people and raise Ottawa's contacts with the organization to the ambassadorial level to encourage it toward moderation and negotiations.

However modest, the proposed Middle Eastern policy was soon in trouble. On reflection, Privy Council Office staff told Shenstone, Trudeau hesitated to address the question of Palestinian self-determination lest it create trouble with Quebec's separatist government. Without the prime minister's support, MacEachen, too, began to waver, and by the end of June, he had decided to shelve the policy review, at least until the fall.[55] A second Middle Eastern tour in October confirmed his fears. MacEachen met an array of foreign ministers and heads of government in Syria, Egypt,

Jordan, and Israel, with an unscheduled stopover in war-torn Beirut. Primarily intended to signal Canadian interest in the Lebanese crisis, the delegation found the trip "immensely informative and enriching."[56] Other Canadians were less convinced. An editorial in the *Ottawa Citizen,* for instance, attacked MacEachen's remarks in Egypt as unfriendly to Israel, while the visit provided grounds for a sustained assault on the government's Middle East policy from pro-Israel members of Parliament from both sides of the House.[57] Stung by the criticism, MacEachen beat a final retreat and reassured Parliament that the government had no plans to upgrade Canada's contacts with the PLO,[58] abruptly ending his efforts to address evolving realities in the Middle East.

The Middle East was a constant preoccupation during MacEachen's two turns, just over four years, as Canada's external affairs minister. Like most other postwar ministers, he divided the job with his boss, the prime minister. Trudeau set the direction, turning south in the mid-1970s, probing for equitable and more just forms of engagement with the postcolonial world in Asia, Africa, and the Middle East. MacEachen handled the detail. The Cape Breton minister shared Trudeau's attachment to a progressive diplomacy, which he combined with a veteran politician's tactical sense for compromise, retreat, and tenacity.

Yet unvarnished success proved elusive. The Middle East was treacherous terrain, where Canada's limited interests and influence forced it to play on the margins. The landscape at home was equally complex, peopled with powerful and vocal stakeholders on both sides of the Arab-Israeli dispute. Rebuked by cabinet in the fall of 1974 for his handling of Palestinian issues at the UN, MacEachen first balked, then rallied to craft new and stronger policies to engage the PLO and the resurgent Arab world. Humiliated again by his prime minister and cabinet in the spring of 1975 over the UN Crime Congress, MacEachen doggedly persisted. He eventually won cabinet backing for his policies edging Canada closer toward recognizing the PLO. After these bruising battles, however, MacEachen changed tactics in the 1980s, eschewing cabinet altogether and concentrating his efforts on the prime minister alone. This strategy faltered on the shoals of Quebec separatism, and when the prime minister's support for Palestinian self-determination sagged, MacEachen retreated, as foreign ministers must when prime ministers look away.

NOTES

1 Pierre Trudeau to Allan J. MacEachen, 4 September 1974, file 22, vol. 21, H.B. Robinson Papers, Library and Archives Canada (hereafter LAC).
2 Allan J. MacEachen, "All Those Years: Practice and Purpose in Politics," in *In Pursuit of the Public Good: Essays in Honour of Allan J. MacEachen,* ed. Tom Kent (Montreal/Kingston: McGill-Queen's University Press, 1997), 16.
3 MacEachen, "All Those Years," 18.
4 John C. Crosbie, *No Holds Barred: My Life in Politics* (Toronto: McClelland and Stewart, 1997), 191.
5 Keith Davey, *The Rainmaker: A Passion for Politics* (Toronto: Stoddart, 1986), 172–73.
6 MacEachen, "All Those Years," 5.
7 Allan Gotlieb, *The Washington Diaries, 1981–1989* (Toronto: McClelland and Stewart, 2006), 93.
8 Michel Dupuy, *Diplomate de Père en Fils* (Montreal: Carte Blanche, 2011), 762.
9 Gotlieb, *The Washington Diaries,* 139.
10 Paul C. Noble, "Where Angels Fear to Tread: Canada and the Status of the Palestinian People 1973–1983," in *Canada and the Arab World,* ed. Tareq Y. Ismael (Edmonton: University of Alberta Press, 1985), 117–18.
11 Permisny to Ottawa, tel 1729, 9 October 1974, file 20–4–4, vol. 9060, RG 25, LAC; Ottawa to Permisny, tel GAM-267, 10 October 1974, file 20–4–4, vol. 9060, RG 25, LAC.
12 John Halstead, Memorandum to the Minister, 17 October 1974, RG 25, vol. 9060, file 20–4–4, vol. 9060, RG 25, LAC.
13 Robert Kaplan, quoted in Ottawa to Tel Aviv, GAM-277, 22 October 1974, file 20–4–4, vol. 9060, RG 25, LAC.
14 John Diefenbaker, quoted in John Saywell, ed., *Canadian Annual Review of Politics and Public Affairs for 1974* (Toronto: University of Toronto Press, 1975), 318.
15 UNO to GAP, 6 November 1974, file 20–4–4, vol. 9060, RG 25, LAC.
16 John Halstead, Memorandum to the Prime Minister, 15 November 1974, file 20–4–4, vol. 9060, RG 25, LAC.
17 John Halstead, Memorandum to the Minister, 19 November 1974, file 20–4–4, vol. 9060, RG 25, LAC.
18 A.J. MacEachen, "The Middle East: The Will to Peace and the Form It Takes Must Be Evolved by the Parties Concerned" (presented in New York, 20 November 1974), in Department of External Affairs, *Statements and Speeches 74/16.*
19 Permisny to Ottawa, tel 2349, 22 November 1974, file 20–4–4, vol. 9060, RG 25, LAC; Ottawa to Permisny, tel GAM-321, 22 November 1974, file 20–4–4, vol. 9060, RG 25, LAC.
20 Cabinet Conclusion, 28 November 1974, PCO Records, Privy Council Office (PCO).
21 PDM to GAM, 3 December 1974, file 20–1–2–Middle East (ME), vol. 8762, RG 25, LAC; GAM to GAP/UNP/UNO, 4 December 1974, file 20–1–2–Middle East (ME), vol. 8761, RG 25, LAC.
22 G.A.H. Pearson to GAM, 31 December 1974, file 20–1–2–ME, vol. 8762, RG 25, LAC.
23 GAM to PDE, 7 February 1975, file 21–3–Arab-Israeli, vol. 10589, RG 25, LAC; Dupuy's marginal notes on the Draft Memorandum to Cabinet, 27 January 1975, file 21–3–Arab-Israeli, vol. 10589, RG 25, LAC.

24 Washington to Ottawa, tel 782, 31 March 1975, file 20–1–2–USA, Foreign Affairs Canada (FAC).
25 Trudeau's marginalia on MacEachen, Memorandum to the Prime Minister, 10 April 1975, file 20–1–2–USA, FAC.
26 H.B. Robinson, Memorandum to GAM, 28 April 1975, file 20–1–2–ME, vol. 8762, RG 25, LAC.
27 A.J. MacEachen, Memorandum to Cabinet, 23 May 1975, Cabinet Document 342–75, MEO, PCO Files.
28 GAP to PDM, 28 February 1975, file 20–4–4, vol. 9060, RG 25, LAC.
29 John Saywell, ed., *Canadian Annual Review of Politics and Public Affairs for 1975* (Toronto: University of Toronto Press, 1976), 190–91.
30 Minutes of the Cabinet Committee on Priorities and Planning, 3 June 1975, PCO Files, PCO.
31 Minutes of the Cabinet Committee on Priorities and Planning, 10 June 1975, PCO Files, PCO. On the ministerial views of MacEachen, see Marcel Cadieux to H.B. Robinson, 15 May 1975, file 8, vol. 25, Robinson Papers, LAC.
32 Record of Meeting between Acting SSEA and Jewish Leaders, 24 June 1975, file 1, vol. 24, Robinson Papers, LAC.
33 Cabinet Minutes, 26 June 1975, PCO Files, PCO.
34 H.B. Robinson, Memorandum to the Minister, 27 June 1975, file 1, vol. 24, Robinson Papers, LAC.
35 Cabinet Conclusions, 3 July 1975, PCO Files, PCO.
36 "Summary of Meeting between SSEA and Representatives of the Canada-Israel Committee on Wednesday, July 9, 1975," 14 July 1975, file 20–4–4, vol. 9060, RG 25, LAC.
37 Cabinet Minutes, 10 July 1975, PCO Files, PCO.
38 Paul Martin, *Paul Martin: The London Diaries, 1975–1979*, ed. William R. Young (Toronto: University of Toronto Press, 1988), 65.
39 Cabinet Minutes, 17 July 1975, PCO Files, PCO.
40 Claude Lemelin, A Report on the SSEA's Meeting with the UN Secretary-General, 18 July 1975, file 8, vol. 24, Robinson Papers, LAC.
41 Mary Halloran, "Multiculturalism and External Policy in the Trudeau Era, 1968–1984," in *Multiculturalism and the History of International Relations from the 18th Century up to the Present*, ed. Pierre Savard and Brunello Vigezzi (Milan: Edizioni Unicopli, 1999), 388.
42 H.B. Robinson, Memorandum to the Minister, 10 July 1975, file 20-Cda-9Exstaff/ME, vol. 9229, RG 25, LAC. See also H.B. Robinson, Memorandum to the Minister, 28 October 1975, file 20-Cda-9-MacEachen-ME, vol. 9282, RG 25, LAC.
43 Draft Memorandum to Cabinet, 3 October 1975, file 20–1–2–ME, vol. 8762, RG 25, LAC.
44 Arthur Andrew, Memorandum to the Minister, 3 October 1975, file 20–1–2–ME, vol. 8762, RG 25, LAC.
45 H.B. Robinson, Memorandum to the Minister, 14 October 1975, file 20–1–2–ME, vol. 8762, RG 25, LAC; A.J. Andrew, Memorandum to the Minister, 16 October 1975, file 20–1–2–ME, vol. 8762, RG 25, LAC.
46 Saywell, *Canadian Annual Review of Politics and Public Affairs for 1975*, 295.

47 The visit is covered in Janice Gross Stein, "Canadian Foreign Policy in the Middle East after the October War," *Social Praxis* 4, 3–4 (1976/77): 288–89. See also Tel Aviv to Ottawa, tel 136, 29 January 1976, file 20-Cda-9-Ext Staff/ME, vol. 9229, RG 25, LAC; and OECD Paris to Ottawa, tel 160, 25 January 1976, file 20-Cda-9-Ext Staff/ME, vol. 9229, RG 25, LAC.

48 Cabinet Minutes, 19 February 1976, PCO Files, PCO.

49 Ibid. On leaks, see Shenstone to Marchand, GAP-201, 24 September 1982, file 20–1–2–Middle East, vol. 8764, RG 25, LAC; Shenstone to File, GAP-210, 1 October 1982, file 20–1–2–Middle East, vol. 8764, RG 25, LAC; and Schioler to LAO/J. Gaudreau, GAM-1736, 23 November 1982, file 20–1–2–Middle East, vol. 8764, RG 25, LAC.

50 Shenstone to PFG, GAP-257, 10 December 1982, file 20–1–2–Middle East, vol. 8764, RG 25, LAC; A.J. MacEachen, Memorandum to the Prime Minister, 16 February 1982, file 20–1–2–Middle East, vol. 8764, RG 25, LAC.

51 Donaghy noted "cite paper drafted for PM" but did not complete this endnote before his passing.

52 Canada, Senate of Canada, *Proceedings of the Standing Senate Committee on Foreign Affairs,* 17 February 1983, Issue No. 37, 9–19.

53 Fowler to Alain Dudoit, 8 April 1983, file 20–1–2–Mid-East, vol. 8764, RG 25, LAC.

54 Shenstone to Marchand, GAP-104, 6 May 1983, file 20–1–2–Mid-East, vol. 8764, RG 25, LAC; Attached Draft Memorandum to Cabinet, GAP-104, 6 May 1983, file 20–1–2–Mid-East, vol. 8764, RG 25, LAC. The memorandum was circulated only to the minister, the undersecretary, the deputy minister of trade, and the deputy minister of foreign affairs.

55 External to Tel Aviv (HOP Only), tel GAP-146, 30 June 1983, file 20–1–2–Mid-East, vol. 8764, RG 25, LAC.

56 Mindel to Beirut, tel 1079, 28 October 1983, file 20-Cda-9-EA-Mideast, vol. 9260, RG 25, LAC.

57 GMD/Elliott to MINA, GMD-240, 16 November 1983, file 20–1–2–Middle East, vol. 8765, RG 25, LAC.

58 Canada, *House of Commons Debates,* 32nd Parl., 1st Sess., Vol. 25, 3 November 1983, 28671–72; Canada, *House of Commons Debates,* 14 November 1983, 28832; Canada, *House of Commons Debates,* 21 November 1983, 29024.

CHAPTER 9

A JOURNEY WITHOUT MAPS

John Hadwen in India, 1979–83

Ryan Touhey

John Hadwen joined Canada's foreign service in 1950 at a time of unprecedented growth and opportunity in Ottawa's diplomatic corps, eventually emerging as one of the most senior diplomats of his generation. Over the course of his forty-year career, Hadwen was repeatedly posted to Canadian missions in postcolonial Asia, where he encountered some of the most pressing and controversial problems of postwar Canadian foreign relations. His final posting as high commissioner to India from 1979 to 1983 was undeniably his most difficult but important one.

Relations between Canada and India were tense and acrimonious for much of the 1970s. The diplomats in the Department of External Affairs were long skeptical of India's Cold War diplomacy of nonalignment. Canadians were outraged when New Delhi used donated Canadian technology to build and detonate a nuclear bomb in 1974.[1] They were hardly reassured when Prime Minister Indira Gandhi suspended democracy between 1975 and 1977. Yet senior officials in External Affairs understood that India could not be ignored indefinitely given its regional status, its size, and its economic potential. Perhaps, they mused, it was time to redevelop the relationship along more practical lines based on trade and investment. In 1979, they tapped John Hadwen to begin rebuilding a new and more modern bilateral relationship.

Hadwen, like many of the men who staffed the Department of External Affairs in the 1950s, was a strong nationalist, whose childhood and youth in middle-class Toronto reflected the gradual transformation of a city and family steeped in a sense of "Britishness" to one whose character became distinctly Anglo-Canadian. His father, Isaac Hadwen, had immigrated to Canada from Lancashire at the turn of the twentieth century. After studying science at McGill University, Isaac Hadwen served as veterinary captain with the Sixth Canadian Mounted Rifles in the South African War. After graduate studies at the University of Liverpool, and at Cambridge where he earned a doctorate, Hadwen returned from England to serve as chief animal pathologist for Canada from 1917 to 1920.

An accomplished scientist, Isaac Hadwen married Alden Godwin, a champion figure skater, soon settling in Toronto as director of the Department of Pathology and Bacteriology with the Ontario Research Foundation.[2] Isaac and Alden provided a comfortable and intellectual environment for their three children, John (born in 1923), Anne (1924), and Theodore (1933), as they came of age in depression-era Toronto. In an era when over 20 percent of Canadians were unemployed and struggled to put food on the table, the Hadwens offered their children stability and uniquely enriching experiences such as driving from Toronto to Vancouver Island before the Trans-Canada Highway was built.[3]

John Hadwen attended Brown Public School, on Avenue Road, in the leafy midtown neighbourhood of Summerhill before enrolling at Trinity College in the University of Toronto. Hadwen enjoyed his university years immensely, thriving academically in an institution that promoted smaller class sizes and offered an environment that granted students and teachers the opportunity to interact with each other closely, a hallmark of the institution since its establishment in 1852. The young man excelled as an athlete, too. Tall, broad, and powerful, Hadwen enjoyed sports, especially boxing, where he fought as a heavyweight, and cross-country running, in which he won the Trinity annual cross-country race.[4]

The outbreak of the Second World War, in September 1939, soon interrupted his studies. Just as his father felt compelled to serve the British Empire in South Africa, young Hadwen rallied to fight against the evils of fascism and Nazism, enlisting in the army and serving overseas from early 1944 to March 1946. All told, 918 men and 97 women from Trinity enlisted, with 66 killed and 37 wounded between 1939 and 1945.[5] The physical and mental demands of boxing and cross-country running undoubtedly helped Hadwen survive tense years with the Royal Canadian Artillery during bloody campaigns in Italy – between July 1943 and June 1944 the Italian campaign produced 13,000 Canadian casualties – and the liberation of Holland.

Following the war, Hadwen returned to Toronto, completing his studies at Trinity College in 1948. Soon after, he travelled to Britain for graduate studies at the London School of Economics. The sojourn in London was memorable: tea at Buckingham Palace with the Queen and holidays in Brittany.[6]

Completing his studies at the London School of Economics, Hadwen looked to the future. An appetite for life and a keen interest in international affairs as well as a desire to see the world prompted him to sit the foreign service exam in London. Successful, Hadwen joined the Department of External Affairs as a foreign service officer in 1950, one of only fourteen candidates recruited that year. Hadwen entered the foreign service during a period of rapid expansion in the aftermath of the Second World War. Between 1946 and 1948, the number of Canadian overseas posts expanded from twenty-six to forty-four, and Canada's diplomatic staff increased by over one third. That expansion continued steadily throughout the 1950s as decolonization accelerated across Asia and Africa. Between 1951 and 1956, the department added another 416 staff, and the number of posts grew from forty-six to sixty-four. There was plenty of scope for advancement.

Hadwen's background reflected that of the majority of the fifty-six foreign service officers recruited between 1949 and 1952. All were university educated, many were Second World War veterans, most had graduate degrees, all were white, and all but three were male. There were eleven francophones, but the rest were predominantly Anglo-Saxon Protestant with English as their first language.[7] For Hadwen, it was a comfortable fit, made easier perhaps by the sizable Trinity College network at External Affairs. Two senior members of the department were distinguished alumni and Rhodes scholars: Escott Reid and George Ignatieff. They were soon joined by Rhodes scholar James George, Blair Seaborn, Geoffrey Pearson, Michael Shenstone, Peter Dobell, and, a few years later, by Dwight Fulford and Tom Delworth, all of whom enjoyed highly successful careers in the Canadian foreign service. This select cohort alone illustrates the extent to which External Affairs recruitment continued to shape and influence Canadian statecraft well into the 1980s despite some suggestions to the contrary that the golden age of the "Ottawa Men" ended precipitously in 1957.[8] And it was in Ottawa that John Hadwen would meet his wife, Shirley Brown, a fellow civil servant from Toronto. With a bouquet of roses in hand, Hadwen proposed to Shirley in a canoe at Lake of Bays in the summer of 1955. A week later, the couple married in Toronto. Work beckoned soon enough; the next week Hadwen flew to Vietnam, where Canada had recently taken up a role overseeing a shaky ceasefire in Indochina, while Shirley returned to the Civil Service Commission in Ottawa.[9]

Hadwen's lively personality and strong work ethic were undoubted assets in his new career. One colleague, Earl Drake, recalled Hadwen as a man with "distinctive traits of boundless energy and a strong sense of humour." That good humour came in handy, Drake said, when Hadwen and junior diplomat George Hampson both ended up working for George Glazebrook in Defence Liaison Division. Scholarly, serious, and far senior in rank, Glazebrook found the similar surnames confusing and responded by addressing "both Hadwen and Hampson as Hadson."[10] Hadwen simply chuckled and took it in good stride. One fellow officer considerably more junior than Hadwen fondly recalled the latter as someone free of conceits, "ebullient, irrepressible, always positive, and up and running all the time with his ideas."[11] Others described Hadwen as a diplomat who never lost the common touch, treating colleagues, family, and friends with compassion.[12]

Over the course of his career, the sizable and gregarious diplomat not only served with the Defence Liaison Division, but also with the Canadian UN delegation in Manhattan, in 1956, where he and Shirley lived in an apartment on bustling Madison Avenue, enjoying the cultural and entertainment offerings of the borough. Other postings brought Hadwen to the Canadian embassy in Oslo. His unflappable capacity for work and astute political judgment were recognized in 1964 when the foreign minister, Paul Martin Sr., recruited him as his special assistant.[13] Hard work, exuberance, seizing the opportunities on offer, and his belief in the fundamentals of Pearsonian diplomacy made these exhilarating years. Hadwen "would go from morning 'til night," Martin recorded in his memoirs, and accompanied the minister on "nearly all" of his travels.[14] Hadwen reciprocated his minister's admiration but remained sufficiently independent to retain the trust and confidence of his colleagues in External Affairs. When it was time to relax, Hadwen enjoyed a solid social circle of departmental colleagues with whom he regularly played low stakes poker. These games were less about the poker and more a means to unwind, laugh, and exchange departmental war stories.[15]

Like many of his generation, Hadwen's first overseas posting was in Asia, setting his career trajectory toward the Asia-Pacific region. From 1952 to 1954, he served as third counsellor at the Canadian High Commission in Pakistan in the early years of the Colombo Plan, and he took a lifelong interest in that foreign aid project. From 1967 to 1971, after a gap of thirteen years, he served as high commissioner to Singapore and Malaysia and as ambassador to Burma. Although he hoped to return to Ottawa in 1971, he was sent off to Pakistan as high commissioner.

This was a tough assignment. Pakistan had just finished a brutal and humiliating civil war in which its eastern wing had proclaimed independence with India's backing, emerging as Bangladesh. Pakistan bitterly watched its rival, India, become ascendant on the subcontinent. Islamabad, however, could not be ignored, as Hadwen well knew. Although Pakistan had refused to sign the nuclear Non-Proliferation Treaty, Canada had provided that country with a CANDU reactor at the Karachi Nuclear Power Plant (KANUPP), believing that Islamabad had agreed to sufficient safeguards. That reactor opened on Hadwen's watch.

From 1972 to 1974, Canada's nuclear relationship with Pakistan dominated Hadwen's time in Islamabad. Hadwen had long been interested in promoting Canada's commercial interests abroad, and he was determined to secure Canada's nuclear presence in Pakistan, acknowledging that one of his central "functions was to make sure that, as the Pakistanis began to consider their long-term nuclear power requirements, Canada benefited as much as possible from the successful operation of KANUPP."[16] Those plans were irredeemably upset when India exploded its nuclear bomb in May 1974. Hadwen glumly understood that any future Canadian nuclear cooperation with Pakistan had come to an abrupt end as Islamabad sought to match India's capability.[17] As Prime Minister Pierre Trudeau's Liberal government registered its anger and sharply curtailed its nuclear exports to the region, Hadwen prepared to return to Ottawa in the summer of 1974 as director general of the security and intelligence bureau.

Hadwen received news in the spring of 1979 that he was again returning to South Asia, again as head of post. He wanted to be ambassador to China, a country that Trudeau and External Affairs considered a key priority throughout the 1970s. But that post was occupied, and since Hadwen regarded himself as an "Asian hand," he was ready to accept a posting to New Delhi.[18] This sojourn would be different, however. Though only small posts, Singapore and Islamabad had given Hadwen experience working with commercial and nuclear files, undoubtedly sharpening his diplomatic skills and his instinct for what was possible. This was crucial for the next stage on his diplomatic journey. New Delhi was challenging, its environment physically taxing, and the central task of rebuilding a strained relationship undoubtedly gruelling. With the election of a minority Progressive Conservative government in Ottawa in May 1979, it was also unclear how the new government intended to proceed on the world stage. Yet, as he later wrote in a short memoir, Hadwen relished the challenge.[19]

As the new high commissioner prepared to depart for New Delhi, he turned to his predecessor and friend, Louis Rogers, for a sense of what awaited him in Asia. The outlook was hardly reassuring. Appointed high commissioner to India in 1977, Rogers was a tough and blunt-spoken diplomat. He was also an India skeptic who yearned for a change of scenery after just two years in India. In an exchange of letters, Rogers mused that perhaps the two colleagues might meet in Ottawa before Hadwen's departure and share a meal, "but not in an Indian restaurant, I think." In the meantime, he unloaded in his letter that the official residence, with its poor air conditioning, poor chef, and worn furnishings, was grim enough. Bilateral relations were worse, warned Rogers.[20]

"In the Indian scheme of things, Canada is pretty small potatoes," Rogers wrote to Hadwen, dismissing the notion that a special relationship had ever joined the two countries.[21] Illustrating why he believed Canada mattered little to the Indians, Rogers pointed to the bureaucratic structure of the Indian Ministry of External Affairs: "the Americas Division … deals with everything from the North Pole to the South Pole in the Western Hemisphere and … most of its energy is absorbed by relations with the United States." The Indians, Rogers continued, "will be satisfied with an appearance of action" whereas Ottawa "is interested in substance." He also cautioned Hadwen not to expect the government of India to take the initiative in developing or recasting the relationship, for "the Indian tactic on almost everything is to sit back and wait for the other party."[22] This downcast assessment of the bilateral relationship must have been disconcerting to Hadwen.

Though Rogers pointed an accusing finger at India, Ottawa was also to blame for poor bilateral relations.[23] By the 1970s, India had few champions in Ottawa in either the bureaucracy or cabinet. China loomed large; India stood in the shadows. No Canadian secretary of state for external affairs had visited India since 1955, and other Canadian ministerial visits were increasingly rare; only two occurred in the 1970s. Though India remained the largest recipient of Canadian foreign aid, the aid program was slowly cut in the aftermath of the Indian nuclear test.[24] Similarly, bilateral trade between the two nations was tepid, with Canadian exports to India dropping sharply from $203,580,000 to $136,194,000 between 1975 and 1977.[25] Whereas India today is the second largest source of immigrants to Canada, immigration in the late 1970s and early 1980s was low, and the rise of militant Sikh nationalism in Canada raised profound concerns in New Delhi and continued to do so as the 1980s progressed.

Hadwen approached his new role in a hopeful but pragmatic frame of mind. Though the special relationship had long been put to rest, he remained an admirer of India's first prime minister, Jawaharlal Nehru. He also considered himself a Pearsonian and a protegé of former colleague John Holmes. For Hadwen, this meant that he understood the necessity of measured respectful dialogue, particularly the application of quiet diplomacy. It also meant acknowledging that there were limits to what Canada might achieve in India. At the same time, Hadwen thought it was paramount to determine the potential to promote Canadian interests and seize any available opportunities. He firmly believed in the "art of the possible."[26]

Preparations for Hadwen's arrival in India unfolded into late August and early September, 1979. There was little time for pre-posting briefing according to Hadwen. Although he received a specific briefing on nuclear issues affecting the subcontinent, he recalled that "no progress" was expected on bilateral nuclear cooperation with India during his posting.[27] Hadwen strongly opposed nuclear proliferation and was deeply disappointed that India had developed a bomb, but he believed in the need to move beyond past tensions and foster communication. One had to be pragmatic.[28] And the department provided him with an objective that Hadwen was already comfortable pursuing from previous assignments. After reassessing the bilateral relationship through much of 1979, External Affairs judged the time ripe to develop a more mature and practical relationship that emphasized the promotion of trade over aid. This message would be delivered in Hadwen's presentation of credentials speech, on 26 October 1979.[29] A second factor influencing Ottawa's decision to pursue commercial objectives was that the longstanding socialist government of Indira Gandhi had been defeated in the 1977 election by a coalition government, the Janata Party. Dominated by a right-wing core, the new government appeared more willing to open up the Indian economy to foreign investment.

***

In contrast to Rogers and many of his other contemporaneous colleagues, Hadwen understood that trade promotion had become an increasingly key responsibility for a head of post.[30] Moreover, he quickly grasped that in a country where the government maintained rigid control of the private sector, it was vital to cultivate close ties with cabinet ministers and senior Indian civil servants. Building constructive relationships with his Indian counterparts came easily to Hadwen, who was naturally affable. He and his wife Shirley were actively engaged in the New Delhi diplomatic scene, hosting and attending social functions. They enjoyed their elegant residence with its sizable rear lawn garden. Contrary to Rogers's forewarnings, Hadwen found the address on Aurangzeb Road "beautiful," and he and Shirley made continued improvements to the home throughout their time in New Delhi.[31] Early in the morning he often golfed with members of the diplomatic corps or with Indian civil servants, including Indira Gandhi's private secretary, before the oppressive heat and smog consumed the city.[32]

In January 1980, the Janata coalition crumbled, triggering fresh elections which returned the Congress Party and its long-time leader Indira Gandhi to power. The actors and power brokers quickly changed, as did government priorities and interests. Three months into his posting, Hadwen prepared to start afresh with a new government whose prime minister had met every Canadian prime minister since Louis St. Laurent in the 1950s. Hadwen's successful pursuit of a dialogue with Gandhi mattered considerably in helping to redevelop relations along the lines Ottawa desired.

Throughout his time in India, interactions with Indian officials convinced Hadwen that "much good work" remained to be done in redeveloping bilateral relations.[33] He began to identify and focus on promoting specific key areas that have become hallmarks of the modern postcolonial Canada-India relationship. First, he believed that opportunities awaited the Canadian private sector. Hadwen lamented the Canadian private sector's inability to see the possibilities of doing business in India. Convincing Canadian businessmen to visit India was like "pulling teeth," he wrote to a friend, but he was encouraged by such developments as the establishment of a fledgling Canada-India Business Council and a rise in the number of joint ventures.[34] These, he hoped, might position Canada for a commercial breakthrough in India.

He also made extensive use of his personal contacts. Within a month of arriving in New Delhi, Hadwen drew India to the attention of Richard O'Hagan, a vice-president at the Bank of Montreal and former prime ministerial press secretary whom Hadwen knew well from the 1960s. The bank, the diplomat argued, should look more closely at India, remarking "how little Canadians seem to appreciate the possibilities for us in India ... [E]veryone's attention in respect of Asia is focussed on China."[35] Bilateral trade was "leaning well" at over $300 million annually. India represented Canada's fifteenth largest export market, placing it ahead of all Eastern European nations save the Soviet Union, and ahead of all Latin American countries except Brazil and Venezuela. Hadwen recalled how in previous Asian posts he had persuaded Canadian banks "to move down from Hong Kong to Singapore and Malaysia. They have made millions as a result. I strongly suspect that there are similar possibilities available to Canadian banks in India."[36]

In contrast to his predecessor, Hadwen was bullish on the economic opportunities awaiting Canada. In a year-end letter to his deputy under-secretary, Robert Johnstone, Hadwen expressed his surprise "at the number of commercial possibilities there are for us here. Some of them are developing rapidly and two of them will I believe require your and perhaps Cabinet's consideration."[37]

Perhaps Hadwen was too optimistic. After all, the government of India had recently banned Coca-Cola and IBM from India. Indeed, the director of the department's Bureau of Economic Intelligence, J.A. Macpherson, politely acknowledged and thanked Hadwen for an earlier letter providing his optimistic insights about India but waved away any interest: "for the time being, India is rather low on the list of priorities given to me by the member departments on the Economic Intelligence Committee." Macpherson offered a slight glimmer of hope, however, in relaying to Hadwen that his unit was severely understaffed and he had "to concentrate ... efforts pretty rigorously.[38] Nonetheless, few, if any, of his predecessors had been this commercially oriented and ambitious so quickly in their tenure as high commissioner, and given the recent tumult in bilateral relations Hadwen chose optimism over pessimism.

Hadwen's bosses applauded his efforts to identify commercial prospects that helped prompt the minister of state for trade, Ed Lumley, to visit India in early February 1981. Hadwen described the visit as an "opportunity for the most important substantive economic discussions between Canada and India for many years." The bilateral meeting between Lumley and prominent Indian finance minister Pranab Mukherjee would "bring to a head a number of ongoing discussions with a fair chance of reaching agreements that might not otherwise be possible."[39] Hadwen was not embellishing the significance of the discussions. The potential projects open for discussion included Met-Chem establishing an iron pellet factory; construction of the Idukki hydroelectric project with Canadian support; PT-6 engine sales; Twin Otter coproduction or purchases; and locomotive sales. Consequently, Hadwen and his team at the High Commission lobbied vigorously to secure a meeting between Lumley and Prime Minister Gandhi given her influence on economic and trade matters.[40]

Tom Delworth, assistant undersecretary for Asia and the Pacific, was impressed with Hadwen's energetic planning. "I am glad the Lumley visit is confirmed and I have been most impressed by the range of Canadian interests that you have identified for pursuing during his visit," he wrote the high commissioner. "I think the visit derives additional political importance as an affirmation of Canadian interest in India."[41] But Delworth, who was an India skeptic since working with Indian diplomats on the Indochina truce commissions in the 1960s, warned him against exaggerated expectations: "I might just note that the range and vigour of your mission's activities contrast markedly with India's performance here. The calibre of the diplomats at the High Commission here is disappointing in the extreme." He dismissed the Indian high commissioner as "almost completely irrelevant."[42]

Between 10 and 13 February, Lumley met with Mukherjee and an array of other Indian cabinet ministers, including ministers for defence, finance, civil aviation and tourism, petroleum and chemicals, and energy. He met with key engineering and business groups, too, including the Association of Indian Engineering Industries and the highly influential Federation of Indian Chambers of Commerce and Industry. Most important, Hadwen secured Lumley a valuable appointment with Gandhi to discuss bilateral economic relations.

Though no concrete deals were inked during the visit, the Canadian businessmen accompanying Lumley received invaluable exposure to the Indian government and private sector. For Hadwen, Lumley's visit was an achievement. Despite a simultaneous meeting of nonaligned foreign ministers in New Delhi, Hadwen had secured meetings with the most important cabinet ministers and the prime minister herself. By meeting with Lumley, the Indians signalled their interest in expanding bilateral trade and direct foreign investment. Hadwen believed a new kind of bilateral relationship might be in the offing, pragmatically pointing out that the only "satisfactory basis for Ottawa to redevelop its underwhelming ties with Delhi was through commercial and development efforts."[43] While high-level political visits were undoubtedly important to champion Canadian business interests, Hadwen insisted that more was required. The Canadian private sector needed advocates, encouragement, and better information before it would consider India a worthwhile market. A nascent Canada-India Business Council, formed in late 1981, would certainly help, and Hadwen aided the establishment of the council and put it into conversation with established Indian counterparts.[44]

Hadwen also mobilized his Canadian contacts to drum up support for the council. Writing to Sonja Bata, director of Bata Shoes, he emphasized that Canada was "the only major trading partner with India that does not have such a council and ... our interests in India and Canada are suffering seriously as a consequence."[45] Announcing the formal establishment of the

Canada-India Business Council to an Indian audience, the Canadian High Commission listed a veritable who's who of Canadian business as core members of the group, including Air Canada, Bata, the Bank of Nova Scotia, SNC Group, and Canadian General Electric.

Hadwen understood that momentum must be maintained in reimagining the bilateral relationship in both capitals. He believed in the need to promote consistent high-level bilateral visits between the two countries, observing that the government of India put great stock in such events, and tight government direction of the economy further necessitated continually cultivating the appropriate official figures that influenced the commercial agenda. This was not a message that Ottawa grasped. Hadwen complained to Escott Reid that he had been in New Delhi for three years and that only two Canadian ministers had visited India. Worse, only one Indian minister had visited Canada, and that was just to attend an international conference in Montreal! "This was simply not good enough," he wrote, especially given that Trudeau and Gandhi were both working closely on the North-South dialogue.[46]

Hadwen's economic ambitions for the bilateral relationship also fuelled an interest in tackling the moribund state of bilateral cultural relations and a sorry lack of media awareness in both countries. Canada's business community still thought of India as deeply impoverished or mired in endless red tape. Moreover, India rarely made headlines in Canada for anything other than corruption, natural disasters or riots. Indeed, Lumley's India visit had received only one meagre reference in the *Globe and Mail* while other media outlets ignored the visit altogether. For its part, the Indian press largely ignored Canada. Hadwen sought to correct this failure. He recognized that Canada needed a continuous cultural presence in India, but he had scarce resources at his disposal – a decades-long weakness for the Canadians in South Asia. In contrast to Canada's paltry promotional efforts in India, the British and other European nations were beating out Canada for trade opportunities because of the time and effort they put into coordinating cultural, political, and development cooperation to advance their commercial interests. Indians attached importance to culture, and he warned that Canada would continue to fall behind Western nations if it did not acknowledge this reality and remedy the situation.[47] Even in something as simple as promoting bilateral sports contacts, Hadwen lamented "the Indians are most anxious" to have some sort of association but "we have reacted with horror." In the meantime, Eastern and Western European nations and the Chinese were already active on that front.[48]

Closer educational ties were also vital for nurturing the new relationship that Hadwen had in mind. Canadian universities and colleges had a negligible interest in India and lagged far behind Australia, Britain, and the United States in educational relationships. Hadwen understood that these connections facilitated practical relationships, and he wanted the binational Shastri Indo-Canadian Institute to assume a greater role in promoting exchanges between Canadian and Indian students and faculty. Yet Ottawa's financial contribution to the Shastri institute had steadily shrunk since the 1960s and had not even kept up with inflation. He unsuccessfully lobbied Ottawa to increase its funding. An exasperated Hadwen confessed to Reid that he found it "hard to believe that we cannot find an additional $10,000 a year for three years to help with a major Canadian bilateral relationship."[49]

Despite the deep personal antagonism that had divided Indian prime minister Indira Gandhi and Trudeau since her nuclear test in 1974, Hadwen worked hard to promote closer relations at the top. Impressed with Gandhi's intelligence, graciousness, and tough-mindedness, he was delighted when she dropped by Hadwen's home one evening for tea. As they watched the sunset, a colony of green nesting parrots flew overhead and Gandhi expressed her enchantment.[50] The formidable and prickly Gandhi was renowned for her lack of social graces, and Hadwen chalked up the visit as a small victory. Indeed, Gandhi's unease with small talk was legendary in Ottawa, prompting former high commissioner Jack Maybee to jokingly describe an exchange about the weather as "something resembling a conversation."[51]

Hadwen and Ottawa worked to woo Gandhi in other ways too. When L.K. Jha, a retired Indian diplomat whom Gandhi made her personal representative for North-South issues, visited Ottawa on 30 June 1980, Hadwen and Canadian foreign minister Mark MacGuigan made sure that Trudeau met him. Both prime ministers were deeply interested in the burgeoning dialogue between the impoverished global South and the developed North, a common interest that might bridge their mutual disregard. A meeting with Jha would not go unnoticed in New Delhi and would emphasize the renewed importance Ottawa assigned to bilateral relations, reflected in the "efforts ... underway to increase very substantially Canada's economic and commercial relationship with India."[52]

Indeed, Hadwen saw the Indian prime minister as an ally in his search for a basis on which to establish a modern relationship with India. Taking advantage of his access to Gandhi, he emphasized his view of the evolving Canada-India relationship to her. "I described the kind of special relationship, built on shared economic interests, which we were now building," he wrote External Affairs in Ottawa:

> Mrs. Gandhi agreed that it should be possible to move in this direction. I told her that there had not been any major new commercial developments for some time and that it was essential we find some basis for this new relationship in the near future. We went on to discuss a series of specific proposals but I think it is fair to say that Mrs. Gandhi is prepared to put some effort into a new closer relationship between our two countries. She recognized that she and Mr. Trudeau had to build links between India and Canada different from those which had existed in period of Mr. Nehru and Mr. Pearson.[53]

Similar discussions between Hadwen and Gandhi followed into the summer of 1982, but Hadwen waited in vain for a stronger signal from Ottawa that it was ready to commit to this new practical connection. Hadwen urged Ottawa to invite Gandhi to visit Canada, pointing out that it had been nearly a decade since her last visit. The Prime Minister's Office and External Affairs were supportive, but the timing proved elusive – to the disappointment of the high commissioner.

Yet Hadwen soldiered on, marking an important achievement in July 1982: a bilateral air agreement allowing for reciprocal flights of Air Canada to India and Air India to Canada. Direct bilateral air links made it vastly easier for businesspeople, immigrants, students, and tourists to flow between each country. In short, it was a new tool for Hadwen to promote cultural and economic awareness. Pointing to recent constructive trends such as the air agreement and growth in bilateral trade, on 4 August the *Ottawa Citizen* noted "what a difference a couple of years can make ... about the only discordant note in present relations ... concerns the pattern of two way trade, which shows a heavy imbalance in Canada's favour."[54]

There was more good news in August 1982, when Hadwen helped prepare transport minister Jean-Luc Pépin, a long-time Trudeau cabinet minister, to lead a trade mission to India to promote Canadian aerospace exports. The visit reflected Hadwen's emphasis on promoting commercial and industrial contacts and featured proposals for major long-term contractual relationships between Canada's De Havilland and Pratt & Whitney with the Indian aeronautical industry. The trade mission began on 13 September and was notable for its length – eleven days. Hadwen's energy and sense of purpose took him to Toronto to drum up interest in the Pépin visit and for the Indian market. Updating the High Commission in Delhi on his activities, Hadwen cheerfully noted that he had been "wheeling with [diplomat Anthony] Vincent" and had secured a meeting with John Alsop, manager of software development for AES Data, which Hadwen encouraged to "contact CIDA to discuss possible study of data processing relationship with India."[55] The successful Toronto meetings reflected Hadwen's comfort and zeal in playing the role of salesman for his country when he believed that such a role was necessary.[56]

Pépin would be hosted by the Indian minister of shipping and transport, Veerendra Patil. Pepin's aim was to help Canadian companies secure contracts for their transportation equipment and systems, and to promote aircraft sales, including the sale of telecommunications services for the Indian rail network. Accompanying Pépin were senior executives of nearly fifteen Canadian companies and a representative from the Canada-India Business Council.[57] In many respects, Pépin was building on the Lumley visit and the contacts made from that trip. As was the case with the Lumley visit, both De Havilland and Pratt & Whitney pressed the merits of their products and abilities with the Indians as part of a Canadian package of transport aircraft and engines competing against Germany's Dornier aircraft. Ottawa watched the visit closely, encouraging Pépin to remind his Indian counterpart that the government attached a great deal of importance "to working out a mutually advantageous agreement … [and that Ottawa] would regard this as the beginning of a new era of technical and commercial cooperation between India and Canada."[58] The Indians gave Pépin a "warm reception" in New Delhi, and Hadwen could take satisfaction that again his efforts had secured a meeting between Pépin and members of the mission with Gandhi. While no agreements were signed, the deputy prime minister and recently reappointed foreign minister, Allan MacEachen, informed his Indian counterpart at the United Nations General Assembly that the Canadian government had been "very pleased" with the "successful mission."[59]

A remarkable shift in bilateral relations appeared to be unfolding just as Hadwen had hoped. By the time he returned to Ottawa for year-end briefings, bilateral ties were arguably in the most positive state in over a decade. Trade figures indicated that Ottawa had made headway in building an advantageous trade relationship. Canadian exports to India had "been increasingly rapidly" approaching $350 million annually, "three times the level of imports." Moreover, Hadwen learned during his visit that MacEachen himself had agreed "in principle" to visit South Asia, including India, in the summer of 1983.[60] Nearly thirty years had passed since a Canadian foreign minister had last toured the region, in 1955. Hadwen's consistent lobbying efforts to secure high-profile cabinet-level visits had paid off.

In the lead-up to MacEachen's arrival, Hadwen stressed "how much [the] post welcomes" the forthcoming discussions "and how willing we are to do everything possible to assist in taking advantage of Canadian interest opportunities that will certainly arise." Just as with the previous ministerial visits, Hadwen cheerfully offered his resplendent residence to host any session that benefited from a more informal environment.[61] MacEachen arrived on 3 July amid the baking heat of the New Delhi summer. The schedule for his two full working days brimmed with high-level meetings. Beginning on 4 July, MacEachen met with his counterpart, foreign minister Narasimha Rao, who welcomed the Canadians by noting significantly "that there had not been a visit at this level for the last twelve years."[62] Rao was well briefed, referencing Pierre Trudeau's state visit in February 1971. In a considerable shift from previous years, MacEachen informed Rao that "he now considered closer relations with India as an important asset ... [The] purpose of his visit ... was to maintain the rapidly developing relationship and strengthen it across the spectrum." This was not only MacEachen's view but also that of Prime Minister Trudeau and the cabinet. In particular, MacEachen emphasized how important it was "to give more substance to the economical commercial dimension of the India-Canada relationship."[63] Hadwen's prescription for the making of a new "special relationship" had gained traction in Ottawa.

The meeting with Rao then expanded into a larger gathering with senior Indian diplomats. Following a broad discussion of bilateral and global issues at the Indian Ministry of External Affairs, MacEachen was whisked away to Raj Ghat, the memorial to Mahatma Gandhi, where he laid a wreath and observed a moment's silence. Within minutes, MacEachen and Hadwen raced through the Delhi traffic to meet the minister of industry, Narayan Datt Tiwari, and the powerful minister of finance, Pranab Mukherjee. MacEachen urged that both countries "should put more flesh on the bones of our economic relations," pointing out that Canada and India "have left untapped the potential for economic cooperation."[64] Mukherjee was receptive to this overture but countered that Canadian firms were simply not competitive. The meeting ended with MacEachen and Mukherjee signing a memorandum of understanding on Canadian financing for edible oils, aid for which the Indian minister expressed deep gratitude.

A long but fruitful day concluded with a dinner in MacEachen's honour, when the Indian foreign minister surprised MacEachen in private by explaining that India wished to "renew" nuclear cooperation with Canada. Both parties treated the delicate conversation with the utmost secrecy. Hadwen and MacEachen agreed that the ball was in India's court.[65] It is difficult to conceive of such an exchange occurring without Hadwen's consistent message that Ottawa focus on promoting mutually beneficial, constructive, but neglected commercial aspects of the relationship. The high commissioner had helped foster an environment whereby positive communications between the two governments had become normalized, transcending the suspicion and accusations of betrayal of previous years.

The next morning, MacEachen met Gandhi. In advance of the meeting, the High Commission had circulated an *aide-mémoire* of topics to be discussed with the Indian prime minister. Gandhi had circulated the document to her cabinet colleagues, and to the delight of MacEachen and Hadwen, they found both the prime minister and her cabinet colleagues well briefed. MacEachen continued to emphasize his plea for closer economic ties, and he found Gandhi supportive of his call for increased bilateral "economic and commercial content."[66] Following an informal lunch at the High Commission, MacEachen spent the afternoon in meetings with the minister for power, the secretary for petroleum, the president of India, and the defence minister. Hadwen was elated. Door after door had been opened for the Canadians, and the Indians had been warm and amenable during their discussions, particularly on the theme of enhanced economic links. The long day ended with a lively press conference attended by over fifty Indian and international media representatives.[67]

In the following weeks, Hadwen scrutinized the visit carefully and provided Ottawa with a thorough assessment. Hadwen heaped praise on the Indian media, applauding their "vigour and enthusiasm." This was in contrast to the Canadian media whose coverage was spotty. The deputy prime minister had reassured the Indians that Canada took domestic support for Sikh separatism seriously and received "maximum publicity in doing so." Ottawa's desire for robust economic links and cooperation on files ranging from aircraft construction and energy projects to mining received front page attention in "all widely read economic newspapers." With a hint of delight, Hadwen observed that MacEachen had received greater "and more generally positive" media attention than his American counterpart, Secretary of State George Shultz, who departed Delhi just before MacEachen arrived. Although Hadwen acknowledged that the minister's visit had produced no major commercial breakthrough, he thought that the visit had "emphasized" to the Indian government "current projects of importance to Canada" and that those "projects have been given strong support and some useful developments [were] occurring." The next steps for Hadwen were obvious. The high commissioner promised to be "aggressive" in following up, and he hoped for the same commitment from Canadian industry. Ottawa, he repeated, had "to continue to develop as much linkage as possible if we are to use these good relations for Canadian interest purposes." Rivals for India's trade were not sitting idly by. The "Europeans, particularly the British, the Russians and Americans" were Canada's "competitors in every field."[68]

Steering that transition along from New Delhi would be the responsibility of someone else, however. Hadwen's journey in India came to an end after four years, in late 1983. Hadwen enjoyed his time in India with many fond memories. In the long arc of bilateral relations, few other high commissioners had worked as diligently or as consistently as Hadwen to transform the relationship – especially through the commercial file. Hadwen was leaving the Delhi post – and bilateral relations – in far better shape for his successor than what he had inherited in 1979. And for that, his positive and pragmatic approach to diplomacy – that John Holmes and Lester Pearson had influenced decades earlier – deserves much credit. He left India hopeful, predicting that the 1980s would bring increased trade, growing bilateral cooperation in the North-South dialogue, and closer relations between Canadians and Indians. But he also noted that "prophets lead dangerous lives."[69] Indeed, change was slow in coming. Relations between the two countries remained correct but distant partly because of the memories of 1974, partly because the incoming Progressive Conservative government of Prime Minister Brian Mulroney emphasized the primacy of close relations with the United States and with NATO allies. And Hadwen had overestimated the appetite for Canada's private sector to embrace the Indian market. Bilateral trade between the two nations remained sluggish into the new millennium, underscoring that officials such as Hadwen faced limitations on what they could aspire toward. Moreover, from the Indian perspective, Ottawa had not done enough to rein in the burgeoning growth of Sikh extremism in Canada – an issue that emerged during Hadwen's later years in New Delhi and culminated in the Air India bombing of June 1985.

A biographical approach to Hadwen's time in India highlights the positive impact a diplomat can have on influencing bilateral policy. It is also important to note that Hadwen kept many of his personal papers from his diplomatic journey. Such individual records can allow historians to better understand the personal story, thereby providing a richer texture to and understanding of this important chapter of John Hadwen's long and distinguished career and providing historians with a glimpse of what life was like in India for Hadwen and his family beyond the daily routine of representing Canadian interests gleaned solely from official government records. Indeed, a careful reading of Hadwen's personal correspondence, juxtaposed with government records, reveals that he candidly expressed his hopes and frustrations in a way that he did not, or could not, in his official correspondence with the Department of External Affairs. Looking back over the past thirty years, however, it is clear that Hadwen accurately identified the niche areas that have come to characterize the contemporary Canada-India relationship. Trade between both countries is steadily growing, and the expectations for continued growth remains bullish as the two countries slowly negotiate a free trade agreement. As India seeks to fulfill the burgeoning aspirations of its youth for higher education opportunities, the possibilities have captured Canadian attention. Postsecondary institutions and provincial governments now consistently travel to India to build relationships and show young Indians what Canada has to offer. Canada still trails behind the Americans, Australians, and the British, but figures show a continued increase in the number of Indian students pursuing their studies in Canada. The Canada-India relationship also benefits from a new generation of enthusiasts in prominent organizations such as the Asia Pacific Foundation of Canada and the Canada-India Business Council, the organization Hadwen helped nurture. Hadwen, who passed away in 2007, would be pleased.

NOTES

1 On Canada's nuclear relations with India, see Ryan M. Touhey, *Conflicting Visions: Canada and India in the Cold War World* (Vancouver: UBC Press, 2015); John Hilliker, Mary Halloran, and Greg Donaghy, *Canada's Department of External Affairs*, vol. 3, *Innovation and Adaptation 1968–1984* (Toronto: University of Toronto Press, 2017); Mary Halloran, "Mrs. Gandhi's Bombshell: Canadian Reactions to India's Nuclear Detonation, 1974–1976," in *Canada's Global Engagements and Relations with India*, ed. Christopher Raj and Abdul Nafey (New Delhi: Manak, 2007), 279–91; and Duane Bratt, *The Politics of CANDU Exports* (Toronto: University of Toronto Press, 2006).

2 "The Troops Coming Home," *Globe and Mail*, 7 July 1902, 2; "Authority on Pathology, Dr. I.S.A. Hadwen Dies," *Globe and Mail*, 21 April 1947, 10.

3 "Linda Anne de Weerdt," *Globe and Mail* obituary, 5 October 2007, S7.

4 "U.T.S. Holds Annual Assault at Hart House," *Globe and Mail*, 14 March 1941, 16.

5 T.A. Reed, ed., *A History of the University of Trinity College Toronto 1852–1952* (Toronto: University of Toronto Press, 1952), 169.

6 Social and Personal Notes, *Globe and Mail*, 28 July 1950, 10.

7 Ibid.

8 See, for example, J.L. Granatstein, *The Ottawa Men: The Civil Service Mandarins 1935–1957* (Toronto: Oxford University Press, 1982); and Andrew Cohen, *While Canada Slept: How We Lost Our Place in the World* (Toronto: McClelland and Stewart, 2004).

9 "Shirley Vivyan Hadwen," *Ottawa Citizen* obituary, 29 March 2017, http://ottawacitizen.remembering.ca/obituary/shirley-hadwen-1066056592.

10 Earl Drake, email correspondence with author, 28 April 2019.

11 Gar Pardy, phone interview with author, 29–30 April 2019.

12 Mary Taylor, "John Gaylard Hadwen," *Globe and Mail,* 19 February 2008, https://www.theglobeandmail.com/life/john-gaylard-hadwen/article1351322/.

13 Greg Donaghy, *Grit: The Life and Politics of Paul Martin Sr.* (Vancouver: UBC Press, 2015), 194.

14 Paul Martin Sr., *A Very Public Life,* vol. 2, *So Many Worlds* (Toronto: Deneau, 1985), 379.

15 Allan McGill, *My Life as I Remember It* (Vancouver: Granville Island, 2004), 230.

16 John Hadwen, "A Foreign Service Officer and Canada's Nuclear Policies," in *Special Trust and Confidence: Envoy Essays in Canadian Diplomacy,* ed. David Reece (Ottawa: Carleton University Press, 1996), 163.

17 Ibid., 164.

18 Tim Hadwen, interview with author, 9 May 2018.

19 Hadwen, "A Foreign Service Officer and Canada's Nuclear Policies," 165.

20 Rogers to Hadwen, 21 May 1979, file 3, box 3, F 2307, John G. Hadwen Papers, Trinity College Archives, University of Toronto.

21 R.L. Rogers to John Hadwen, 6 June 1979, Ibid.

22 Ibid.

23 See Touhey, *Conflicting Visions.*

24 See Touhey, *Conflicting Visions,* chap. 10; and Touhey, "From Periphery to Priority: Lessons of the Canada-India Relationship 1976–2009," *International Journal* 64, 4 (2009): 911–25.

25 See Statistics Canada, *Canada Year Book 1978,* chap. 18, https://www66.statcan.gc.ca/eng/1978-79-eng.htm. Indian imports to Canada in 1975 stood at $46,650,000, climbing to a still underwhelming $55,677,000 in 1977.

26 John Hadwen, "Opportunities for Canada in South Asia" (paper presented to Conference Workshop on Canadian-South Asian Political and Strategic Relations, University of Toronto, 27–29 October 1988), 17. The author is grateful to Gar Pardy for providing him with a copy of this paper.

27 Briefing for Mr. J Hadwen, High Commissioner Designate to India, 22 August 1979, file 20–1–5–Delhi pt. 1, vol. 5055, RG 25, LAC.

28 Tim Hadwen, interview with author, 9 May 2018.

29 Ottawa to Delhi, Presentation of Credentials Speech, 7 September 1979, file 22–9–INDIA-I pt. 2, vol. 204606, RG 25, LAC.

30 Not all of Hadwen's colleagues were enamoured by the emphasis on trade promotion. For example, see Bill Warden, *Diplomat, Dissident, Spook: A Canadian Diplomat's Chronicles through the Cold War and Beyond* (self-pub. 2017), tellwell.ca.

31 Hadwen to Escott Reid, 27 April 1982, file #37 Hadwen, John (4), vol. 33, E46, MG 31, Escott Reid Papers, LAC.

32 I am most grateful to Sylvia Lassam, Trinity University archivist, for bringing the anecdote about Gandhi's secretary to my attention.

33 Hadwen to Reid, 28 February 1982, file #37 Hadwen, John (4), vol. 33, E46, MG 31, Escott Reid Papers, LAC.

34 Ibid.

35 Hadwen to O'Hagan, 25 October 1979, file 3, box 3, F2307, John Hadwen Papers, Trinity College Archives.

36 Ibid.

37 Hadwen to Robert Johnstone, 20 December 1979, file 3, box 3, F2307, John Hadwen Papers, Trinity College Archives. The two commercial possibilities he referred to were Canadian Met-Chem for the development of an iron ore mine in Bangalore and the joint production of the PT6 engine of Pratt & Whitney, also in Bangalore.
38 J.A. Macpherson to Hadwen, 4 March 1980, file 3, box 3, F2307, John Hadwen Papers, Trinity College Archives.
39 Hadwen to Ottawa, 13 January 1981, file 20-CDA9-IT&C (1) pt. 11, vol. 33734, RG 25, LAC.
40 Ibid.
41 Delworth to Hadwen, 30 January 1981, file 4, box 3, F2307, John Hadwen Papers, Trinity College Archives.
42 Ibid.
43 Hadwen to Delworth, 5 March 1981, Ibid.
44 Hadwen to B.M. Gupta, 29 April 1982, file 5, box 3, F2307, John Hadwen Papers, Trinity College Archives.
45 Hadwen to Sonja Bata, 23 June 1982, Ibid.
46 Hadwen to Escott Reid, 27 April 1982, file 37, vol. 33, E46, MG 31, Escott Reid Papers, LAC.
47 Ibid.
48 Ibid.
49 Ibid.
50 Tim Hadwen, interview with author, 9 May 2018.
51 Touhey, *Conflicting Visions,* 232.
52 M.R. MacGuigan to Prime Minister, June 1981 (no specific date provided), file 20–1–2–India, pt. 19, vol. 8741, RG 25, LAC.
53 Hadwen to Ottawa Subject: INDO/CDN Special Relationships, 25 May 1982, file 20–1–2–India, pt. 21, vol. 4727, RG 25, LAC.
54 See Patrick Best, "Relations between Canada and India Improved since 1980," *Ottawa Citizen,* 4 August 1982, 46.
55 Ottawa to Delhi, Message from Hadwen, 5 August 1982, file 20–1–2–India, pt. 21, vol. 4727, RG 25, LAC.
56 See John Hilliker, Mary Halloran, and Greg Donaghy, *Canada's Department of External Affairs,* vol. 3, *Innovation and Adaptation 1968–1984* (Toronto: University of Toronto Press, 2017), chaps. 8–9. It is worth noting that Hadwen also met with members of the engineering firm SNC Lavalin to learn about their interest in procuring work in Rajasthan, as well as with General Electric Canada.
57 "Minister Heads Mission to India," *Globe and Mail,* 13 September 1982, B11.
58 Canada-India Bilateral Issues, 25 August 1982, file 20–1–2–India, pt. 21, vol. 4727, RG 25, LAC.
59 Delhi to Ottawa, SSEAS MTG with Indian Foreign Min, 24 September 1982; PRMNY to Ottawa, SSEA Bilateral with Indian FM Rao, 29 September 1982, Ibid.
60 M.G. von Nostitz to PSS/GPP, 29 November 1982, Ibid.
61 Delhi to Ottawa, 5 April 1983, file 20-CDA-9-EA pt. 6, vol. 33683, RG 25, LAC.
62 Hadwen to SSEA, DPM/SSEA Visit 3–6 July 1983 Verbatim Notes, 29 July 1983, file 20-CDA-EA pt. 8, vol. 33684, LAC.

63 ISBAD to Ottawa, India/SSEA Visit: Meeting with FM Rao 04 JUL, 6 July 1983, file 20–1–2–India, pt. 22, vol. 4727, RG 25, LAC.
64 Minutes of Meeting between DPM/SSEA Allan J. MacEachen and Government of India Finance Minister, Pranab Mukherjee, 4 July 1983, file 20-CDA-9-EA pt. 8, vol. 33684, RG 25, LAC.
65 Delhi to ISBAD/MINDEL, DPM/SSEA Visit: Nuclear Discussions, 8 July 1983, Ibid.
66 Delhi to Ottawa, SSEA Visit Thank You Notes, 14 July 1983, Ibid.
67 Hadwen to SSEA, DPM/SSEA Visit July 3–6, 1983 Verbatim Notes, 29 July 1983, Ibid.
68 Delhi to SSEA, DPM/SSEA Visit: Retrospective Evaluation, 1 August 1983, Ibid.
69 High Commissioner's Message on the Occasion of the Special Supplement, 25 June 1982, file #37 Hadwen, John (4), vol. 33, E46, MG 31, Escott Reid Papers, LAC.

CONCLUSION
The Academic as Activist

John Milloy

Individuals matter. Prime ministers and ministers, hustlers and lumberjacks, senators and diplomats, all have their stories to tell. And as the notes to the chapters in this collection make clear, how they are told in Canada today owes much to John English. First as a biographer of Lester B. Pearson and Pierre Trudeau and then as editor of the *Dictionary of Canadian Biography,* English has almost single-handedly moved biography to the core of contemporary Canadian historiography.

But what is especially remarkable about English's career has been his ability to move beyond the academy and contribute significantly to public life in Canada as a political activist, a deeply engaged citizen working at the coal face of politics. Political activists are not afraid to enter the fray and get their hands dirty, and they become involved in issues, movements, and campaigns to influence public policy. They are the people who run for office, join political parties, hold advisory appointments with governments, and offer formal and informal advice to elected officials and senior public servants.

This is obviously not the only way that academics contribute to politics and public policy. Professors and scholars are often at the vanguard of change, and their work can inspire policy makers, broaden their perspectives, and challenge conventional thinking. Like water on a rock, academic critiques of society can slowly change our thinking, setting new courses for our country. The academy, in short, can serve as a prophetic voice.

Yet, academics often play an equally important and more direct role in Canadian political life. John English's long history of active participation in local, regional, and national politics is an outstanding example. My perspective on his life – his political biography – is unique. Although I have an academic background and teach in the university system, I spent close to twenty years working in and around politics, spending roughly half that time as a member of provincial Parliament and cabinet minister in a Liberal government at Queen's Park. My relationship with John English spans both these worlds.

John has been an academic mentor. Though never formally my supervisor, he was generous with advice and guidance as I pursued a doctorate and published my thesis. However, I first met John through his activist side, encountering him when I was a young Liberal at the tender age of fourteen. Later, he gave me my first job on Parliament Hill. Soon after completing my doctorate, I spent a week in John's office – he was a member of Parliament at the time – answering letters from disgruntled constituents. He paid me one hundred dollars and a nice lunch.

John English has a rich history of political activism. The span of his political career is impressive and includes stints as the member of Parliament for the Ontario riding of Kitchener, parliamentary secretary, member of the Special Joint Committee Reviewing Canadian Foreign Policy, special advisor to the Canadian minister of foreign affairs on landmines, principal reviewer of the mandate and future roles of the National Library and National Archives of Canada, chair of the board of the Canadian Museum of Civilization, and special envoy for the election of Canada to the UN Security Council. He has frequently provided advice to candidates at all levels, elected representatives and cabinet ministers, and premiers and prime ministers, along with senior public servants on countless public policy issues. He has worked alone and with any number of nongovernmental organizations to shape public policy, drafting countless speeches and policy documents.

Clearly, John English has made his voice count. One anecdote illustrates just how well connected he was: when I was first elected to the legislature, I followed the intergovernmental affairs beat for the Ontario government. In the course of a few days, my travels allowed me to meet both the premier of Ontario, Dalton McGuinty, and Prime Minister Jean Chrétien. Both greeted me with the same question: "How is John English?"

How did English do it? What lessons does his career – his political biography, if you will – have for academics who want to be successful political activists and who want their advice taken seriously? After reflecting on John's political biography, I would like to offer a workable framework for success for those in the academy who want to make a difference. I call them the four *R*s of successful academic activism: relatable, respectful, realistic, and relevant. And each reflects a quality that John English demonstrated in spades.

RELATABLE

For an academic to be taken seriously in political and public policy circles, ordinary people need to be able to relate to them. The academic needs to be seen as someone who is, for lack of a better word, "normal." Decisive political leaders determined to bring about significant change need the trust of ordinary Canadians and earn that trust by being "one of them." This extends to their academic advisors. It is difficult for a policy maker to accept advice from someone far removed from the reality of everyday life.

Examples of academics who inhabit different planets are plentiful. I was once struck, for instance, by an outlandish comment from historian Niall Ferguson in an interview with the *New York Times Book Review* section. "Everyone has at least one vice," he explained. "Mine is reading (and re-reading) 19th-century novels. It's hard to pick just a couple of favorites but I unreservedly adore Wilkie Collins (e.g., 'The Moonstone') and Theodor Fontane ('Der Stechlin')."[1] Reading nineteenth-century novels is not a vice. Going through sixty-three quarts of Ben & Jerry's Chunky Monkey ice cream in twelve months and never using a bowl is a vice! This kind of false modesty greatly limits the effectiveness of academics to really make a difference in the here and now – to be taken seriously by people whose goal is to convince Main Street, not the faculty club.

John English's approach to politics and people is markedly different. What is the most common thing people say about John English after they finish commenting on how pleasant he is? They speak about his approachability and down-to-earth character. In any setting, with any group of people, including the most humble, John English will be quick to engage them, to exchange ideas and insights, and to make them feel heard.

As a member of Parliament, English did not represent upscale Waterloo with its two universities and high income and education levels. Instead, he represented the blue collar neighbouring riding of Kitchener, a riding with lower education levels and incomes and one of the highest concentrations of new immigrants and refugees in the country. They related to John.

And John English had a way of presenting ideas and concepts – of teaching and explaining, in fact – that allowed him to relate to them. Defending the secrecy of negotiations between an Indigenous community and the federal government in the House of Commons in 1995, for instance, John English did not resort to a long legal explanation. He instead explained to the Commons that there is an element of secrecy in most negotiations, even when you buy a car.[2] Similarly, his Plattsville roots showing, John English happily launched into an earthy back and forth in the Commons with Alberta Reform Party member Ken Epp on tractors and cow milking, and their use as a metaphor for the government's policy toward agencies, boards, and commissions. Perhaps John's academic training did come through a little when he won the debate with a quote from novelist George Orwell's *Animal Farm*.[3]

In short, as an engaged political activist, John English was the real deal. Despite his extraordinary abilities, experience, and background, he always came across as an ordinary guy. Most important, it was never an act. John was truly and genuinely interested in people from all walks of life.

RESPECTFUL

Successful activists need to believe in the wisdom of the people, valuing their views and understanding that voters get the last word. Activists must tailor their advice and perspectives in ways that respect the ultimate wishes of the governed. They must realize that there will be many others who hold different views. And although they might well disagree with the people, political leaders must acknowledge that voters have every right to those views, which are usually legitimate and always deserve to be heard. This is not always common in the academy, where individuality and originality are prized above collective wisdom, and yet it is so crucial to making public policy and advising political decision makers.

John English's passion for education and dialogue went far beyond the university classroom. As a political actor, he enjoyed engaging with the public and has a long history of moderating town hall meetings, giving public lectures, and serving as a panellist at public discussions, always trying to explain his viewpoint but also trying to understand the other side. Typically, as on one cold night in February 1992, John could be found moderating public meetings in downtown Kitchener on the Charlottetown constitutional accord or addressing nine representatives of the local Chinese Canadian community on behalf of the Kitchener–Waterloo–Woolwich Yes Committee. The newspaper reported passionate remarks from John on behalf of the *Yes* campaign. He told the group that should the *No* side win, everyone who felt excluded from this round would show up at the next with more demands. As English put it, if the *No* side wins, "the next thing you know we'll have people who wear pink hats at Christmas wanting a place in the Constitution."[4]

REALISTIC

These events and this role are aspects of activism in their own right, but they also build the skills and insight needed to offer advice that is practical and realistic. Unlike many of his fellow academics, John gets it. Maybe it is a combination of his study of history and his political experience, but he knows that politics and government do not always work the way one wants them to. He knows that the reality is messy, complicated, and chaotic. He understands that one cannot simply wish all these things away and start over.

As a cabinet minister, I often worked with academics who provided helpful insights. But I remember, too, consulting those whose advice often began with a suggestion that the first thing we needed to do was to change the basic structure of society – economically and socially – and then proceed from there. When I pressed these people for advice on what I should do then and there with all the financial and political pressures I faced, the room usually fell silent. The sounds of crickets could be quite overwhelming.

Several years ago, the *New York Times* asked a series of Americans what they would do if elected president of the United States. One prominent academic and public intellectual responded:

> With my staff, I would decide what my administration was for. Once I had clarified that, I would write several speeches on how to cope

> with a stagnant economy, how to deal with countries (such as Iran and Syria) that harass their own populations, and how the United States is committed to the survival of Israel. These speeches would not attack the other party or previous presidents but would describe the views I supported … People would disagree with some of what I said, but they would know where I stand. After delivering the speeches, I would submit to Congress my specific proposals, on which I would ask them to vote.[5]

Several speeches and a vote? Hardly the practical advice that politicians need.

RELEVANT

Finally, advice has to be useful and applicable – whether accepted or not, it ought to add value to the discussion.

This can sometimes be tricky when it comes to history. There are always moments when historians are tempted to simply show off and illustrate the way that what is happening today echoes events fifty or one hundred years earlier, and leave it at that, adding little to the conversation. But that has never been the case with English and his use of history. He understands that if you want to address current challenges, you need to understand them as fully as possible. And part of that understanding involves appreciating their historical context: What came before? How did previous events shape where we are today? And are there lessons from the past that might help us shape an appropriate response?

In a piece published in the journal *Policy Options*, in 1999, aptly entitled "What do we do about history today?," English outlined his approach. Quoting the old maxim that history may not repeat itself, but it does rhyme, he warned that a "generation drowned in detail, imbued with nostalgia, and intoxicated by future technology would do much better if it remembers those old rhymes sometimes."[6]

Most important, John English always remembered those old rhymes in his speeches and writings and in the advice that he gave. As a member of Parliament during the turbulent 1990s, he often drew on his scholarly training to place contemporary events within their historical context. His maiden speech to Parliament, for instance, was during an important debate over Canada's role as a peacekeeper in the former Yugoslavia. His remarks gave a robust overview of the history of international peacekeeping, including the correction of a number of myths. He was able to analyze the post–Cold War situation within the historical context of international relations and come up with some excellent advice on how to move forward while still managing to make several references to his constituency and constituents.[7] He pursued a similar strategy during the crisis surrounding the Quebec referendum of 1995, and his insights into that tumultuous period were insightful and drew on his vast understanding of the development of our nation. He added much to a national discussion where many felt lost.

***

Academia and activism: bridging the two roles is never as easy as it appears. On the one hand, political actors and government officials are often prejudiced against the work of the academy, fearing that it is too grandiose and theoretical. Academics, on the other hand, often see the realities of politics and public policy as unseemly and beneath them. This is unfortunate. Both sides have much to contribute to the other. Those with time and expertise to explore complex issues often bring a fresh perspective to some of our most challenging problems. A healthy dose of political reality, on the other hand, can inject a needed dose of practicality into the work of our centres of learning. John English was the quintessential academic activist. His recipe for success – be relatable, respectful, realistic, and relevant – empowered him in both political and historical contexts. Like the other biographical studies in this collection, John English's story represents a vibrant dialogue between the individual and their times, shedding light on both.

NOTES

1 Niall Ferguson, "Niall Ferguson: By the Book," *New York Times,* 11 January 2018, https://www.nytimes.com/2018/01/11/books/review/niall-ferguson-by-the-book.html.

2 John English, Canada, *House of Commons Debates,* 35th Parliament, 1st Session, 7 December 1995, 17374.

3 John English, Canada, House of Commons *Debates,* 35th Parliament, 1st Session, 7 February 1995, 928–91 (reference to Orwell's *Animal Farm,* 9290).

4 Liz Monteiro, "Referendum Still Confusing despite Local Yes Meeting," *Kitchener-Waterloo Record*, 23 October 1992.

5 James Q. Wilson quoted in Jesse Kornbluth, "If I Were President ...," *New York Times Sunday Review*, 21 August 2011, https://archive.nytimes.com/www.nytimes.com/interactive/2011/08/21/opinion/sunday/20110821_Kornbluth_President.html.

6 John English, "What Do We Do about History Today?," *Policy Options*, March 1999, 51.

7 John English, Canada, House of Commons *Debates*, 35th Parliament, 1st Session, 25 January 1994, 370–72.

CONTRIBUTORS

Stephen Azzi is professor of political management, history, and political science at Carleton University. He is author of *Walter Gordon and the Rise of Canadian Nationalism, Reconcilable Differences: A History of Canada-US Relations,* and (with Barry Gough) the third edition of *Historical Dictionary of Canada.*

Jennifer Levin Bonder was one of John English's last students, whose research explores the economic angle of the Canada-US relationship. She has taught Canadian history on both sides of the border. She got her first taste of policy research working for Greg Donaghy in the Historical Section at Global Affairs Canada and continues this work as a researcher at the Munk School of Global Affairs and Public Policy.

Robert Bothwell was for fifty-one years a teacher in the History Department of the University of Toronto. He is the author of various books on Canadian foreign relations and of *The Penguin History of Canada.*

Penny Bryden is professor of history at the University of Victoria and past president of the Canadian Historical Association. Her books include *Canada: A Political Biography* (2016), *"A Justifiable Obsession": Conservative Ontario's Relations with Ottawa, 1943–1985* (2013), *Framing Canadian Federalism* (co-edited 2009), *Canada and the New World Order: Facing the New Millennium* (co-edited 2000), and *Planners and Politicians: Liberal Politics and Social Policy, 1957–1968* (1997).

Greg Donaghy was a historian with the Department of Foreign Affairs and then Director of the Bill Graham Centre for Contemporary International History at Trinity College, University of Toronto. He edited six volumes in the *Documents on Canadian External Relations* series and wrote *Tolerant Allies: Canada and the United States, 1963–1968* (2003) as well as the biography *Grit: The Life and Politics of Paul Martin Sr.* (2015).

Norman Hillmer is Chancellor's Professor of History and International Affairs at Carleton University. Among his books is a biography of O.D. Skelton, the architect of Canada's Department of External Affairs.

P. Whitney Lackenbauer is Canada Research Chair (Tier 1) in the Study of the Canadian North and a professor in the School for the Study of Canada at Trent University, where he leads the North American and Arctic Defence and Security Network (NAADSN). He has written or edited more than fifty books related to Canadian history, security, and politics.

Asa McKercher is assistant professor of history at the Royal Military College of Canada. He is the author of *Canada and the World since 1867* (Bloomsbury, 2019) and *Camelot and Canada: Canadian-American Relations in the Kennedy Era* (Oxford, 2016).

John Milloy is Director of the Centre for Public Ethics at Waterloo Lutheran Seminary and the inaugural practitioner-in-residence in Wilfrid Laurier University's Department of Political Science. From 2003 to 2014, John served as a Member of Provincial Parliament for Kitchener Centre, holding several cabinet posts, including that of Minister of Training, Colleges and Universities.

Galen Roger Perras is a professor in the History Department at the University of Ottawa. His major publications include *Mike's World: Lester B. Pearson and Canadian External Relations* (co-edited 2017) and *Stepping Stones to Nowhere: The Aleutian Islands, Alaska, and American Military Strategy, 1867–1945* (2003).

Angelika E. Sauer has spent the past twenty-eight years researching and teaching international and transnational history, first at the University of Winnipeg and, since August 2000, at Texas Lutheran University, a liberal arts college in Seguin, Texas. Now retired, she has published numerous journal articles and book chapters on Canadian-German relations, nineteenth- and twentieth-century immigration history, and the construction of North American borders through immigration law enforcement.

Ryan M. Touhey is an associate professor at St. Jerome's University, University of Waterloo. He is the author of *Conflicting Visions: Canada and India in the Cold War World 1947–1976* as well as co-editor of *Reassessing the Rogue Tory: Canadian Foreign Relations in the Diefenbaker Era.*

INDEX